The Bird and The Fish

Memoir of a Temporary Marriage

MIRIAM VALMONT

Copyright © 2016 Miriam Valmont.

All rights reserved. No part of this book may be reproduced, stored, or transmitted by any means—whether auditory, graphic, mechanical, or electronic—without written permission of both publisher and author, except in the case of brief excerpts used in critical articles and reviews. Unauthorized reproduction of any part of this work is illegal and is punishable by law.

Grateful acknowledgement to:

Another Sundown Publishing for permission to print Kate Wolf's lyrics to *Give Yourself to Love*, Copyright 1982

Coleman Banks for permission to print an excerpt from *The Essential Rumi*, copyright 1995.

Excerpt(s) from GIFT FROM THE SEA by Anne Morrow Lindbergh, copyright © 1955, 1975, copyright renewed 1983 by Anne Morrow Lindbergh. Used by permission of Pantheon Books, an imprint of the Knopf Doubleday Publishing Group, a division of Penguin Random House LLC. All rights reserved.

Excerpt(s) from THE PROPHET by Kahlil Gibran, copyright © 1923 by Kahlil Gibran and renewed 1951 by Administrators C.T.A. of Kahlil Gibran Estate and Mary G. Gibran. Used by permission of Alfred A. Knopf, an imprint of the Knopf Doubleday Publishing Group, a division of Penguin Random House LLC. All rights reserved. Any third party use of this material, outside of this publication, is prohibited. Interested parties must apply directly to Penguin Random House LLC for permission.

http://mvalmont.blogspot.com/
miriamvalmont@gmail.com

ISBN: 978-1-4834-4846-6 (sc)
ISBN: 978-1-4834-4847-3 (e)

Because of the dynamic nature of the Internet, any web addresses or links contained in this book may have changed since publication and may no longer be valid. The views expressed in this work are solely those of the author and do not necessarily reflect the views of the publisher, and the publisher hereby disclaims any responsibility for them.

Lulu Publishing Services rev. date: 07/14/2016

Contents

Dedication vii

Section 1   Part 1 xi

Chapter 1 1
Chapter 2 9
Chapter 3 16
Chapter 4 26
Chapter 5 34
Chapter 6 41
Chapter 7 51

Section 2   Part 2 61

Chapter 8 63
Chapter 9 68
Chapter 10 77
Chapter 11 86
Chapter 12 94
Chapter 13 105
Chapter 14 111
Chapter 15 118
Chapter 16 127
Chapter 17 132
Chapter 18 138
Chapter 19 143
Chapter 20 154
Chapter 21 161

Chapter 22 166
Chapter 23 174
Chapter 24 186
Chapter 25 192
Chapter 26 200

Section 3   Part 3 .... **215**

Chapter 27 217
Chapter 28 230
Chapter 29 240
Chapter 30 247

Author's Note 253
Acknowledgments 255
Reader's Guide 257

Dedication

In memory of Marshall Rosenberg, creator of Nonviolent Communication. Through his dedication to developing and spreading an effective communication tool, my life has been enriched in ways I never suspected were possible.

During the time described in this story, I was a newbie to Nonviolent Communication. Yet even the little I knew kept me in touch with the reasons prompting me to choose anew, every day, to continue a relationship that sometimes left me puzzled or heavyhearted. I was connected to a deep yearning I've had since childhood—to understand people of other cultures and, in this case, a person I loved who was different from me in many ways.

Marshall Rosenberg often quoted J. Rumi's poem:

"Out beyond ideas of wrongdoing and rightdoing,
there is a field. I'll meet you there.

When the soul lies down in that grass,
the world is too full to talk about.
Ideas, language, even the phrase *each other*
doesn't make any sense."

When my heart was open to Afshin, I walked with him in that field.

Author's Note:

Names of people and locations have been changed
in order to respect people's privacy

Part 1

My Tenant: The First Three Months

Chapter 1

Afshin and I had been married six months, according to an Iranian Shiite Muslim tradition. Although most couples would still see themselves as newlyweds at this point, we knew our marriage would end at midnight, as planned from the beginning. With only two hours left, I yearned to make love with Afshin one last time, knowing that this would be the single act forbidden to us in the new roles we were about to assume. When he trotted down the stairs, though, I realized it was too late. Weeks earlier we'd agreed to end our marriage with a dance. And now he was wearing his dance shoes.

Afshin turned on the CD player, and the Cajun music of Beau Soleil reverberated throughout the room. A sob erupted from him as he clasped me to his chest. I was surprised by my own calm. After composing himself, he gathered me in waltz position. We danced for a moment at half time, our bodies swaying as one. Suddenly he stepped away, and his feet started beating the full rhythm into the wood floor. I willed my feet to join his. With tears coursing past his lips, he smiled at my attempt to keep up, and I smiled back at the face I'd come to love ferociously.

Only nine months earlier Afshin's friend, Milad, answered the usual ad I had placed with the local university's housing department. He explained that his friend was not in town yet, and he was making the rental decision in Afshin's stead. After examining the room, Milad told me that Afshin could move in the following week.

Meeting Milad reawakened in me a desire to understand Iran. The images I had seen on television in 1979—thousands of fists punching through a sea of billowing black fabric, from women within who thundered "Death to America"—usually came to mind when I heard the country's name. I was shaken and wondered why they hated us. Through my new tenant I might have a chance to learn, first-hand, about the real Iran.

A week later I answered the clang of the Swiss cowbell at my front door to find a young man in well-worn jeans, an orange T-shirt molded to his chest. His sparkling eyes met mine. With a day-old beard and curly black hair, he matched my image of an Iranian man.

I invited Afshin to join me for a chat on the patio around the side of the house. We sat across from each other in the shade of tall white pines—their fragrance freshening the sweltering summer air.

"So, is this your first time in Girton?"

"No, I lived here last year with two friends. But we left for the summer, and when we came back we were not able to find a place together. They have each found rooms." A shadow of sadness passed his eyes. "I'm going to miss living with them."

"I'll be your friend." The words spilled out, surprising me. I had never before offered friendship this way to a tenant.

He glanced at me, smiling.

"You're studying mathematics?" I asked, quickly filling the silence.

"Yes, I'm a doctoral student at NYU, but I live here to be near my friends. I have to be in New York only two days a week."

I explained my usual schedule, working from eight to four-thirty at a psychiatric hospital, going to the gym four times a week, and pursuing various hobbies in the evening. Afshin told me that on days he didn't go to New York, he'd be working on his dissertation most of the time, but also playing soccer and spending time with his two friends.

"I think we'll make out fine." I rose and he sprang to his feet. When we reached the front door, he stepped ahead to open it. Normally I disliked such formalities, but his politeness, I liked.

While he lugged his suitcase upstairs to his room, I retrieved a copy of the house rules from the buffet drawer in the dining room. The rules simplified life. I had reviewed them and made adjustments over the years, as I learned from experience what had to be spelled out for students from Japan, Brazil, Indonesia, China, and other faraway places.

Afshin returned a few minutes later, and I handed the document to him. "If you're not comfortable with anything on this list, please let me know."

"This is your home and I will respect it," he said, bowing his head.

After only a few days I noticed that when Afshin wasn't doing research at the university library or teaching in New York, he often worked at the dining-room table, papers spread in front of him and pencil in hand, ready to work out a new problem. I usually preferred that my tenants study in their rooms, but I enjoyed watching Afshin at work. When he squinted at some point in the distance, scribbled his calculations, and then resumed his concentrated gaze, I felt vicarious pleasure in his discovery process.

That first Sunday Afshin cooked a large pot of chicken and rice stew, enough to last for a few meals. I tasted its fragrant aroma in the air. Three days later he prepared a spinach dish with flour and eggs. Compared to my other tenants—male students who usually ate meals requiring minimal preparation—Afshin cooked like a chef.

One day, not long after he moved in, he stood at the kitchen counter slicing onions and peppers as I cleaned around the cabinet handles. I thought it might be a good time to satisfy my curiosity.

"Afshin . . . you're a Muslim, aren't you?" I had seen the prayer rug in his room.

He turned to me with raised eyebrows. "Yes, I am."

"I've been curious about Islam for a long time, and more so lately." I hesitated, but what I had first heard in the Baptist church as a teenager still bothered me. "Is it true that Muslims think of Americans as blue-eyed devils?"

He looked surprised. After a moment he said, "America is sometimes referred to as 'The Great Satan,' but that's in reference to the government, not the citizens."

"Can you separate them?" I asked, leaning back on the counter.

"Of course," he said, with a puzzled expression. "The government often does things that citizens don't know about." He paused. "For example, do you know about Mossadegh?"

I shook my head. He explained that early in the twentieth century the British had bought the rights to Iranian oil fields from rulers who had no idea what they were selling. British companies prospered while Iranians remained in poverty.

In the fifties, however, a politician named Mossadegh was democratically elected prime minister of Iran. Mossadegh tried to regain control of the oil fields. Average Iranians finally had hopes of getting out of poverty. But then the British turned to the Americans for help—and they got it. The CIA staged a coup to overthrow Mossadegh and put the Shah back in power. Then the Shah allowed the British to take back control of the oil. Once again, Iranian laborers in the oil fields had to work and live like slaves.

The oil in the frying pan started to smoke. Afshin spun around, swept the vegetables into the pan, and stirred the spattering mixture.

"I didn't know," I said, wondering whether the story was accurate. I felt encouraged to ask more questions. "And what about women? Do they still have to keep their faces covered in public?"

His head dropped, and he shook it slowly before looking up. "No, no, no. They don't cover their faces, only their *hair*. And at home women dress the way you do here, but more feminine."

"But when it gets hot out, how can they stand to wear those big . . . uh, robes?"

"They are called *chadors*."

"They must be terribly uncomfortable. Don't women want to choose what to wear in such hot weather?"

"I never heard women complain. They were the ones who wanted the *chador* back after the Shah banned it in the 1930s. He wanted them to dress like Western women, and they resented it. They wanted to keep their cultural identity. After the ban on the *chador*, religious women never left home."

He sounded confident of his opinion. Surely many women resisted the *chador*. But, given my desire to learn more from him, I decided not to challenge him.

My hunger stirred. I took pea soup from the refrigerator and placed it in the microwave. I almost offered some to Afshin, but then remembered that it contained ham, a definite no-no for Muslims. While the soup was heating up, I watched Afshin sprinkle curry powder and pour a jar of marinara sauce over the vegetables. The sweet aroma made me salivate. I wished we shared meals, yet I was happy to simply share his company.

I grabbed a piece of whole-grain bread and carried my food into the dining room. A moment later Afshin brought his plate and settled into a chair catty-corner to my left. His eyebrows joined just above his nose in a wisp of vertical hairs.

I studied my soup deliberately: the shade of green, the bits of ham poking through the surface. I hoped he hadn't noticed me staring at him.

"Do men still have more than one wife?" I asked, turning to him again. I hoped that he'd appreciate my interest. As for me, the hunger pangs for information coming straight from the source wouldn't let me feel satisfied with the morsels he'd already shared.

Afshin put his fork down, and I caught him scowling. He took a deep breath and his dark eyes softened, but I felt uneasy. Had my questions started to feel like an interrogation?

"No," he said. "Having more than one wife is no longer well accepted although, in the villages, it still happens."

"I'm glad to hear that. But marriages are still arranged, aren't they?"

"It's true that mothers search for suitable mates for their children, but these days many people find their own." He scooped up some food, chewed quickly, swallowed, and added, "Parents must still approve."

"But isn't that limiting? My mother didn't want me to get married when I did, and yet my marriage was good."

"Maybe yours was, but look at the high divorce rate in the U.S. It's terrible," he said, his voice rising.

"Is that so bad? Is it worse than staying with someone who doesn't treat you well or doesn't love you?"

"When you marry, you make a commitment. Marriage is about devotion. I believe being devoted is the most important thing a husband can give to his wife. God requires it." He twirled spaghetti around his fork and sauce spotted the tablecloth. "I think parents can choose a mate for their child with more wisdom. I see many happy marriages in Iran. My mother was not in love at the beginning, but my father is a good and faithful husband. Her love for him grew, and thirty-three years later they are still happy together."

How refreshing to hear a man speak of devotion to a woman, and of love growing in a marriage. The men I'd dated squirmed when they heard the "m" word, and people in general mentioned "devotion" only when referring to saints or sports heroes.

I sipped the last of my soup. "You may be right. Perhaps it is a better system, but convincing American young people of that would be impossible. Besides, many girls these days are in no hurry to get married or have children."

He leaned forward with a crinkled brow. "Why not? In Iran we have the greatest respect for a mother and wife. What career can compare to it?"

"Maybe not many in Iran. I've heard that women are only allowed to work as secretaries or teachers, or in other typically female jobs."

Afshin threw his head back and laughed.

"*Where* do you get these ideas? A woman can be almost anything except a clergy person or a judge. Being a mother is still at the top of the list, but many girls today want to be scientists, doctors, or businesswomen." He glanced away, then turned back to me with a quizzical look. "May I ask *you* something?"

I nodded, wondering what was coming.

"What happened to your husband?" he asked, his voice softening.

I was touched that he wanted to know.

David. My dearest David. The scene of that morning replayed in my mind's eye.

I'm preparing the children's lunches for school when David pokes his head in the kitchen and says, "See you later, babe." I hug him, and my cheek lingers in the warmth of his neck. Then he's off to a prayer meeting with his friend Dick. I call David "the mobile minister." He's always ready to go help a person in need.

Greg, our fifteen year-old, had left for school a few minutes earlier.

I spread hummus and alfalfa sprouts inside two pitas and place one in each lunchbox. Cal and Beth still have forty-five minutes before their school bus picks them up at the end of the driveway.

A distant siren sounds. Cal rushes to the picture window, hoping to see a fire truck zoom by, but none does. After a few minutes he walks away, lips in a pout. Beth calls him into the family room to play.

I slide onto the built-in bench at the kitchen table, reach for the Bible, and begin reading chapter three in Romans. When I next check the clock, I call to the children, "The bus will be here in five minutes." Beth moans. Even after two and a half months in first grade, she still wants to stay home with me. I open the door and, after kissing each of them goodbye, I notice turbulent gray clouds and a ground cover of red, orange, and yellow leaves.

Back inside I kneel next to the sofa and have just begun sorting a pile of magazines when a knock startles me. What on earth is David's mom doing here? Even though she lives next door, she rarely drops in. She stands immobile, paler than I've ever seen her.

"What's the matter, Mom?" I ask with concern, assuming something has happened to my father-in-law, who is eighty-one.

"You better sit down, honey," she says as she takes my arm and leads me to the sofa.

I sit down, feeling ready for news about Grandpop.

She slips an arm around me. "A policeman just came to tell us . . . David's gone to heaven," she says, her voice weak.

I gape at the clock—the strongest urge to slap the hands back runs through me. "David? No, it can't be. He just left."

In the distance her voice continues, "The police think that someone failed to make a stop, and David's truck slammed into a telephone pole when he tried to avoid them. It happened just down the road." She's quiet for a moment. Then, without letting go of my hand, she stands. "Come," she says. "Let's go see Dad."

Three days later I stand behind the pulpit of the church David and I have attended for eleven years. Greg, Cal, and Beth sit in the front pew between me and Grandmom and Grandpop. I can still hear Beth's cry upon learning of David's death, and an ache spreads through my chest. I haven't seen Greg or Cal cry yet. They're staring at the closed casket. How are they feeling? Our eyes meet, and they send me a pale smile. Behind them people are pressed into pews like participants at an old-fashioned revival meeting. In the back, the standing crowd overflows out the doors.

I'm amazed at my own calm. Will people think I didn't love David? How appearances can lie. I open the thick, well-worn Bible to the book of Ephesians and read, "Husbands, love your wives, just as Christ also loved the church and gave himself up for her . . . so husbands ought also to love their own wives as their own bodies." I close the Bible. "This is how David loved me. I have been blessed."

In the days that follow I don't eat; I pick at food. I don't go to sleep at bedtime; I stay up for hours after the children are in bed and read from <u>The Prophet</u> *by Khalil Gibran. I read,*

> *"But if in your fear you would seek only*
> *love's peace and love's pleasure,*
> *Then it is better for you that you cover*
> *your nakedness and walk out of love's*
> *threshing-floor,*
> *Into the seasonless world where you*
> *shall laugh, but not all of your laughter,*
> *and weep, but not all of your tears."*

I read it again and again, and pencil beneath it: I want to know ALL of love.

"My husband?" My eyes focused back on Afshin. "David died sixteen years ago in a car accident."

He shuddered and glanced away. "I'm sorry."

"It's OK," I said, starting to put my hand on his arm, but catching myself. "David was a wonderful husband and . . . my best friend. His death was my worst fear coming to pass. Yet the way we lived prepared me to bear that loss. Knowing of his strong faith in God and an afterlife comforted me." I took a deep breath. "I've always made the best of difficult situations. And of course, our three children kept me busy."

"You have *three*?" His brow lifted.

I understood his surprise—he'd met only Beth, who still lived at home—although one would hardly know it since she was usually at work or hanging out at her boyfriend's house.

"Yes, I also have one son, Calvin, who lives here in town, and another, Greg, in Florida." I walked over to a collage of family photos on the wall. "This is Greg, the oldest, and here's David. Greg's a good blend of the two of us, with his fair features and curly hair." I touched another picture. "Cal is now twenty-four, a year older than Beth."

He came closer and examined the pictures.

"Calvin and Beth don't resemble you."

Indeed, their caramel complexions and straight black hair didn't match my coloring. "That's because we adopted them in Guatemala when they were babies."

I pointed to a towheaded toddler, "That's my grandson, Jacob."

"What!" Afshin stepped back and scanned my face. "You don't look old enough to have a grandson."

His surprise pleased me, though I'd grown used to that reaction from people.

"I guess eating a good diet and exercising pay off," I said, looking at him with a self-satisfied smile. "Well, I better get going. It's time for my French group."

"You speak French?" His eyes lit up. "It's a beautiful language."

"I grew up in Belgium, speaking French. And I used to teach it before I decided to become a nutritionist. At times I wish I'd stayed in teaching. I miss those summers off."

"Why did you stop?"

"Nutrition seemed like a more practical field. In this country, people rarely use French, but everybody has to eat. I also thought I could help people more by being a nutritionist, since what we eat is extremely important to our health."

"Do you think I eat well?" he asked, a glint in his eyes.

"Mostly. I never see you eat sweets, but you do drink a lot of Coke." I tilted my head and peered at him from the corner of my eye.

"Oh, it tastes so delicious," he said, stepping back toward the table and picking up his glass. He gulped down the rest with eyes closed, smiling his pleasure.

I raised my hand in a goodbye. "I better go or I'll be late."

As I pedaled my bicycle toward my French group with extra vigor, I smiled. My desire to learn about the real Iran would be fulfilled, and I wasn't the only curious one. Though my tenant didn't pepper me with questions about the U.S., he did ask a lot of questions—about me.

Chapter 2

Sunday afternoon, I rode my bike to the local orchard where I picked a half-bushel of apples. The scent of apples signaled autumn's arrival. On the way home, I stopped to borrow a video from the library.

"You are watching a movie tonight?" Afshin asked, as I set the video on the table.

"Yes, *Double Happiness*. Would you like to see it? A friend recommended it."

He picked up the case and read the synopsis on the back. "Maybe."

Around nine o'clock I called up the staircase, inviting him to join me. He came down right away and followed me to the family room. We sat at opposite ends of the contemporary sofa, and I started the movie. Usually I'd dim the lights, but that night I decided to keep the room bright.

A few minutes into the movie, a young Chinese-American woman and her boyfriend undressed and had sex. I grew uneasy as I imagined Afshin's probable embarrassment at watching this scene with me.

He got up. "Thank you for inviting me, but I'm going back to study."

I continued watching the movie, though I kept wondering why he'd left. After the movie ended, I walked up the short staircase to the dining room, where Afshin sat with his books.

"Did you like it?" he asked. His question was simple, but through the filter of my worry, I heard, *Did you actually like that shallow movie?*

"It was all right," I said. "I wanted to see how the differences between the Chinese parents and their Americanized daughter would get worked out."

"Hmm," he muttered, returning to his math scribbles.

Though my explanation was true, I realized I was emphasizing my interest in cultural differences in the hope that he wouldn't judge me as immoral and want to keep his distance.

I climbed the steps toward my bedroom and shut the door behind me. After dropping into my favorite chair in the corner, I spotted *Happiness Is a Choice* in a stack of books beside the bed. I reached for it and glanced at passages I'd marked. Barry Kaufman wrote that we had control over our feelings. That seemed right. I didn't have to let Afshin's reaction to the movie get me down. Even if he thought it was immoral to watch a movie with sex, I doubted our talks—almost nightly by now—would stop. Afshin clearly made time for them.

※

While the oatmeal cooked, I took my three-ring notebook from the credenza and opened it to a section I'd titled "Gratefulness." I wrote:

73. I'm grateful I've learned how to change my attitude in unpleasant situations.

74. I'm grateful Afshin helped me fix the drawer of my filing cabinet when he saw me struggling with it.

Afshin came down and, after putting the teakettle on, brought bread and cheddar cheese to the table.

"I'm going to visit friends in Boston for a few days," he said.

"Who will I talk to?" I threw my hands up in mock exaggeration.

He grinned. "Yes, I know. I will miss you, too."

He can express his feelings! I thought. *What a sweet soul. If only he were older . . .*

※

After six years of working as a nutritionist at a psychiatric hospital, I moved through my days there with ease. In the morning, I retrieved my list of patients from the printer and read the reasons they needed nutrition consultations. On that September day, I had four diabetics, one vegetarian, one anorectic, and one elderly person refusing to eat.

I loved talking to patients and listening to their stories. Again and again they expressed appreciation for an attentive ear, and I was gratified to provide it. In fact, providing nutritional advice felt secondary.

The day flew by and I drove straight home.

That evening, I was reading a Spanish edition of *Reader's Digest* in order to improve my fluency in that language when the phone rang.

The clipped "Hi" told me right way that it was Ana. My dear friend. She'd been away for most of the summer, attending one music and dance festival after another. Fortunately, I'd managed to get some time with her by joining her on a weeklong camping trip in the Adirondacks.

I was glad she was home for the fall. That meant she'd be available again for bike rides in the country or preparing dinner together and watching foreign films. We always had things to talk about—especially our relationships with men. "Well, not much is new here," I said. "Oh, wait. I gave that speech, 'Cookie Cutter People,' at Toastmasters and won a blue ribbon. I'm excited. I'm hoping I can apply experiences like this to developing presentations about self-esteem."

"Fantastic. I know how much that means to you," she said. "And what about Mark? Have you heard from him?"

Ana had been with me from the beginning of a saga that had started in January and was continuing—even though Mark and I weren't dating anymore. He'd recently started calling me again. I hoped he was finally ready for a serious relationship.

I told her I'd had dinner with Mark a few nights earlier, but he was no more ready to commit than before. Anyway, I had lots to do. Where would I find time for a relationship? Hearing my question, I realized it wasn't completely honest. Otherwise, why was I still repeating my daily affirmation about the perfect partner?

I paused. "Guess what? Remember that Iranian I mentioned? He is *so* nice—and funny and very smart. We talk almost every night. Right now he's in Boston for a few days, and I actually miss him."

The background noise, of dishes being washed, stopped. "Could he be the one?"

"Are you kidding? He's twenty-five years old."

"Too bad," she said. "That *is* a bit young."

We made a date for a twenty-two mile bike ride before saying goodnight.

Two days later, when Ana and I rolled into the driveway on our bikes, I saw Afshin's car there.

He greeted me with a slow nod and a smile. "I missed this home," he said, in a soft tone. He rummaged through his backpack and handed me a cassette tape. "This is for you—Persian music."

A while later, I found myself still smiling.

The following morning I sliced half a banana on top of my Cheerios. After folding the extra banana skin over the other half, I placed it on Afshin's shelf in the refrigerator. The outdated clothes he wore, the car he drove, and the type of food he ate made me think he didn't have much money. I wanted to let him know I cared, even in this small way. Every other time I'd done this, the banana had disappeared by evening.

"Thank you very much for the banana," Afshin said when I saw him later that morning. "In Iran, we used to save for a month to buy a banana for each person." He smiled. "When I came here, I stuffed myself with bananas and then had problems—you can imagine..."

Knowing of the constipating effect of bananas, my smile widened.

He smiled back at me. "But I didn't care."

A couple of days later, I went to the gym right from work. I rode the exercise bike for twenty-five minutes and then headed for the weight room. Intermittent grunts erupted from the five men lifting free weights and using the machines. I lifted two fifteen-pound dumbbells and stood in front of the mirrored wall, watching my biceps form well-defined bulges. Not bad for a fifty-one-year old.

I drove home rejuvenated and bounced into the house. Afshin nodded hello from the dining-room table and, as I walked past him on my way to the kitchen, I saw him drawing an unusual shape. What strange math, I thought.

I ate my dinner of brown rice and beans at the far end of the table so I wouldn't disturb him. Through the picture window, I took in the last of the summer foliage on the dogwood and maples. How I loved my neighborhood—quiet and populated with smart, friendly people.

Selling my house in Allentown eight years earlier so I could buy one in Girton had been one of the best decisions of my life.

I fell in love with Girton the first time I saw it. The tree-lined streets, the university atmosphere, the people from all parts of the world, and the magnificent houses whose architecture spanned three centuries all whispered, "Come live here. This is where you belong."

Realizing I could earn the extra money by renting out a room, I'd given up a mortgage-free home to live in my dream town even though it meant taking on a new thirty-year mortgage. After the closing on the bi-level built in the 1950s, my realtor said, "I've never seen a single woman on a limited income buy a house so calmly." I stood taller.

Afshin looked up from his work. "May I teach you some math for a few minutes?"

"Math . . . uh, why?"

"We mathematicians don't have to have reasons." He grinned.

"Sure. Why not?" I pulled my chair close to his.

He stepped briskly to the credenza drawer where I kept scrap paper, and he pulled out a few sheets. Sitting back down, he rested his chin on his fist and gazed toward the ceiling for a few seconds. I found myself staring at his profile: thick eyebrows, a sturdy straight nose, and a lower lip curling above a rounded chin.

He sketched a triangle, a rectangle, a circle, and an oval. "I love geometry," he said. "It's the reason I became interested in math." He pointed his pen at the shapes. "What do you know about these?"

"They're two-dimensional figures?"

"That's right," he said and then drew a few three-dimensional figures. "These are called Platonic bodies." He wrote a simple algebraic formula. "Go ahead. Can you solve this?"

I didn't want to appear stupid. My mind dug back thirty-five years to high-school algebra and, to my surprise, the process resurfaced. My grip on the pencil relaxed.

"Very good," he said. "Now see, you can apply this one formula to figure out the total surface of all the shapes."

"I wish you'd been my teacher in high school. Algebra wasn't my favorite, but I loved geometry."

He raised his eyebrows, looking pleasantly surprised.

"Do you know about the fourth dimension?" he asked.

"Time?"

"Wow! And do you know how Einstein showed it?"

I shook my head.

"He said that Time and Space are not absolute, but relative to the observer and the object being observed. We cannot go as fast as the speed of light. The more we try, the more distorted we appear to the outside observer." My puzzlement must have shown, because he added, "I will show you with this picture."

He sketched a train and a man standing on a platform. I had seen the picture before in a textbook. I listened to Afshin with all the focus I could muster, but when he glanced up with a questioning look, I told him I needed further explanation. He provided it, more deliberately, sketching again as he talked. His enthusiasm, combined with his Persian accent, delighted me.

"This is interesting, but it sounds more like physics than math," I said.

"The two are married."

I grasped only part of the concept, but I loved the way Afshin taught it. "I love learning this, and you're a good teacher."

Afshin leaned back with an expression of satisfaction. I glanced at my watch. More than a half hour had passed, and I had no desire to stop.

"When did you realize you wanted to be a mathematician?"

"In high school. My father wanted me to be an engineer, but my mother stood by me when I chose math."

"What made you come to the United States for a Ph.D.?"

"Two American professors who came to visit our university. I was impressed by their knowledge of math. One of them visited my home. He dressed in jeans and talked to everyone as equals. I liked that. Two years later, I applied to a few universities here. When I received a letter of acceptance, I danced *so* hard." His face glowed with the memory, but then gradually grew somber. "My best friends, Javad and Milad, came here a year before I did. That was a terrible year for me." He spoke as though he still carried the pain.

"You missed them?"

He gave a sharp, short nod.

He clearly didn't want to linger on this topic. After a moment, I asked, "Tell me . . . when you first came here, what did you think of the way women dress?" I wondered whether he'd been shocked.

His face brightened. "Oh . . . the girls here are so beautiful. To see girls without *chadors* was heaven."

"Beautiful enough to make you stay here after you get your Ph.D.?"

"Oh, no. My dream is to teach at a small university in Iran, and make their math department the best in the country. I hope that someday students will not have to come here to study math." With two fingers, he drummed his lips for a few seconds, and then asked, "Would you come teach English in Iran someday?"

"I'd love to, but I don't know how I'd get enough time off from my job."

"It won't be for a few years. First, I have to teach in Tehran for two years, and then it will take a while before I could make the arrangements for you to come. By then, maybe you can retire."

Retire! How old did he think I was?

That night I pulled the covers to my chin as the autumn air wafted in through the window above my bed. How exciting it would be to teach in Iran. Afshin had spoken of the high standard he had for teachers, so I took his invitation as a compliment.

Images of Afshin teaching me math waltzed by as I drifted into sleep. I dreamed that I reached for his hand and led him in another dance—a dance in which *I* was the teacher.

Chapter 3

Saturday morning, after cleaning my room, I had carried the vacuum cleaner down only a few stairs before Afshin came rushing toward me from the dining room.

"It's too heavy for you," he said, trying to take it from my grasp.

"Thank you. I appreciate your offer, but if I'm able to do something, I'd rather do it myself."

He shook his head and compressed his lips. "My mother would let me help."

Mother! But moments later, reality tapped me on the shoulder: *Excuse me, but remember the age difference?* I took a deep breath and focused on that fact. A grain of gratitude sprouted as I realized that at least he'd compared me to a woman he loved.

Later I stepped outside to retrieve the empty trash cans from the curb, but they were gone. I lifted the garage door and there they stood. Afshin must have brought them in. Never had a tenant looked for ways to help me. Perhaps he'd noticed that Beth rarely helped with household chores. In fact, we hardly saw her.

It gave me an idea. I'd started painting the wood shingles on the exterior of the house. But with winter weather arriving in a few weeks, I'd never complete the job in time by myself. I'd resigned myself to the fact that I'd be able to finish only part of the house before winter. But now I had an alternative: I'd ask Afshin if he'd like to paint the rest of the house. He could earn extra money, and I could get the help I needed.

That evening we came out of our respective bedrooms and arrived at the top of the stairs at the same moment. Afshin gestured for me to go ahead.

I hesitated a moment. "Would you like to earn money by painting the outside of the house?"

The Bird and The Fish

"I will do it for nothing." He sounded as though the thought of getting paid repulsed him. "Would you pay your son?"

How sweet. Was he an angel in disguise visiting my home?

"For a big job like that, yes. I want to be fair. I accept help with little things, but I don't want my children to feel obliged to help with larger projects."

"You're their mother!" he said with a tone of indignation I hadn't heard from him before. "They should help for nothing."

In the days that followed, Afshin painted the shingles on the back of the house. I didn't get a chance to see his work the first couple of times he painted, but one day when I came home from work early, I walked around to the side of the house. There he was, teetering near the top of the ladder, brushing paint with gusto. His once white T-shirt, the windowsills, and the plants below were spattered with maroon dots.

"How do you like it?" he asked with obvious pride.

"The shingles look great." My eyes fixated on the polka-dotted air conditioning unit. "But did you notice that paint is also landing everywhere else?"

He climbed down, leaving a series of maroon handprints beside the rungs. I'd always prided myself on how neatly I painted, and yet I wasn't perturbed by Afshin's sloppiness. He worked with such enthusiasm—and for me.

He scanned his artwork on the ladder. "Don't worry. I will wash it. Would you paint with me tomorrow?"

"Sure," I said, jumping at the chance to be with him.

※

The next morning, after breakfast, I pulled on a raggedy pair of jeans and a sweatshirt marked with paint from the past twenty years. Afshin followed me to the garage, and we gathered our equipment. Soon I was busy painting the trim while he continued with the shingles. The rectangular backyard was bordered by tall spruce on two sides and Norway maples in the back. From the cloudless sky, the sun's gentle rays warmed us through the crisp October air.

I glanced at Afshin now and then. When our eyes met they sparked a mutual smile.

I lifted the ancient ten-foot wooden ladder to reach the second-floor windows, and Afshin darted over. "No, no, no. Let me move it." He picked it up with ease, set it where I indicated, and held it steady as I climbed to the top. A moment later I felt him holding my ankles.

"Please be careful," he admonished.

I heard concern in his voice. Although I prided myself on being independent, I had to admit I liked having someone who wouldn't let me do everything for myself. I felt protected, like a child who does not yet have to worry about the burdens of life.

As I painted, I remembered that in the evening I planned to attend a monthly dinner held by a of Baha'i group in a private home. Usually about seventy people attended, many of them Iranians who had fled Iran after enduring religious persecution. Their prophet, Baha'u'llah, had revealed his message from God in the mid-19th century. He is considered a heretic by Muslims who believe that Mohammed was "the seal of the prophets," that is, the last prophet.

Non-Baha'i guests, including me, attended because we enjoyed the discussions. For me there was also a special connection with my grandmother, who had been one of the first Baha'i converts in Antwerp while in her seventies. That was my *Bonne-Maman*—never too old to try something new if it reflected her values: equality for the sexes, universal education, and world peace.

As I rinsed out the paintbrushes in the kitchen sink, I realized the dinner would be a great opportunity for Afshin to get to know Baha'is and see them as human beings, rather than as "heretics." I doubted he'd had a chance to socialize with any Baha'is in Iran.

Just then he came in and poured himself a tall glass of Coke.

"Tonight I'm going to a dinner with a group of Iranians, including some Baha'is. Would you like to go with me?" I feared he'd decline the invitation. "They'll serve lots of delicious Persian food," I added, hoping to sway him.

"I have no interest in meeting Americanized Persians," he said firmly. "I have nothing in common with Persians who left when we had our revolution. I would rather spend time with you."

With me? So, the feeling is mutual. My heart smiled.

"Please come. I think you'd enjoy it." I wanted him to meet—and maybe even like—these "forbidden Persians." Since childhood I had nurtured a dream of seeing people from dissimilar backgrounds connect, in spite of their differences.

He thought for a moment. "All right. I will go. But only because you ask." I wanted to throw my arms around him.

When it was time to leave that evening, Afshin was waiting near the front door. The black and white pin-striped shirt he wore, with black pants, looked thin from many washings, but he had the stature of a prince. He bowed slightly from the waist as our eyes met. My heart fluttered; I was nineteen again, watching Omar Sharif in *Dr. Zhivago.*

I drove. Twenty minutes later we parked near a new two-story mansion. We entered through a double doorway of carved mahogany, flanked by columns. In the foyer, where two winding staircases led upstairs, Mr. and Mrs. Asadpour greeted us warmly.

"This is Afshin, a student from Iran who's living at my house until May."

They switched to Persian, and I stepped away so they could talk freely.

I wound my way through pods of chattering guests in the long dining room and adjacent open kitchen. I found the snack table and picked up some cruditées, crackers, and cheese, and then meandered with ease, greeting people I'd met at previous gatherings.

I peered through the crowd. Afshin, arms crossed against his chest, stood out like a sapphire in a box of pearls. A young man who had made a daring escape from Iran stood talking with him, hands sculpting the air.

Mrs. Asadpour announced dinner, and a line formed at the kitchen island, where the food had been laid out. Huge bowls of chicken and rice with red currants, lamb and eggplant stew, and salad waited to please our palates. I filled my plate and found a seat in the main dining room. Afshin was still engaged in conversation. Assuming he'd found common ground with his fellow Iranian, I didn't save him a place at my table. When I got up for a second helping, I spotted him seated in the second dining room.

After we finished eating, everyone gathered in the main room for the evening's talk: "The Equality of Men and Women." I caught sight of Afshin weaving his way toward me through the crowd. He darted for the empty chair next to mine. During the talk, he stared at the floor, and every couple of minutes his leg went into jackhammer mode. Was he bored with the topic? Or feeling guilty for attending a Baha'i event?

A question-and-answer period followed the talk. I was impressed by the men born in Iran who expressed how hard it was to undo the sense of superiority over women that had been instilled in them for generations. Afshin made no pretense of interest in the topic. I was relieved when that part of the evening ended.

After dessert, Afshin led the way to the front door, where Mr. Asadpour was saying goodnight to his guests.

"Please come again," he said to Afshin.

"Thank you very much," Afshin replied, sounding more polite than grateful.

"Did you enjoy yourself?" I asked as we rode home.

"No, I didn't. A Persian man wanted me to say that things in Iran are terrible. I don't agree."

"I'd hoped you would enjoy yourself."

"I have different views," he said, staring at the road.

"You mean religious views? Don't you have the same God and culture?"

"I have more in common with you." I felt his eyes on me. "Do you believe in God?"

I thought for a while. "I used to. Now I'm not so sure."

"*Please* . . . don't say that," he pleaded, as though it pained him to hear my doubt.

But I meant it.

As we rode in silence, I reflected on the changes in my beliefs over the years.

My mother and grandmother were Catholic in name only; I rarely heard them mention God. When I was seven, Bonne Maman and I started attending a tiny Methodist church where people not only talked about God, but also provided a community that demonstrated Jesus's message of love. The warmth of the community satisfied a hunger in me of which I hadn't even been aware. However, I stopped attending church when I was thirteen and moved to the States with my mother.

These were not the biggest changes in my life, however. The most significant one occurred when Mamy found a job as a waitress on a cruise liner. Because she'd be away for two weeks at a time, she had to find a place for me to live. That was how I wound up at the Baptist boarding school where I had two life-changing experiences: I was born again and I met David.

I sighed contentedly and glanced over at Afshin. He was staring into the night.

David's mother and minister father had welcomed me into their home and church. I found affection there that I hadn't known in my own family. No wonder I gravitated to the whole package offered by David.

For most of our fifteen years of marriage we lived a sheltered life, following Christianity as we thought Jesus wanted us to. We even gave away our television and stopped reading newspapers. We had more important things to do—like saving the world. Looking back, I wish we'd stayed more in touch with the world we wanted to save.

Even so, I started questioning the Baptist "one-way-to-heaven" doctrine, and after David's death I cut the cord to the community that had been a haven of security. Two months after David died, I told his mother that the children and I would no longer attend her church.

She told me that I had always been a doubter. If, by "doubter," she meant that I had always wanted to examine the beliefs on which I based my life, then she was right. Doubt was the trowel I used to unearth the pieces of spiritual pottery I hoped would someday hold my faith. I wished she could understand the importance of doubting, but I never heard her question her beliefs.

I had to trust my mind, as well as my heart—how could I ignore it? In the years that followed, I devoured books that explored life's questions, but I relished my freedom from the rules of religions instituted by men. And now here I was, brought face-to-face by my heart with a firm believer in Allah and his rules.

As I turned into our street, the car clock showed 9:49. I wasn't tired and hoped that Afshin would be willing to stay up for conversation. His background intrigued me. He had been shaped, not only by an ancient civilization, but also, from early boyhood, by a major revolution.

"Would you like a cup of tea?" Afshin asked as soon as we stepped into the house.

"Oh, yes, thank you," I said, grateful to have a wish granted before I could even voice it.

He filled the kettle with exactly two mugs' worth of water and flashed a smile at me. He knew I'd be pleased that he didn't waste water.

We stood near the stove, facing each other with our arms crossed, waiting for the kettle's whistle. The ceiling light cast a shadow beneath his lower lip, setting it off from his chin, chiseled with a shallow cleft. His eyes were pensive; I waited for him to express his thoughts.

"That guy at the dinner said that news censoring in Iran is wrong. I don't agree," Afshin said, his voice brittle.

What could I say? For me, freedom of expression was like water to a fish. "That's a tough topic. I don't like some people's ideas, but I prefer letting them share their opinions over censorship."

"Most people don't have the wisdom to express what is good. I've seen TV programs here that are terrible for the mind. How can parents allow children to watch these?" He shook his head.

"I don't know. David and I used to control what our children watched, but we finally gave away our television. We worried that even a few good programs weren't worth the risk of exposing the children to the rest."

"So you see my point—it has to be controlled." He took a deep breath and leaned back against the counter. "Our religious leaders have more wisdom than the people, and they can decide what is good for us. We are like children. We need their guidance."

"That might be fine if the leaders are truly wise, but I wouldn't want to give up my freedom of choice, even to people who supposedly know what's good for me. What if they're wrong?"

He squinted in thought for a second. "Isn't it better to take *that* chance?"

"I wouldn't risk it." Afshin's question seemed logical enough, but didn't he see the danger in giving away his power of choice to another human being?

With the limited vantage point he'd had in Iran, I could understand how he'd formed his opinion. But I couldn't pretend to agree with it, although part of me wanted to—for a closer connection with him. Did I really need to? His strong desire for a society that protected its citizens resonated with my yearning for one that truly valued the well-being of each member.

We carried our cups to the dining room, and Afshin pulled out the captain's chair for himself. I'd noticed how he gravitated to it. Was it the unconscious act of a man who grew up in a place where men were in charge?

In the dark window I saw our reflection under the warm glow of the Tiffany shade. I realized that neighbors walking their dogs could see us sitting inside. I wasn't in the mood to share the moment with passers-by. I drew the drapes.

"So," I asked, "with all that censorship, what were you taught in school?"

"We had classes in math, science, Persian, and English," he said, holding up a finger for each. "Also Arabic and, of course, religion." At the mention of these last two, his face scrunched in distaste. He crossed his arms and stared at the table. "Every morning at the entrance to our school we had to walk over an American flag painted on the floor and shout, '*Marg bar Amrika!*'—'Death to America!'"

"That's harsh!"

"Yes, but after years of having the Russians, the British, and then the Americans telling us how to run our country, our new leaders wanted to make sure we would never again allow another government to control us."

"I'd want to find a kinder way to do that."

"You are so American," he said, with a chuckle.

"Wait a minute! Didn't you just say that we try to tell other countries what to do?"

"Your government, not you. Not the people."

Ah, yes. That distinction made by me and, according to Afshin, by many Iranians. But didn't he know that many Americans still identified with their government? For Americans who had had it drummed into them since their first history class, that the government of the U.S. had been created by the people and for the people, there was little distinction.

He added another teaspoon of sugar to the three he'd already stirred into his tea, and I held back my warning about the harmful effects of sugar.

"So even though your leaders tried to make you hate America, it doesn't sound as though they succeeded."

"No. Our opinions came after we received news from family living in the U.S. and from American movies. When I first came to New York, I was shocked to see people living on the street. I thought everybody here would be rich." He massaged his mustache with his thumb and forefinger.

"That's a common misconception. I had a funny idea, too, when I first came here. When my ship docked in New York City, I started looking for cowboys in the streets. Can you believe it?" I was happy that I could share an immigrant experience—though hugely different from his. In fact, he wasn't an immigrant; he didn't intend to stay.

It was getting late, but I was entranced by learning about his experiences and—well, by him.

"After high school was it difficult to be admitted to a university?" I asked.

"To a free university, yes. I had to take a big exam we call the *concours*. Thank God, I passed." He glanced toward heaven for a second.

"I'll bet you did more than just pass," I said, shaking a finger at him.

He lowered his eyes. "I placed forty-first in the country."

"You were accepted, of course."

He nodded.

"How do universities there compare to the ones here?"

"University in Iran is nothing like here. We had to sleep eight in a room. And the food! It was not different from prison food. But the worst thing was that we had almost no books. We were hungry to learn, but how could we?" His hands curled into fists. "Students here are in heaven, but they don't realize it."

"We *are* fortunate." It bothered me that we had so much, compared to others.

"Our universities were closed for a while after the revolution. Then we had the war with Iraq, and even boys went to defend the country. Our knowledge fell behind." His face turned solemn.

I cradled my head in my palms. "I remember the war, but not why Saddam attacked you."

"He wanted control of Shatt al-Arab, a river going to the Persian Gulf in southwest Iran." Afshin sketched an outline of Iran on a napkin and pointed to the river.

"To go to war right after the revolution must have been hard for people."

"Yes, it was terrible, but we *had* to defend ourselves."

"Of course. And yet, after eight years of war there wasn't a real winner, was there?"

"No, but if the U.S. hadn't helped Saddam, we would have beat them." He spat out the last words.

"The Americans hated Khomeini after the hostage situation," I said, wanting him to have a little understanding of U.S. support for Iraq.

"You can hate Khomeini, but that's no reason to shoot down an Iranian plane and kill two hundred ninety people, including more than sixty children."

"What?"

He stared at me. "You don't remember? It was a regular flight traveling from Iran to Dubai."

"I can't be sure. Tell me."

He shook his head for a moment and let out an exasperated throaty growl.

"It happened in 1988, near the end of the war with Iraq. The U.S. said it was an accident, but it was not. They knew they were shooting down a commercial plane. The American ship that sent the missile was in Iranian waters, but the captain lied and said it wasn't. Later he admitted that it was."

"I can't believe it. Why would he shoot at a commercial plane?"

"I did not make up this story," he said, flattening his palm on the table in front of me. "We can go to the library. I will show you on the internet."

"All right."

Even though I didn't sense that Afshin was blaming me for the actions of my government, I wanted to leave war behind us and end the evening on a lighter note.

"Could we switch to another topic?" I asked. He nodded faintly. "What about the universities? When did they open again?"

He glanced away before responding. "In 1982," he finally said. "But they had few professors because most had left the country after the revolution." He paused again. "How could they leave us?" he snapped. "I respect those who stayed. They had courage."

"Maybe the others were afraid they wouldn't be allowed to teach freely."

"That's *not* a reason to leave your country," he said, smacking his fist into his palm.

Though I understood that he'd wanted professors to stay and help build the new Islamic Republic, it disturbed me that Afshin showed no compassion for those who left. I imagined they had fled under duress.

The silence was a third presence.

Like a driver avoiding the next pothole, I diverted the conversation again. "Does your government pay for your tuition here?"

"No. I earn it by teaching," he said, a trail of anger in his tone.

The urge to drop my head on my arms alerted me that it was time to stop. "I've enjoyed our conversation very much, but I better say goodnight," I said, getting up slowly.

"I liked painting with you today," Afshin said softly, as I started up the steps.

His eyes held mine and I flushed. Why did he look at me that way?

Closing the door behind me, I perched on the edge of my bed. *Could he possibly be attracted to me? What! Am I crazy?* I thought. *I'm twice his age.*

Chapter 4

I woke up cold and dragged myself to my knees so I could reach the open window above the headboard and close it. The somber sky drove me back between the cozy flannel sheets. Dry leaves, like cupped brown hands, drifted by the windows. How sweet it would be to wake up next to someone I loved.

I remembered the day Mark had phoned, back in April, to say that we had to stop seeing each other. He wasn't ready for a serious relationship—even though I was a wonderful woman, he added. Since David's death I had grown tired of trying one relationship after another, only to have each one end, either by my choice or someone else's. I was ready for a mutual, wholehearted commitment.

I lingered in the warm bed a little longer as I recalled a conversation I'd had with Ana a month after the breakup with Mark. Would the prediction she'd made—"You'll soon be with a man of substance"—actually come to pass? Ever since that conversation, I had often repeated to myself, "In six months I'll be in a relationship with a warm, loving, affectionate, intelligent, interesting, down-to-earth, honest, humorous, sexy, passionate man who has depth to his soul." I wondered whether I was asking for too much, but I chased the thought away. Why ruin a good affirmation?

Yet that Sunday morning as I lay in bed, the affirmation didn't bring the same relief it had provided five months earlier. I bunched up my pillow and turned on my side. My knees came up automatically. No. Feeling sorry for myself wouldn't help. I swung my legs to the floor and reached for the phone. Ana answered and I asked her if she'd like to go dancing that night. She agreed. We both enjoyed swing dancing, and we weren't required to bring a partner.

That night Ana arrived around eight, and we hugged at the door. Her curly chestnut hair reached just below her earlobes and flared out like a crinoline skirt, framing an attractive face with dark eyebrows, a Roman nose, generous lips, and a square chin. Her eyes carried a lingering sadness, masked by her vivaciousness.

"How've you been? Sorry I'm late. Ready to dance?" she asked, her words spilling forth in a high pitch.

We started out the door, but I stopped and backed up two steps. "Afshin, I'd ask you to go with us, but you don't dance, do you?"

He leaned back in his chair, smiling, but didn't answer.

When I came home later, Middle Eastern music was flowing from the house. I stepped inside and there was Afshin, arms extended to either side, palms up, while he vibrated alternating shoulders back and forth. I stood transfixed. He watched me with amusement before demonstrating the next move. His head darted horizontally, moving from one shoulder to the other.

"This is how we dance in my country," he said with evident pride.

"Do it again," I said, clapping. "It's amazing."

He danced with a contagious energy that left me frustrated; I wanted to join him.

"Would you like to go dancing with us next Saturday?" I asked, when he stopped. "There's a new dance spot in Philadelphia. Ana's friend, Ben, is going, too."

"Yes, I can go," he said, beaming.

Afshin going to a nightclub with me—it didn't match my mental picture of the post-revolutionary Iranian, I thought, as I got dressed the following Saturday evening. I stood in front of the mirror and wondered if the purple, scoop-neck top and the multicolored Indian skirt I wore would fit a nightclub setting. No matter. I twirled twice and caught glimpses of the flowing skirt.

On the way to the club Afshin and I rode in the back seat. With Ana and Ben in front, we could have been double-dating, but I reminded myself that the man next to me probably felt as though he were out with his mother. Thirty minutes later, as we pulled into the parking lot, I recognized our destination: the old paper factory had been renovated as a club.

I hadn't gone to a nightclub in at least thirty years. I suddenly realized I felt uneasy and made up my mind to try and enjoy myself anyway. As we walked into the hall, music slammed my ears. People covered the dance floor, while on the periphery, men and women stood sipping drinks. I wondered whether the sight of so many people drinking alcohol would make Afshin want to leave, but when I glanced at him I saw the hint of a smile and a raised eyebrow. Apparently he felt amused and curious, rather than uncomfortable.

Ana gave me a little wave as she and Ben found a space among the dancers. I glanced at Afshin standing near me. Like a new swimmer standing at the edge of a pool, he watched people dancing. I hesitated. Then, finding the beat, my feet pulled me into the sea of swaying bodies. A few seconds later Afshin joined me. He danced like a regular—a regular who'd had two cups of coffee. His exuberance was contagious. The song ended and, barely pausing, the band played on. We continued dancing, never touching. I respected the distance he kept, yet I could feel the magnetism his body exerted.

I leaned toward his ear. "Are you having a good time?" My question wasn't necessary; his broad smile, sparkling eyes, and vigorous easy movements had already spoken for him.

Suddenly he turned his palms up and started shaking his shoulders, Iranian style, as he had shown me the week before. As he moved his head from side to side, I caught furtive glances from fellow dancers. A few stared, wide-eyed.

I was not bothered. Finally, here was a man who wasn't self-conscious.

I tried imitating him, but my neck moved only an inch in either direction, and when I tried shaking only my shoulders, like Afshin, my whole torso followed. Oh, well. I gave up on Iranian dance moves; it was time to walk like an Egyptian. I bent one arm in front of my chest; the other, behind my hip. Afshin burst out laughing.

The music stopped again, but neither of us made a move to leave the dance floor. We stood smiling at each other, like two teens at their first dance.

The band played a slow tune, and we made flowing motions with our arms while swaying our hips. Perspiration had dyed Afshin's royal-blue polo shirt a new shade of navy, and sweat streamed down his face. The soles of my feet ached, and my toes were being tortured by my shoes, but I couldn't stop. Afshin moved his body with confidence while gazing steadily at me from under a tilted brow. Again I felt a magnetic pull, but I fought to repel it and stay at arm's length.

Near the end of the night a young African-American man break-danced his way toward us to the sound of rap music. The crowd cleared a path for him. When he came within ten feet of us, Afshin started to dance in the Iranian style he'd demonstrated earlier. I moved out of the way and found Ana and Ben. People formed a widening circle as the two young men danced their cultural hearts out. The music stopped and wild clapping broke out. The

African-American man and Afshin exchanged a series of fancy handshakes before Afshin sprang back toward me, his face a picture of joy.

"You're an amazing dancer," I said. "I had such fun dancing with you."

"And Miriam was afraid you didn't dance in public. Ha! What a show that was," Ana said, looking at Afshin as though he were a performer she'd come backstage to congratulate.

"That was great," said Ben, "but I'm ready to call it a night. How about you?"

We agreed and headed for the parking lot.

During the ride home, Ana glanced up to catch Afshin's eye in the rearview mirror. "Where did you learn to dance?"

"At home with my mother and sister. We often danced."

"So this was different for you—dancing in a public place?"

"I danced at weddings, but only with the men. We are not permitted to dance with women outside the home." He turned to me, looking uncomfortable. Perhaps he dreaded more questions from Ana. His fears were not unfounded; once she started exploring a topic, Ana asked numerous questions. But I'd been an unrelenting questioner, too, when I first met Afshin. Hungry to know more, I hadn't considered that he might have been tired of being asked the same questions by one person after another.

"Why is that?" she asked.

I sent him a sympathetic smile.

"We want to avoid the type of thinking that can lead to bad actions," he said, with a hint of impatience.

Guessing Ana's next question—*And did you have harmful thoughts tonight?*—I interjected, "All I know is that we had fun dancing, and I hope we can do this again soon."

Ana and Ben dropped us off at home. At the foot of the stairs, we hesitated before saying goodnight. I didn't want the night to end and hoped he felt the same. However, it was nearly two in the morning. Other evenings and other talks lay ahead.

A few evenings after the dance, I nonchalantly walked into the kitchen as Afshin was washing dishes. I noticed I had new feelings of self-consciousness around him.

He gave his plate a quick rinse and then turned to me.

"You said you would like to learn more math. Would you like a lesson tonight?"

I wondered why he would take time to teach me and could only imagine that he enjoyed my company. Ever since our night of dancing I had been on unfamiliar ground with Afshin. I was drawn to him and had to remind myself, constantly, of the difference in our ages.

"Sure. What's the topic this time?"

"You will see," he said, in a tone that promised a surprise. "Please sit down."

He hurriedly dried his hands and joined me at the dining-room table. He tore a sheet from his notepad, folded it, and ripped off a strip about a half-inch wide and eight inches long. "Would you have some tape?"

Just as I stood to get it, the phone rang.

My heart broke into a trot at the sound of Mark's voice on the line. Talking with him now and then had kept alive my hope for a relationship, although as time passed, his frequent complaints about his life had made him less attractive.

"How've you been?" I asked. For the next few minutes he rambled on about his boss's constant criticism.

I signaled to Afshin that I'd be right back. I expected an acknowledgment, but he didn't respond. A minute later, he started to get up.

"Excuse me, Mark. When you called, I was about to get a math lesson from Afshin, the student you met here in September. Could we talk later?"

"Sure. I just called to ask if you'd like to go bird-watching on Saturday. There's a stop-over in Briganteen for birds flying south. We could get some good pictures."

I was delighted. Here was the Mark I enjoyed being with. "I'd love to," I said. It sounded like a real date—for which I'd been hoping for months. "Let's talk about the details Friday evening, all right?"

When I hung up, I wore a big grin and flashed two fingers in a victory sign.

"Why are you happy?" Afshin asked.

"Well, remember Mark? You met him at my party in September. He's the man I told you about. I dated him for a while, but then he withdrew because he said he wasn't ready for a serious relationship. He just invited me to go birdwatching. Who knows? Maybe he's ready now."

Afshin frowned for a second before reminding me that he needed tape. I found a roll and brought it back to the table.

"How many sides does this have?" he asked, holding an open cylinder he'd made from the strip of paper.

"Two." *Where was this leading?*

He nodded and then carefully removed the tape. Holding it between his teeth, he twisted the strip once and then taped the ends together again. "This is a Möbius band." He handed it to me. "How many sides does it have?"

His smiling eyes alerted me. Was this a trick? I turned it over, and over again, but still came up with the same answer. "Two."

Afshin took the strip back. With a pen, he drew a cross on one side near the tape.

"Put your finger here, on the side behind the cross, and slide it along the band."

My finger traced the twisted strip. I did a double-take. My finger had reached the cross—but on the other side of the strip. How had *that* happened? I hadn't lifted my finger from the paper. I turned to Afshin for an explanation. He just grinned.

"It's a non-orientable surface. There's no left or right."

He explained a little more but I didn't understand. Usually I had no problem asking questions. This time, though, I nodded along, wanting to look as smart as I could in his eyes. My behavior amused me. After a while, I realized that Afshin had gone from giving me a math lesson to telling me about his favorite mathematicians. I didn't mind—I liked the math facts, but learning about what Afshin liked interested me more.

The next evening Afshin joined me at the dining-room table, carrying a plate of rice and chicken, along with the inevitable Coke. After a few bites he said, "I'm worried. You remember my friend Milad? The one who came here to look at the room for me?"

I nodded.

"He just gave a thousand dollars to a nun who said she was collecting money for an orphanage. He saves so carefully, but then he gives it away. I hope he will have enough left to survive when he returns to Iran."

"I'm surprised he's giving to a non-Muslim group." I couldn't imagine anyone from my former church donating to a Muslim orphanage.

"Milad has a soft heart. He gives money to anyone who needs it."

Noticing that my bowl of vegetarian chili was already half empty, I slowed the pace of my eating. I was ready to win a contest for the slowest eater.

"I have a sore throat. Maybe it's from staying up late last night," I said.

"Because you were excited about your phone call?"

I thought I detected irritation in his voice. "Maybe."

"I'm jealous." His spoon smacked the table, and I startled. "Does he care enough about you to paint your house?"

What did he mean? I was speechless.

"May I ask you two things?" His serious tone intrigued me.

"Of course."

"What do you look for in a man?"

His question surprised me. I felt self-conscious, but I spilled forth my memorized requirements. "Someone who's warm, loving, affectionate, intelligent, passionate, not materialistic, honest, spiritual, and who has a good sense of humor. How's that for a list?"

"That should not be hard to find."

"Ha! You're not a middle-aged woman living in America. All my single friends and lots of personal ads can attest to the difficulty of finding such a man. Plus, most men of my age are looking for younger women," I said, hoping he'd refute my assertion.

"Are you interested in getting married?"

"Yes. My marriage to David was good. I never felt truly loved until I met him." My voice faltered. "But what about *you*? Have you ever dated?"

"No." He paused. "You're the only woman I love in this country."

An electric sensation ran through me. My God! What does he mean? Was there a woman in Iran who he loved? He had never mentioned anyone—aside from his mother. Was he saying he loved me like a mother? But no, his gaze felt amorous. I looked away.

I stared at the brown and white swirls in the tablecloth as I struggled to respond. "You're special to me, too," I said, raising my eyes to meet his.

Afshin held my gaze for a moment with a twinkle of delight in his eyes. Without further comment, he returned to eating.

I savored our delicious exchange in the booming silence between us. He finished eating and bowed slightly before leaving the table and going to his room. Was he as stuck as I was about what to say next?

As I scrubbed the chili pot I recalled that a month earlier, after a conversation with Afshin, I'd said to Ana, "I love talking to Afshin. He gives me a new perspective on things and he's so enthusiastic. You know . . . he fits the image of the man I want. If only he were my age . . ."

Now, after what he'd just said, hope, like a freed horse, leapt from its corralled enclosure. I couldn't believe he could be attracted to me. Perhaps he'd never had the opportunity to get to know a woman outside his family as well as he'd gotten to know me. We had such a good time together—could he have fallen in love? I knew how *I* felt. I wanted to caress him and feel him thrill to newly discovered sensations. We had made love in my dreams—and my daydreams. Could these dreams become real?

After Spanish class I drove to French group. As soon as I entered the living room lined with francophiles, I made eye contact with Ana and nodded slightly toward the kitchen. She met me there, and I told her what had happened the night before.

"Who knows what he means?" I said. "He's from another culture. I could be misreading his signals."

"I doubt it. You're an attractive woman, and he's said very complimentary things to me about you. Why don't you follow your heart?"

"I'd love to. I connect with him in so many ways. But . . . he's twenty-five."

"Miriam, you always complain that men just want younger women. Now you can prove to yourself that it doesn't always have to be that way." Her eyes, open extra wide, stayed on me.

"Yes, but he's going back to Iran. That rules out a long-term relationship." I paused and lowered my voice. "You know . . . I don't think he's ever had sex."

A man who had grown up without the influence of *Playboy* magazine and a dozen preconceived ideas of what sex should be like; what a sweet experience it would be to teach him how to love a woman.

"Go for it," Ana said, eyes wide in her smiling face.

"But what about Mark?"

"He's not ready."

Chapter 5

The following night I was home alone reading. Like a banner behind a bi-plane, Afshin's words—"You're the only woman I love in this country"—fluttered through my head and kept me from concentrating on my book. Afshin had once told me that if you love someone, it's especially precious to keep the feeling to yourself and savor it. So what had made him tell me about his feelings?

The phone's ring startled me. Mark explained that rain was predicted for Saturday; we'd have to abandon our plan to go bird watching. Would I like to attend a dinner and Halloween dance, instead? I would. The new invitation sounded cozier than the original.

Although Saturday would not be our first get-together since breaking up (we'd met for coffee once), I was looking forward to a real date. My level of enthusiasm, however, had downshifted a gear or two.

The next evening, as I ironed a vintage dress for the dance, Beth came into the family room.

"Did you do something to your hair?" I asked. The style and color of her hair had been changing every couple of weeks since she started a new job at a styling salon.

"Yeah, I stayed after the shop closed, and one of the other stylists gave me a haircut and new highlights."

She stopped in front of me. I remembered a little girl with long ebony pigtails, but here she was, looking like a model in her tight-fitting black outfit and four-inch heels. Did she have any idea how stunning she looked? Men gaped when she walked by.

"What do you think, Beth?" I asked, holding up the dress. "Is this all right for a Halloween dance?"

Her face puckered. "No way! Why don't you wear the lacy black dress you bought at the church fair?"

"Are you sure? It's awfully revealing."

"Mom. It's a Halloween party. You'll be fine," she said, with a downward flick of her wrist.

"Are you staying at Mike's again tonight?"

"Uh-huh, and I'm going shopping with his sister tomorrow." She continued to her room.

Beth clearly enjoyed spending time, not only with her boyfriend, but with his whole family. Sadness wrapped my heart. Would we ever again enjoy each other's company as much as we had before she became a teenager?

Around five-thirty I heard the clang of the bell at the front door. I rushed to open it, and Mark greeted me with a self-conscious smile. As we hugged, I noticed my hands couldn't meet around his quarterback frame. Two Afshins would fit into one Mark. I looked up into smiling eyes. Closely cropped gray hair suited his round Irish face. He was warm, intelligent, and passionate. No wonder I liked this man. If only he had the self-confidence I admired in Afshin.

The self-confident one stood at the kitchen sink, washing dishes.

"Bye, Afshin. Have a good time in New York," I said, while Mark helped me with my coat.

Afshin turned and nodded at Mark without smiling—a big change from the friendly greeting he'd offered when he first met Mark soon after moving in. Was he still jealous, as he'd said a few nights before? I hoped so.

As we drove to the high school where the dance was being held, Mark kept smiling at me suggestively. We walked into a gym filled with people wearing costumes. I didn't feel out of place; my dress felt like a costume. Mark looked quite appealing in a black T-shirt and matching jeans. After eating at the potluck supper, we headed for the dance floor and found ourselves between Count Dracula with his victim, and the queen of hearts with her king.

I loved the familiar tunes, but even with Mark's firm hand on my back as we swung around, I missed the scintillating energy that had propelled me while dancing with Afshin.

After an hour and a half, Mark said, "You want to call it quits for tonight and go back to your house?"

"Sure. Let's go."

Back at the house, we carried cups of tea into the living room, and Mark followed me to the loveseat. Setting his mug on the coffee table, he swung his arm along the back of the sofa behind me. He told me he was "flammable at the sight" of me. I was still taking in the compliment when he told me that an attractive local woman had invited him to accompany her on a buying trip to South America—and he was considering accepting.

I wanted to scream. Did he think I had no feelings? If he thought I was interested in hearing about another woman while sharing a loveseat with him on a Saturday night, then I doubted he'd be able to hear anything I had to say. Ana had been right to warn me—Mark was just out of one serious relationship and not yet ready for another.

Forget it, Mark, I thought. *Last spring, you'd be all over me one moment, and pulling away the next. And now you bring up traveling with what's-her-name! I want a man who takes my feelings into consideration. Afshin would never play with a woman's emotions this way.*

I leaned forward.

Mark took his arm down from behind my shoulder. After finishing his tea, he said he was exhausted and needed to get home.

I skimmed his lips with a goodnight kiss and closed the door behind him. The lightheartedness of the early evening had vanished.

I returned to the sofa, tucked myself into its warmed corner, and pulled a fuzzy throw over my shoulders and lap. I longed for consistency. Mark's confusing messages teased my heart. Comfort would not come from Afshin; he was in New York, with Ana and her friends, watching the Halloween parade in Greenwich Village. Snuggling under the throw, I knew one thing for sure: Mark's presence drained my energy—Afshin's fed it.

***

Afshin didn't ask about my date with Mark and that was fine. Over the next few days he ate his meals whenever I had mine, and he continued to study in the dining room, even though he had a desk in his room.

Perhaps he missed his mother and saw her in me. From what I'd noticed at Baha'i dinners, Iranians are physically more affectionate than people with a Northern European background. I could be blowing Afshin's actions out of proportion. Yet, the way he looked at me made it difficult to believe.

During supper one night that week, I watched him drain a large glass of Coke and immediately refill it.

"You know, Afshin, soda is full of calories, but has no nutrition. Orange juice or water would be much better for you." I hesitated. "And with less sugar, your pimples might clear up."

His eyebrows arched and his fingertips ran back and forth across his forehead. "OK, if you quit ice cream, I'll quit Coke."

He'd noticed my weakness. "Hmm . . . I'll have to think about that." If I said yes right away, he'd know I cared for him a lot.

A couple of days later he was taking a soda bottle from the refrigerator as I came into the kitchen.

"I decided to quit ice cream," I said, sounding like an adolescent to myself.

He looked at me for a moment. "OK, this will be my last glass."

The next evening Ana and I were talking in the kitchen when the front door opened, and Afshin bounded in, carrying a grocery bag. He pulled out two quarts of ice cream in my favorite flavors—mocha chip and coffee. "You can enjoy these before you quit," he said, grinning.

I wanted to hug him. Instead, I grabbed three glass bowls from a nearby shelf.

"No, thank you. It's for you," he said, as I handed him a bowl.

"Come on—just a little."

He accepted, and I scooped ice cream into the bowls. With spoons clinking against the glass, the three of us sat around the table. I savored each mouthful.

"Would you like a little more?" I asked, seeing Afshin's empty bowl.

"No, thank you."

"Don't you like ice cream?" Ana asked.

"I do, but I don't want to get fat like some of my friends have since they came here."

"I see. You like thin," she said in a teasing tone.

He nodded emphatically.

A little smile appeared at the corners of Ana's mouth. "So how does an Iranian man find a thin woman? If you see a woman on the street in Iran, how do you know what shape is hiding under her chador?"

"We men have our ways." He leaned back in his chair, amusement dancing in his eyes. "Can you guess?"

"Do you peek in the windows of public bathhouses?" I asked.

He laughed. "No. But we *love* windy days." His eyes darted between Ana and me.

She and I looked at each other, puzzled, but two seconds later we laughed simultaneously as we envisioned wind pressing a chador against a woman's body.

"Iranian men seem so macho," said Ana.

"Macho?" He looked quizzical and then threw his head back. "Oh . . . you mean that we are real men: we don't cry."

"That's not what I was thinking. But why can't a man cry? What's wrong with crying?"

"Women cry because they're weak," he said, stating his opinion as though it were law. "Strong men don't cry."

"What?" Ana exclaimed. "I don't think so. Women cry because they're in touch with their feelings, and in my mind it's the strongest men who can express their emotions."

I cheered her on by nodding emphatically.

He stared at his empty bowl for a second. "Men should control their emotions. If they cannot, they are weak."

His certitude disturbed me.

"Afshin, are you saying that men should never cry?" I asked.

"Only for a serious reason." He paused. "And maybe not even then."

"I'm afraid that if men don't cry, they'll explode in anger or get sick," I said.

Afshin's lips tightened, and he shook his bowed head.

Ana's eyebrows shot up and she glanced at me. "Well, it's late. I better go. I have a rug design to finish."

I followed her to the door. "He sure is a typical man, isn't he?" I whispered. "But he gets me—right here," I said, knocking on my heart.

A few days later, I sat in the living room playing the flute. The lamp on the bookshelf beside me illuminated the sheet music. With ten years of practicing and playing behind me, I was able to do justice to the melodious tune, "The Duke of Kent's Waltz."

The front door squeaked on the other side of the bookcase. A second later, Afshin appeared. I rested the flute on my lap.

"Please go on," he said. "It's so beautiful."

I brought the flute to my lips, but my fingers trembled. "Some other time," I said, annoyed at my fingers for revealing my nervousness.

"I hope it's soon." He pulled an envelope out of his backpack. "My mom sent photos of the family. May I show them to you?"

He pulled a chair near mine and handed me a picture as though it were priceless porcelain. A woman with full lips and black shoulder-length hair smiled coyly at the photographer.

"That's a picture of my mother soon after I was born."

"She could be a movie star. How old was she here?"

"Twenty-six."

She and I must be the same age, I thought, after a quick calculation.

"This is a photo of me when I was a boy."

I saw a young man with a downy mustache, not a boy. The lips and expressive dark eyes he'd inherited from his mother captured me for a moment.

As Afshin held out another picture, his knee grazed mine and tingles scurried up my thigh. He went on introducing me to his grandmother, brother, and sister. I studied each one—as well as the hand holding the photos. Listening to Afshin's descriptions, I detected sadness in his voice.

In the next picture, I recognized his mother, in spite of her golden hair. She wore a long-sleeved sheer black coat over a sleeveless V-neck dress in matching black, with a red floral print. She held her head high with the air of a woman who knows she's beautiful. What a contrast to the chador-clad women I'd seen on television. A balding gray-haired man held her waist. His benign smile spelled contentment.

"That's my father," Afshin said matter-of-factly. "The photos came today, and I haven't been able to study since then. It is now three years since I've been home."

"You haven't gone back for a visit?"

"I can't afford it. And even if I could, the U.S. might not give me a visa to come back."

His eyes glistened. He shot up and marched to the kitchen.

He must feel homesick. My heart ached for him. I followed him into the kitchen and watched him scour a pot from the previous night's dinner with more effort than necessary. "May I give you a hug?" I asked tentatively.

"Yes," he murmured, turning toward me but looking down. "I have to dry my hands." With a trembling hand, he reached for the towel hanging on the side of the refrigerator.

He kept his eyes down as my arms encircled his chest. His hands lay on my back. Neither one of us stirred for a moment. Then I stepped back, my legs unsteady.

"Since you don't have family here, . . ." I began.

"I do," he insisted.

Did he think of me as family? Was this his way of saying he felt close to me?

"I care about you," I said, and a smile surfaced on his face for an instant.

How could I ask, "Am I like a mother to you?" But I didn't want to hear him say "yes," and I doubted he'd be able to say "no," even if that were the more truthful answer.

We stood for a long moment in silence.

"I have to go," I finally said, giving his arm a quick squeeze. "I'm having dinner with friends."

He raised his eyes, and they met mine with warmth.

When I came into the house three hours later, Afshin stood up from the table and gathered his papers. He said goodnight with only the briefest glance toward me before going upstairs.

My eyes lingered on the empty staircase and a sense of emptiness filled me. Was he embarrassed? Had I overstepped a boundary? Afshin would be in New York for the next two days, and I'd be away all weekend at an annual swing dance festival in the Catskills. I'd have to wait until Sunday to find out.

Chapter 6

Shortly before nine o'clock on Sunday night, I pulled in the driveway. The house was dark. I went inside and flipped a light switch. On the table a note in Afshin's handwriting read, "Welcome home." So he wasn't upset, after all. Behind the note I saw the lamb puppet I'd recently bought for my grandson. Afshin had slipped it over a vase, and its outstretched arms greeted me. I laughed out loud.

Later, sitting at the dining-room table reading *Growing Young* by Ashley Montague, I heard the rumble of Afshin's car. I sat up straight. A few seconds later Afshin appeared. His face lit up when he saw me, and I beamed back at him in delight.

He slumped into the nearby captain's chair. Seductive Yul Brynner eyes held mine for a couple of seconds. A ballet company of flutters pirouetted from my belly to my chest.

"How was your weekend?" he asked.

I was grateful for the small talk that followed. After a long pause I asked, "Was it all right for me to hug you?"

"Of course." His seductive eyes held me again.

"I was afraid you might be uncomfortable. I don't know if hugging is acceptable in your culture, but when I saw that you were homesick I felt sad."

"I wasn't homesick," he blurted, like a child caught in a forbidden activity.

Then what had made him unable to study that whole day?

He leaned forward, smiling. "So . . . are you going to take the hug back?"

Another flutter ran through me. I shook my head.

We talked until midnight. The room sparkled around us. When I finally made myself go to bed, I imagined him near me – for the night. It took a long time to fall asleep.

Two days later, a headache and the whistle of the teakettle awakened me an hour before the alarm clock. Strange. Afshin was up early. I whisked a brush through my hair and slipped into my clothes.

In the dining room, Afshin was just sitting down to breakfast. We exchanged a smile. After cooking my oatmeal just enough to make it edible, I joined him. He was making the open-faced sandwich he ate for breakfast every day. First, he cut domino-sized slices of cheddar cheese and arranged them on whole-wheat toast. Next, he plopped a heaping tablespoon of strawberry jam on top and smeared it to the edges. Though I'd seen this procedure many times, I still enjoyed watching him make the cheese fit on the bread, his love of geometry spilling over into everyday actions. He bit into the toast, took a gulp of tea, and returned his attention to the newspaper with Arabic script he'd been reading.

"That's in Persian?" I asked.

He nodded. "I'm reading about the International Mathematical Olympiad. Iran has been getting better scores every year. Many of our high-school students have won gold medals."

"You must be proud of them." I squeezed more honey onto my oatmeal. "As your family must be proud of you. They encouraged education, didn't they?"

"My father did. He made sure that we went to university." He scowled. "Our education was the only thing that concerned him about us." His lips tightened and he gazed outside.

"You sound angry."

"If we were playing ball in the street when he came home from work, he would yell at us to go study. Other fathers didn't do that."

"He may have been afraid you'd have a hard life without an education." I didn't wait for his reaction. "How about your grandparents? Were you close to them?"

"To my grandmother—my mother's mother. She's a strong woman and knows the meaning of love."

"How do you mean?" I asked, curious to hear his definition.

He poured himself another cup of tea and added four rounded teaspoons of sugar.

"When my grandfather was young, he took a second wife in another town but didn't tell my grandmother. When she found out, it broke her heart, yet she kept on loving him. He gave her a hard life in other ways, too, but she prayed that one day he would be happy at home." He stared at a point on the tablecloth and his face brightened. "It took years, but it finally happened."

"That's a happy ending but . . . I wonder. Could it be that your grandmother was afraid to leave him because she'd have no one to take care of her and the children?"

"Oh no, he was *required* to take care of them," he said, as though my concern had no basis in reality. "I admire her strength and the way she stayed with him all those difficult years. That's love."

I wondered what had made her stay, and whether *she'd* received the love she needed. Yet her story touched me. I wanted to be loved like her husband—in spite of my shortcomings. But secrets? No. "That may be love," I replied, "but his lies must have hurt her deeply. I think it's important to be truthful—otherwise love can't grow. My husband David and I talked things over, even if they were unpleasant. Our trust in each other grew, and it made our love deeper."

Afshin leaned back and nodded slowly. He was quiet for a few long seconds.

"A husband should be truthful with his wife, but my mother told me that a man should not bring his work problems home. He should do what he can to protect his wife."

I sent him a dubious look. Although I would welcome protection from physical harm, I wouldn't want my husband's problems hidden from me. David and I had been companions in solving problems, and we treasured the closeness that came from sharing hard times.

"I think it's important for partners to know each other fully," I said, kneading my aching neck. "When couples hide unpleasant parts of life to protect each other, they wind up as strangers."

"I would appreciate a wife who would try to protect *me* from pain, too. Life is hard enough. We don't have to know everything." He downed the last of his tea. "But, I agree, it's important to be honest."

We were quiet for a minute, and I flushed under his gaze.

"I was in the library last night and I missed you," he said, "so I came home, but you had gone to bed. I felt like knocking at your door."

He missed me? *Missed* me? I wanted to say, "I missed you, too," but the words met a barrier between my heart and my mouth.

"I'm glad we enjoy each other's company," I said, instead, though reducing our relationship to good cameraderie felt like making a bread pudding out of a gourmet cake.

He stared at his plate for a second but said nothing. When I didn't continue, he excused himself and cleaned up his breakfast dishes. Minutes later he left for the university.

That evening I was sitting at the dining-room table when Afshin came home. He dropped his tattered bookbag on the chair beside me and said hello.

"Hi," I replied. My greeting paled in comparison with the welcome tune played by the band marching in my heart.

He sat down and, after a moment, pulled a writing pad from his bag. He scribbled some notations. I tried refocusing on my speech but found Afshin's quiet presence distracting me as much as any baby's insistent cry.

I struggled with ideas for natural-sounding ways to start a conversation.

"At the hospital last week," I said, "we had a career development workshop. The instructor asked us to identify the four things we value most. It wasn't easy, but I decided on these: growing—emotionally, intellectually, and spiritually; being loving; passing knowledge on to others; and being compassionate. These are the things that motivate me. What about you? What four things do you value most?"

He must have thought it odd—the way I started on a topic out of the blue—but after a moment a smile spread on his lips. "Well . . . my hopes for my work, my friends, my soccer playing, and the many interesting experiences I've had. Not many boys have these chances."

"You're not a boy. You're a man."

He paused, ignoring my assertion. "I have a question for *you* now," he said. As though he sensed my anticipation, his pause stretched out like a gentle tease. Finally he spoke. "What do you think is the greatest sin?"

"Sin? I don't like that word. It reminds me of the guilt it conjures up in people. But if you're asking my opinion about what causes harm, I'd have to put dishonesty at the top of my list."

"The prophet's follower, Ali, said it was fear."

"Oh, yes. I forgot that one. Fear harms us by keeping us from doing what we really want to do in life. It's better to act out of love," I said.

He nodded. "And what do you think is the greatest treasure?"

I took more time before answering. This was important. "Peace of mind," I finally said.

He leaned back in his chair, folded his arms, and nodded again. I could tell he was pleased.

"According to Ali, it's contentment. That's the same thing, isn't it?" he asked.

"It sounds that way to me."

"And what do you think is the greatest inheritance?"

"What I've learned from my mother—to be compassionate."

He cocked his head. "For me, it's what we call politeness, but it's not exactly what your English word means. It's more a way of being kind." His eyes stayed on me; I said nothing. Though I wanted to understand Persian politeness more clearly, I could wait.

"I like your answers," he added in a lower tone. My breathing and heart rate quickened.

"What do you see as your best attributes?" I asked, trying to calm my agitation.

He didn't answer.

"You are the most considerate tenant I've ever had," I said.

"And you are an excellent person, and . . . the best landlord," he said, motionless in his chair.

I smiled to myself at his gender mix-up, but didn't correct him. I loved his mistakes.

"The landlord I had before smoked and watched television all day. She was a weak woman."

He probably meant weak in character, but I pretended to misunderstand.

"Weak?" I planted my elbow on the table. "Would you like to arm wrestle? I'll show you how strong this landlady is."

He stifled a laugh, hesitated, and clasped my hand. For a second I doubted I could muster any strength, but I took a deep breath and pressed with all my might. He resisted and without difficulty brought my arm to the table. With our hands still clasped, he curled his free hand over mine and bowed his head. A kettledrum beat throughout my body. Could he feel it in my hand? Unsure about what to do, I started to push up on his hand, but with his eyes, he stopped me. He rose from his chair and bent toward me. His lips brushed my forehead, and as I rose my arms encircled his chest. When my cheek rested against the slope of his neck, I felt his pulse beating. Afshin was trembling.

For an eternity, I stood motionless, savoring heaven.

"Let's go downstairs. Beth is staying at her friend's house tonight," I said, grateful for Beth's second home.

Afshin kept his head down for a long moment. Then, from under his brow, his eyes met mine.

On the sofa, he lifted my hand and kissed each of my fingers, then the rim of my palm and its hollow. I shuddered. He continued to my ear, neck, and cheeks. As his lips approached mine I anticipated their softness, but he pulled back and, instead, I felt their gentle pressure on my eyelids. Circling his mouth with tender kisses, I hungered for his lips, but held back. If he hadn't kissed a woman this way before, I feared scaring him off.

After a while he patted the cushion at the head of the sofa, inviting me to lie down, and we lay facing each other. His leg hooked over my thigh and drew me close. We gazed at each other in the faint moonlight. Suddenly his lips covered mine, and I melted into his embrace.

Through the nighttime stillness I heard him murmur, "I love you," so softly that I wasn't sure he meant it for my ears.

We caressed each other's faces, hands, and cheeks. I let him lead with the kisses and was reminded of my first kisses with a boy in eighth grade—tender with trepidation. Hours later, we finally sat up. "I've learned something," I said. "Age doesn't matter when there's love between two people." He said nothing. I wondered what he was thinking.

Hand-in-hand we climbed the stairs and, after a drawn-out goodnight, headed for our respective rooms.

This could complicate life, I thought. Guilt might grab him by the throat in the morning, and he might leave. If we continue, how will it end? Broken hearts? So be it. I pulled the blanket to my chin. Why stop such a sweet expression of love?

Khalil Gibran's words came to me:

"But if in your fear you would seek only love's peace and love's pleasure,

Then it is better for you that you cover your nakedness and pass out of love's threshing-floor . . ."

The next evening I went to the local playhouse, where Ana and I ushered in exchange for free viewings of performances. I trotted down the wide marble steps to the coatroom and found Ana there, stuffing her gloves and hat into the sleeve of her jacket.

"You'll never guess what!" I said, knowing that she surely could.

"What?" She grabbed my shoulders. "Don't tell me!"

"Yes. He *does* love me—and *not* as a mother. We kissed and . . . Oh, my God, I feel like, like . . . I can't even describe it." Ana looked at me expectantly. "I'll tell you more later. We better get upstairs."

When I arrived home around ten-thirty, Afshin's car was gone. Had religious guilt made him change his mind?

By the time I went to bed, he still hadn't returned. I curled up on my side and pulled the comforter to my ear. Maybe he saw me as a seductress, an American without morals. Would he pull away because he no longer felt safe around me?

I woke up early and tiptoed down the stairs to the living room. Looking outside, I saw Afshin's old Honda Civic and felt lighter, knowing he'd returned.

Before leaving for work, I scribbled a note: "Thank you for that most precious time on Tuesday night. I hope that you're feeling OK about it and, if not—that you'll tell me. OX Miriam."

I slipped the paper under his door.

In the evening I came home to find my little lamb puppet sitting on my bedroom doorknob with a note pinned to his chest. I read: "Dearest Miriam." *Dearest*, he'd said. I sighed and relaxed even more. I continued reading: "I *do* feel OK. I left some precious thing in the freezer. That's all yours. But don't finish it quickly. XXX, Afshin."

I opened the freezer and a quart of ice cream fell at my feet. I stared at it with a pleased smile before picking it up and helping myself to its smooth sweetness.

Friday evening I delivered a speech at Toastmaster's about dancing. My stomach was fluttering as I walked to the podium, but my nervousness faded as I described how dancing benefited body and soul. At the end I nodded to my assistant, and the song "Shall We Dance" from *The King and I* burst from a cassette player at his feet. I whirled around the stage with an invisible partner, and an outburst of clapping followed me back to my seat.

As soon as the meeting ended I raced home, recalling another time I had stood and spoken with passion.

The room barely holds four long tables for ten. I sit among other sixth-grade girls, but even after two months here, I don't fit in. I don't belong in this boarding house.

Madame Devroux, the owner of the home, sets two bowls of stew on our table and returns to the kitchen. We help ourselves. I take a bite but nearly gag. I hold the food in my mouth, afraid to swallow. The faces of the girls around me carry their own looks of disgust.

The next moment I stand up.

Miriam Valmont

"We need better food," I say. "Our parents pay for us to live here. Why don't we protest by eating only the bread tonight?"

The younger girls gape and the older ones grin. I sit back down, trembling, and they burst out clapping, continuing until Madame Devroux comes dashing from the kitchen. I stare at the red-and-white checked oilcloth on the table. Finally I glance up. Her hard eyes search the room for the source of the commotion, but she doesn't see and doesn't ask.

I reach for a slice of country bread and push my bowl aside. My companions follow suit and we chew in silence. The bread tastes sweet, coming after my honest words.

The glow of my bravado fades as night falls, and I get ready for bed. I pull a flannel nightgown over my head and draw a white cotton curtain along the metal rod separating my space from that of the other girls. Just as the lights go out, I slip between the sheets, but quickly draw my feet up from the biting iciness below. The darkness pushes me under the covers, and the springs beneath me creak. A sob rises from my chest and grips my throat. I tighten my lips. My body quakes and tears flow into my ear.

Closing my eyes tightly, I try to picture home. But where is home? It's not in New Orleans with my mother and her new husband. I hate him. He's the reason I'm here. But is it with Bonne Maman in Antwerp, only an hour away? No . . . she's too busy. I create my own room: a sunny room, filled with flowers—on the wallpaper, the curtains, and the bedspread. On the bed I stretch out and read my favorite children's book: The Orphans of Simitra. I am entranced by the story of a brother and sister forced to make their way in the world after losing their parents in an earthquake. Someday, I decide, I'll adopt children.

I open my eyes and the light from the streetlamp shines through the folds of the curtain. In nine more days I can visit Bonne Maman for the weekend. Then six more months until summer vacation. I'm tired of crying every night these last two months.

Thank God those days are over, I thought, as I pulled in the driveway next to Afshin's car. Since he usually walked to the train station when traveling to New York, I couldn't tell whether he was home. The house was quiet. I picked up the latest issue of Town Crier from the dining-room table and started reading. About fifteen minutes went by. Suddenly I heard Afshin's bedroom door open, and my insides buzzed. He came downstairs and joined me at the table. But rather than sitting to my left, as usual, he sat across from me. He smiled faintly and then stared at the salt and pepper shakers between us. I reached across the table and he took my hand. We remained silent as his thumb kneaded my fingers. The hum of the refrigerator grew louder.

His lips parted and closed. I waited.

"You may not want to hear what I'm going to say," he said.

I found it hard to breathe. "That's OK," I whispered.

"I cannot give you what I think you want," he said, still holding my hand but staring at the table. "I felt guilty after the other night." He looked up and my heart went out to him. "I would do anything to make you happy, but I think I should move."

A miniature forest fire in my heart spread throughout my chest. "No, don't move. I would miss you too much. We can work it out."

He didn't respond right away, and then an impish smile appeared. "Well . . . if you keep my security deposit, I *can't* move." He got up and came around to me. "Come, let's sit downstairs."

We faced each other on the green velvet sofa.

"I love you like a mother. I love you with the purest love."

A mother? . . . I gaped at him for a moment. *Then why do you look at me with bedroom eyes? Why do you say you're jealous of Mark? Or that I'm the only woman you love in this country? Is this how you talk to your mother? No, I felt your desire in our embrace the other night.* But I couldn't bring myself to say these things out loud.

His left arm pulled me closer. I took his hand and examined the veins, the long fingers with hairy patches between joints, and the nails, trimmed and clean. I loved hands, and Afshin's were perfect.

"I would marry you in a minute," he said.

I sat up with a start, but then froze. Hadn't he just said that he loved me as a mother?

"The age difference doesn't matter to me," he added. "What matters is that I have to go back to Iran."

I hadn't thought about marriage to Afshin, but of course—for him marriage was the only way he could love me the way I wanted to be loved.

"I'd rather have six months with you than thirty years in a ho-hum relationship," I said.

"Ho-hum?"

"Yes. You know, boring, not special."

His arms encircled me, and he gently brought my head to his shoulder. His face burrowed in my hair and he inhaled, as though trying to take my scent into every part of his being. Lifting my chin, he kissed the corner of my mouth.

"You wouldn't do this with your mother, would you?" I asked, trying to show him he had more feelings for me than he acknowledged.

"Of course I would," he said. "Even fathers in Islam are instructed to kiss their daughters a few times a day so they will learn to be affectionate wives."

But the kisses Afshin gave me, though not French, felt sexual rather than affectionate. I doubted he kissed his mother the way he kissed me. Perhaps without an outlet for his sexuality, he still had a young boy's attraction toward his mother. Yet, however Afshin and his mother demonstrated affection, I saw no evidence of harm. No signs of his being a "Mama's boy." At eighteen he'd happily left home for the university, and four years later, she gave her blessing when he came to the United States. She'd even told him it would be fine if he fell in love with an American girl, as long as it brought him happiness. His mother's actions didn't sound controlling, but loving; she had given him wings.

Afshin lifted a stray strand of hair from my face.

"Affection is fine, but sometimes it goes too far," I said, thinking of the many adult patients I'd known who were still dealing with the traumatic impact of sexual advances made by their fathers or mothers in their childhoods.

Afshin's eyes grew wide. "Oh, no! It's never more than kissing on the cheek."

"'Never' seems impossible," I said. "Maybe less sexual abuse takes place in Iran because of the strong religious sanctions, or maybe you never heard about it because it's a taboo subject. Years ago it wasn't mentioned here either."

"I *never* heard of anything like that in Iran," he said, his face scrunching in disgust.

"How would you act differently with a woman you'd want as your wife?" I asked.

"Passion would play a bigger role."

A bigger role? He exuded passion. His every word and movement shouted passion. I couldn't be *that* far off the mark. Could I?

Chapter 7

I was vacuuming the kitchen when two hands landed on my hips. "Afshin!" I screamed. He picked me up and carried me downstairs to the sofa. I felt like Maureen O'Hara in *The Quiet Man*, a Hollywood movie from the 1940s.

"Why can't you love me like a son?" he asked, again, as we snuggled.

I stiffened and stared at him, thinking, *Are you out of your mind?* In a way, he was. I took a deep breath. "My feelings for you are *not* the feelings of a mother for a son. Besides, I already have two sons."

He glanced at Beth's door. "Is Beth working today?"

"Yes, and I think she's staying at Mike's tonight."

He looked troubled. "Why doesn't she spend more time with you?"

"She'd rather hang out with Mike and also his sister, who's her best friend. Besides, Beth thinks it's too quiet here. Mike's family is from Puerto Rico and they are anything but quiet."

"But you're her mother. You should spend time together," he said.

I recoiled at 'should.' "I don't want us to spend time with each other out of a sense of duty, but because we'd enjoy it, and right now that wouldn't be the case."

"That's wrong," he said. "God requires devotion. I do many things I don't want to do if I know it will help someone."

Hearing his desire to help people softened me, but I could see that right now we'd get nowhere discussing our different ways of interacting with family.

Afshin, however, wasn't ready to drop the subject.

"Even Calvin," he continued. "You hardly ever see him."

"We talk on the phone at least once a week," I countered, "and get together twice a month—or more."

"That's nothing. I don't understand. Is this how it is in America? Don't you know how important it is for children and parents to be close?"

"But we *are* close," I said, my fist slamming my thigh. I wished he understood the stages of development between parents and children. How do children learn to become self-respecting, independent adults if they are coming home to Mama all the time?

Afshin said nothing. I took a breath. Maybe he had a point. Maybe I *could* be closer to my children. "Let me think about it," I said.

He kissed my temple as though saying, "That's a good girl." For some reason I didn't resent it.

For the following minute, he was lost in thought. "Tell me about your childhood," he said, inviting me to take his other hand.

He sounded sincerely interested. Where should I begin?

"My mother and father met in France, at the end of the Second World War. He was an American soldier and she was performing with a ballet company. It's strange . . . I never found out how they actually met. My mother was a very private person. She said they lived together for a while. When he left, he promised to send for her, but he never did. I was born a few months later."

Afshin's eyes darkened and his hands gripped mine. "No! That's terrible! How could he do that?"

"Who knows?" I shrugged. "War makes people do crazy things." The intensity of his reaction surprised me. Didn't he realize men abandoned pregnant women all the time?

I hadn't missed having a father, since other men had doted on me—Mamy's friends and Bonne Maman's tenants. But something about Afshin's reaction—"That's terrible!"—rang true. The absence of a father had first struck me one day in first grade when a schoolmate brought me out of my innocence. She asked about my father and I said I didn't have one. Oh, how upset Mamy was when I told her what I had said. I can still hear her admonishing me, "Don't *ever* tell anyone you don't have a father. You have one. He lives very far away—in America—but he's still your father."

I continued my story. "Anyway, I lived with my mother and grandmother, but when I was seven my mother left Belgium and came to live in the U.S."

"She left you?" His body sprang forward.

"Yes, with my grandmother." A familiar sadness constricted my throat. "She was looking for a new life. Maybe she wanted to get away from being judged for being an unmarried mother. In any case, it took two years for me to join her, and it wasn't until I was thirteen that I first met my father."

Mamy and I walk up the city street in Jackson, Mississippi. She looks pretty in her sky-blue sleeveless dress with tiny white flowers. I strut along in my new plaid Bermuda shorts. We round the corner and she points to a tall brick building with a sign spanning the roof: Hotel Heidelberg.

"Your father should be waiting for us there."

My feet slow down and my heart speeds up.

My father. Is he kind? Do I look like him? Will he like me?

My hand starts to reach for Mamy's. No. I'm thirteen now—too big for that.

As we get close to the hotel, I keep my eyes on the main doors, which seem to move in waves through the August heat rising from the pavement. We push through the doors and go to the elevator. As we step out on the fourth floor, Mamy pulls a compact and lipstick from her handbag. With a shaky hand she shapes her lips in red and presses them together. I watch her take out a tiny blue bottle of Je Reviens and dab a drop behind each ear. We walk down a long hall. Mamy stops in front of a door. She looks at me and raises her eyebrows as though saying, "This is it!" Her knuckles rap three times.

A man opens the door and his frame fills the opening. "Hey! Come on in, y'all."

A few minutes later, I watch them on the settee, talking as though they know each other. I feel invisible. My hand runs back and forth on the smooth wooden table. In the middle of it, on a round lace doily, sits a white vase of flowers, embossed with small half-bubbles, like raised polka dots. I trace each porcelain bubble with my fingertip. Rivulets of sweat trickle down my chest.

"You can come live with me," a man's voice is saying. "I have horses. You'll like that, won't you?"

My eardrums pound. I look at Mamy, but she's smiling. How can she smile? I sit back in the chair, hoping its arms will hold me back from the giant in front of me. Tears spill.

"You don't want to come with me?" He puts his hand on Mamy's back. "Don't worry. I don't think your Mama here would let you go."

Afshin drew me tightly to his chest. "You missed a special and important relationship. A girl learns to love by loving her father."

He caressed my back as though trying to compensate for the affection I didn't get as a child. Neither of us spoke for a while, and I pondered the possibility that my ability to love had been diminished by my father's absence.

Afshin clasped my arms and looked at me with glistening eyes. "Why haven't you found a man to marry?"

An uneasy feeling rose in my gut. Afshin would disapprove of the dating I'd done since it went beyond holding hands. It took a few years after David's death for me to decide that marriage was a good idea, after all. I missed the springboard of emotional security it had once given me, as well as the time for activities I loved. I was tired of expending energy in dating.

"I tried to find a husband," I said, "but either the man wasn't interested in marriage, or I wasn't interested in the man. Now, at my age, my choices have dwindled."

"They were not able to love you unconditionally, and that's what I want to do." He held my chin and met my eyes. "Can you believe that?"

"It's difficult." Who could love unconditionally? I thought. But Afshin wanted to, and a yearning stirred in my heart. "I can try," I told him.

"Believe me, I mean it," he said. "There are only two smart men in your life—your husband and me. We love you and know that you deserve the best."

How idealistic he sounded. But did it matter? He compared his love to David's, and I was hooked.

Afshin fell silent. His gaze seemed to turn inward, as though he were wrestling with a math problem. When he spoke again, his voice was soft. "Tell me. How was it with David?"

I pressed my eyes shut for a few seconds.

"We had a great marriage—even though my mother was unhappy when I married at nineteen. But David was a special man. I never doubted for a moment that he loved me. And because of that, I could put my energy into raising the children and getting my bachelor's degree. Our home felt secure and I enjoyed life." I paused. "The marriage didn't start out wonderful, especially not the first year. David liked to watch television a lot more than I did, and he spent money freely. A few years later, though, he changed. He started meditating and following the teachings of Jesus. He became a pleasure to live with."

"You said he was a priest?"

"A minister, but not the usual kind. He had long hair and a beard, and he drove an old van; he didn't fit most people's image of a church leader. Fortunately, David found a group of people who appreciated him: prison inmates. He taught them spiritual awareness. They loved him because he didn't pretend to be better than they were. He loved his work."

"He must have been a good man," Afshin said, as though talking to himself.

A moment later, he circled my face with gentle kisses. For a second, he hesitated, and then his lips met mine. Sparks scurried from my navel to my thighs. Still uncertain of his intentions, I reined in the impulse to devour his lips with my own kiss. An instant later, he sat back and, with his fingertip, traced the veins on the back of my hand.

What had made him kiss me that way?

We finally got up and went for a walk in a nearby nature preserve, where we spent the afternoon. Later that night, after we enjoyed watching *Chariots of Fire*, Afshin said, "You look tired. I will walk you to your room."

We reached my bedroom. "*Shab Begher,*" I said, hoping I'd pronounced "goodnight" correctly in Persian.

"Don't. Don't do that for me," Afshin said, taking my hands in his. "My English is fine. You are a flower, and I am the butterfly. You don't have to change your perfume to please me."

How poetic. Never had a man spoken to me this way.

"Thank you, but I want to keep learning your language," I said, protective of what I'd already learned. "I love the sound of it."

We stood straddling the threshold of my room. Afshin was holding my hands and moving them nervously. His gaze alternated for long moments between my eyes and my hands.

"If you don't go, I'll have to ask you to sleep with me," I said, wearing an impish smile.

He didn't say anything but paused only an instant before coming in and shutting the door behind us. He picked me up and laid me on the bed with reverence. Then he lay down beside me. Our breathing grew audible as we lay face to face in the moonlight.

Suddenly, Afshin knelt and peeled off his shirt, revealing a lean chest covered with black curls. My breath caught. Slowly, I unzipped my jeans and pushed them down my thighs. We faced each other on our knees. Although in good shape, I knew I didn't have the body of a twenty-five-year-old. Yet I didn't feel embarrassed—Afshin had said he loved me unconditionally.

With trembling fingers, he unbuttoned my blouse. "Miriam, you're an angel," he said, as he bent down and kissed my breast.

I soared.

A moment later we slid under the sheet. "This is the first time I'm making love to a woman," he whispered in my ear.

My God . . . I'm in a dream.

For a few seconds, neither of us moved.

"Should we use birth control?" Afshin asked.

"No. It's OK," I said, recalling the beginning of perimenopause four months earlier.

Afshin's lack of experience was evident, but he showed no sign of embarrassment. He allowed me to guide him, gently. For the next few hours we expressed our love in ways I'd been dreaming about for weeks.

Finally, we lay still. "I love learning from you," Afshin said. My parents didn't teach me, and what my brother taught me isn't useful."

We were silent for a moment and then I asked, "Are you happy?"

"Do you need to ask that of someone in heaven?"

We lay contented in each other's arms until Afshin stirred. "I have to take a shower now."

"This late? Why don't you wait until morning?"

"It's a requirement for Muslims to wash completely after lovemaking. We wash away the animal part and keep the spiritual part—inside."

I cringed at the inference that sex soiled our bodies, but embraced the latter assertion.

"What about with a wet dream? Would you have to wash then, too?"

"Oh, yes. When I was a teenager, it was embarrassing for me to shower in the middle of the night because my whole family knew the reason. My brother teased me because I took showers so often."

"Did you masturbate?"

"Oh, no, that is forbidden," he said with alarm.

"Why?" I asked, suppressing the impulse to add, "And sex outside of marriage isn't?"

"Because it can take something away from the one you make love with. Also, it can be habit forming."

"That makes more sense than telling boys that it would make them blind. That's what happened in this country."

He kissed me and then groped, in the dark, for his clothes. I heard him slide into his pants and smiled at his modesty.

"I better sleep in my room," he said. "I move all night, and you wouldn't get any sleep."

A part of me wanted to say, "Stay," but my need for sleep silenced that voice.

I opened my eyes. When I realized I'd slept only five and a half hours, I tried going back to sleep but felt as wired as I would after three cups of espresso. I got up and headed downstairs in my flowing Indonesian gown.

Mid-morning brightness lit the dining room where Afshin sat with a smile that lit my heart. He held his hand out and pulled me onto his lap. I molded my body to his as I sensed no guilt in his actions.

I started. "Oh, no, it's Sunday. I almost forgot. I'm having some friends and new acquaintances over for dinner." I paused for a second. "Will you join us?"

He shook his head. "I really have to study."

"That's too bad, but I guess you better get back to work. You've been a little distracted lately," I said, looking at him with a grin. As much as I wanted him to be part of the special occasion, I knew better than to pressure him.

We had a leisurely breakfast, and then he left for the university library.

As I cleared the table, I thought about what Afshin had said the day before about how little contact I had with my children. It bothered me. I liked the way I related with them, especially Greg and Cal. I didn't need to talk to them every day. And when we did talk, I sensed an open connection. Not so with Beth. She'd clammed up in her mid-teens and hadn't opened up to me since.

I glanced over the trifle recipe to make sure I had all the ingredients, but I couldn't get Afshin's admonition out of my head; my confidence was shaken. I had tried to make my children independent so they could develop into adults who could take care of themselves. Had I pulled back too much?

On impulse, I called Calvin and asked whether he was free to visit.

He arrived a half-hour later. Soon after, Beth came home and joined us around the table. I kept the recent development with Afshin to myself, even though I usually shared news of my romantic interests with them. How would they react to my being with someone their own age?

"How's work?" I asked Cal.

"The customers are great, but the new servers don't do their share of the prep work and I end up doing it. I don't get it—why can't they see what needs to be done and do it?"

Beth, to my right, studied her nails as though reading a fortune on each one.

"What's up with you, Beth?" Cal asked. "You're spending a lot of time with Mike these days, huh?"

A faint smile and a glance told us she'd heard. We waited for an answer, but none came.

At least I wasn't the only one in the family with whom she barely conversed.

Cal mentioned a book he was reading, and Beth got up and went to her room. Cal and I looked at each other questioningly. Once again, we'd failed at our attempts to engage with her.

She returned, after a while, carrying her travel bag. "I'm staying at Mike's again tonight," she said, holding her cheek to me for a goodbye kiss. Good thing I'd learned this was about keeping her lips glossy, rather than about not wanting to kiss me.

Now that Afshin and I were spending hours in the family room—the room adjacent to hers—I was grateful that she had a second home.

Cal left a little later, and I got busy with dinner preparation, singing while I worked. As I stood layering ladyfingers, custard, and fruit for a trifle, it dawned on me that today was the anniversary of David's death. Dearest David. How sweet life was with you. It seems like another lifetime when I was your wife. Did you send Afshin my way?

As I finished preparing dinner, Afshin came home and bounced into the kitchen. "I told my friend Milad about us, and he said, 'Congratulations.'"

"Are you kidding? Was he surprised?"

"No. He knew how much I liked you."

Afshin pulled the keys off his key ring and slid the empty ring on my finger, saying, "I want us to be married."

I gaped at the ring and then at Afshin.

"We have special marriage vows in Iran. Would you say them with me?"

A knock at the door interrupted us, and the first dinner guests stepped inside. What timing!

"I better go." On his way out, Afshin greeted the guests with a nod.

At the dinner table, I enjoyed stimulating conversation with two old friends and three new ones—a philosophy professor, a holistic physician, and an anthropologist. At a lower volume, the chatter in my head distracted me. What would Afshin's proposal mean to my life? Would it mean moving to Iran? I loved him, but . . . marriage?

When he returned around ten o'clock, my guests were still with me. I fingered the key ring, which I'd slipped onto my watchband. A long half hour followed. Finally, everyone left.

My heart pounded as Afshin and I climbed the steps to my room.

We sat on the edge of the bed, and he repeated, "Would you say the vows with me?" He paused and then added, "We can have a temporary marriage until May. That's when I am going back to Iran."

I stared at him with mouth agape. "A temporary marriage? I've never heard of that."

"It was allowed by the Prophet. And when Rafsanjani was president he encouraged it— under special circumstances."

The story of Betty Mahmoudy, who had married an Iranian, came to me. In her book, *Not Without My Daughter,* she describes how her husband changed after their marriage. He became *especially* controlling after they went to Iran. I once heard that an Iranian husband has all the power in a marriage. Would Afshin change? It didn't seem possible. So even though I didn't believe Afshin would abuse his marital power, I asked, "Will you want to change my present way of life here in the U.S.?"

His brow furrowed. "What do you mean?"

"Will you object to my spending time with friends? Especially if they're men."

"Of course not."

"And can I still hug them, as I do now?"

"Well . . . yes. In Iran, a woman cannot hug or kiss a man unless he's a family member. But since it's different here, please do as you wish."

I noticed my legs trembling. "Why do we have to marry at all?"

"In the Qu'ran, God recommends marriage, and I believe it's the right way for us to be together. I know that couples in the U.S. live together without marriage, but then the relationship lacks something important. I want to marry you because I love you, but it has to be temporary—you have your children who need you here. Our marriage may be for only six months, but I want it to be significant."

I didn't disagree. It wasn't only my children who would keep me in the United States, but my friends, my town, my way of life. Yet I saw no reason not to marry Afshin for six months—I even found the idea intriguing. I wanted to know him deeply, so why not do it his way?

"Yes, I'm happy to say the marriage vows."

Afshin clasped me in an embrace and then took my hands in his. "Please say this with me: 'In the name of the Merciful, Compassionate God, we, Afshin Nahari and Miriam Valmont, agree to be husband and wife. We agree never to lie to each other and to stay together through happiness and sorrow until May.'"

I repeated the vow. It felt right.

Afshin pulled a square-inch piece of folded notebook paper from his shirt pocket and handed it to me as though it were a delicate rose.

"It's from the Qu'ran," he said.

I unfolded it and read the words he'd written: "O, Mankind! We created you male and female and put you into nations and tribes that you may know each other. The noblest of you in the sight of God is the one who is best in conduct, and He knows the best."

I liked the words, "that you may know each other." I longed to know this man—a man so different from any I'd known. We would be tribe mates for six months.

Our lips pressed together in a fervent kiss. Then we drew back, gazing and smiling at each other. Afshin's hands trembled, and every few moments he lowered his head and shook it as though he couldn't believe what we'd just done.

I turned and lit the candle on the shelf nearby. Afshin switched off the lamp.

He lifted my dress over my head, and I did likewise with his shirt. After dropping the rest of his clothes to the floor, he held himself above me. Candlelight and shadows danced across his face and chest. His eyes locked on mine.

"I can't look into your eyes too long. They are like the bluest ocean without boundary," he said.

Long after midnight we lay in each other's arms, warm from our lovemaking.

"In Islam they say that a man has only half the faith until he is married, and now I understand what that means. When I experience this with you and see how a man and woman fit together, I am convinced of God."

"Your love convinces me," I whispered.

Part 2

My Husband: The Next Six Months

Chapter 8

In the morning I dialed Greg's number.

"Hey Mom. How ya doin'?"

I pictured Greg on his patio, his muscular frame stretched the length of a lounge chair, as he overlooked the boats in the canal. The casual lifestyle of the Florida Keys matched his personality.

"Are you sitting down?" I asked.

"Yeah. What's up?"

"I got married yesterday," I said, relishing the shock waves this news would send through Greg. He had shocked me a year ago by announcing he was moving to Florida a month later. Now it was my turn.

"You're kidding, right?"

"No. It's Afshin—the tenant I told you about. We made a six-month commitment. After that, he'll be going back to Iran. But don't worry, I'm not planning to go with him."

Dead silence.

Finally he said, "Don't tell anyone. This is too weird."

"It's only weird to you because we don't do temporary marriages here, but it makes sense to me. Anyway, it's the way Afshin wants us to be together. We love each other, and I'm extremely happy."

"All right," he said, after a long pause, "but I need time to process this before saying 'Congratulations.' I know I have an unusual mother, but this time I'm in shock."

Good, I thought, appreciating Greg's accidental confirmation that I was taking a path less traveled—often my preferred route through life.

After I hung up, I called Cal.

"I'd like to talk to you, but not over the phone. Will you be home tomorrow night around eight?" I asked.

"Sure. Anything wrong?"

"No, no." *At least not in my eyes*, I thought. "I'll invite Beth, too."

After saying goodbye, I leaned back in my chair and stared outside. How precious Cal and Beth were to me. How could anyone have questioned my plans to adopt? But some had. "Can't you have more children?" How surprised they'd looked when I replied, "Yes, but we *want* to adopt." What a day it was when I finally realized my dream of adopting—the dream inspired by my favorite book from childhood.

Later, I was similarly moved by reading Pearl Buck's books about adopting her Amerasian children from China. I admired Pearl Buck; intelligence and compassion shone through in her writing. Her stories, as well as *Les Orphelins*, inspired me to give a home to children who didn't have one. Why should I produce babies when ready-made ones needed love?

❀

"Take it easy on them," Afshin said the next evening as I left for Cal's apartment. "It will be hard news for them to hear."

I arrived at Cal's around eight. He handed me a mug of steaming tea and then opened the cupboard. "Here, Mom," he said, handing me a bag of my favorite chocolate-chip cookies. His thoughtfulness touched me.

The door opened and Beth strode in.

"Hey," Cal said, "you made it. Let's sit over there." He pointed to the small sectional sofa nearly filling the living room and then turned down the volume of U-2 on the stereo. "Well, go ahead, Mom. What's this about?"

"It's hard to know where to begin, so I'll just tell you. I met a man who has all the qualities I want in a mate, and I love him very much."

They stared at me with quizzical expressions.

Let's hope this will prepare them for the rest of the story, I thought.

"It's Afshin, the graduate student. We've committed to a marriage—just until May."

Even the walls emanated shock.

"I'm going to be sick," Beth said, clutching her waist.

I clasped her knee. "What's the matter?" She didn't respond, but tears spilled. "Don't worry," I continued. "I'm not going anywhere." I knew that since David's death, she'd feared losing me.

"I know, but . . . I don't feel good," she whispered.

Cal spoke up. "I don't see it as a marriage. Why not get married forever if you love each other?"

The Bird and The Fish

"Afshin's going back to Iran. My life is here, and yet we want to feel totally committed to each other, even for this short time."

Cal moved to the edge of his seat, leaning toward me. "I'm not persuaded by that explanation."

Was I? But did it matter? Afshin and I would do it our way. We'd *make* it work.

Cal offered Beth a box of tissues. She plucked a couple of them and blew her nose.

I rubbed her arm but she didn't look up. Minutes passed. I didn't know what else to say.

Cal took a deep breath. "I want you to be happy, so even though I don't understand or agree with this 'marriage,' I support *you*."

"Thanks." I squeezed his hand, grateful for his words of support.

"Let's go home, OK?" I said, turning to Beth. Though Cal could override his emotions with logical thinking, Beth would need more time to dig out from the avalanche of her emotions.

As we walked up to the house, Andean music blared from inside. Afshin, his shirt drenched in perspiration, stopped dancing and rushed to the stereo when he saw us. Beth went downstairs to her room without a word, and I followed. She plopped on her bed and scooted back toward her pillows, propped against the wall. I leaned on the doorjamb, wondering what I could do.

"I need time to think," she said, lifting her hand and waving me out of her space.

I kissed her goodnight and went up to the dining room, where I found Afshin slumped in his chair, gnawing on his lip.

"Beth is upset, isn't she?"

His fearful tone shook me. "Yes, but she'll be all right. Give her time." I stood behind him and kneaded his neck and shoulders.

"Would she like for you to sleep with her tonight?" he asked.

"No way! She's not used to that." I could just imagine Beth's shocked response if I made that suggestion, yet Afshin spoke as though it were perfectly natural. Was it something his mother would have done when one of her children was upset? "Don't worry. Beth will feel better soon."

He shook his head. "We're responsible for her sadness."

His guilt tightened a net of fear around my chest. I took a deep breath, trying to dispel the pressure.

"No. We're not responsible. We're not trying to hurt her." I wished he would stop thinking we had done something wrong. "I'll talk to her tomorrow."

He didn't respond, but held prayerful hands over his mouth.

"It's almost ten-thirty. Let's go upstairs," I said, touching his shoulder.

He followed me. We lay down side by side and clasped hands. But he didn't caress me. All I could hear were the hot-water pipes in the baseboard, pinging more and more loudly.

"I feel toward Beth as I do for my sister," Afshin said, "but it's better not to tell her."

Hmm . . . why a sister? Because she lives in the same house? Or to protect himself from feeling sexual? No, he wouldn't entertain such thoughts. His strong commitment to marriage protected me from betrayal. I couldn't let jealousy take root; it could grow into a monster. Besides, I doubted that her serious demeanor in front of him or the huge amount of time she spent on make-up and hair would appeal to him.

"She's probably worried about what will happen to me when you go back to Iran. David died when she was six, and she'd run to my side whenever she sensed my sadness."

Afshin propped himself up and looked at me. "Please, promise me you will take the time to show her you love her."

"I promise," I said, laying my hand on his cheek.

Why was he so agitated over Beth's reaction? I knew she'd be fine.

He gripped my shoulder. "When I go back to Iran, I don't want you to be sad."

"I *want* to be sad. If I weren't, it would mean I didn't care." My throat tightened at the thought of his absence.

"But your family and friends will be hurt by your sadness. In Islam it's a serious sin to make someone sad." He looked worried—even scared.

"Well, in Christianity that's not a sin. We're not doing anything wrong," I said, irritated by a religious belief that discouraged the expression of genuine emotions, including sadness.

"You've caused me immense joy; sorrow will be a small price to pay. Don't worry, I won't *stay* sad."

His expression didn't change. I stared at the shadows on the ceiling. Maybe his agitation was caused more by fear of Allah's judgment than by concern about Beth.

We lay down again. My breath caught as his thigh crossed over mine and his arm slid below my breasts.

"I know someday you'll come to Iran and see what is now only in my dreams. I'm sure of it," he said. I knew he meant that someday I'd go to Iran and see the mathematics program he would develop in a university. Teaching English there could be interesting, but it would take a while before I could bear seeing him with a permanent wife.

In the light of dawn I awoke to Afshin's caresses. Sleep saturated my limbs but I didn't resist him; his pleasure thrilled me and soon my desire matched his.

Coming home from the grocery store in the afternoon, I waded through a sea of leaves as I carried bags of food to the house. On my way to the kitchen I saw a cream-colored envelope addressed to 'Mom' on the dining-room table. I dropped the bags and ripped open the envelope. The handcrafted card inside read, "If you can be happy with the decision you've made, I'll be happy, too. I can't say my emotions agree with it, but only you can live your life. I've seen you get hurt and pick yourself up many times, and that's why it's hard to understand why you're taking this route. You're my mother, and I want to protect you. I also see the happiness in your eyes, and I want you to know I'm not mad at you. I love you and will try not to be afraid for you. Love, Beth."

Through tears, I re-read the card. I knew it. She *was* worried about me. *How blessed I am to have such a daughter,* I thought.

Afshin came in a little later. I handed him the card.

A smile grew as he read. "I'm glad she can say this. I'll wait patiently. Maybe someday she'll be friendly to me."

Chapter 9

I opened the oven door and jumped back as a blast of heat struck my face. The aroma of roasting turkey wafted through the room. The sacrificial twelve-pound bird would provide more than enough for Cal, Beth, Mike, and me for Thanksgiving. Afshin was meeting some of his Iranian friends in New York. He had accepted their invitation before he had known his life would take a detour on the scenic route—marriage to his landlady.

"It's nice to have a quiet Thanksgiving, for a change, without your friends and tenants," said Beth, "but I wish the rest of the family was here."

I, too, was sorry that Greg and my grandson, Jacob, weren't with us, but I also missed friends and tenants. They added fresh ingredients to our family stew and, for my taste, interesting flavors. "Money is tight for Greg right now," I said. "You know they won't be up for Christmas, either, right?"

"Yeah," she sighed. "And you and Cal are lucky—you'll get to see them in January. Wish *I* was going to Florida."

I was sorry she hadn't accrued enough vacation time at her new job yet. "Next year, Beth."

Later, while we ate pumpkin pie with whipped cream, the phone rang. Walking back to the kitchen, I picked it up and heard a warm Southern drawl greet me with, "How ya doin', Sis?" My half-brother, Jim, was calling from Mississippi. After we exchanged Thanksgiving greetings, I shared the news about Afshin and me. He congratulated me, but I heard an edge in his voice. I wondered whether he thought I was crazy.

"I hope he'll join you when you come down for my little girl's weddin' next month."

I'd almost forgotten. "I hope so," I said. "I'll let you know by this weekend."

When I sat back down at the table, Cal, Beth, and Mike were discussing a movie they had seen. As I finished my pie, the voices around me faded. Eight years ago, when Jim first called to introduce himself, I had been thrilled. Now, remembering his invitation to stay in his home for a few days, my heart swelled. I had jumped at the chance to meet him—and to see my father again.

Greg is with me when I arrive in Jackson, Mississippi. We are both excited and nervous about meeting new relatives. When I park and throw open the car door in front of my brother's house, he strolls toward us. He's shorter and stouter than I expected. Sparse reddish hair and a ruddy complexion serve as a backdrop for eyes squinting a smile under sun-bleached eyebrows.

I take a few steps toward him and his husky arms encircle me and squeeze. My whole torso trembles, my legs weaken, and I feel like laughing and crying.

"Sis, you are a sight for sore eyes," he says, stepping back and taking me in like a newfound treasure.

He doesn't look like me, or even my father, but who cares? His warmth envelops my family-hungry soul.

The next morning Jim's wife, Emily, serves us a traditional Southern breakfast: eggs, grits, sausage, and biscuits with gravy. Then we head out to see Jim, Sr. After a short drive we turn onto Chester Avenue, where my father and his wife still live in the house where they raised five children. I try to read the house number on each ranch house we pass, but everything grows blurry. I blink hard.

"Here we are," says Jim as he stops in front of a brick ranch dwarfed by two pecan trees.

Greg puts his arm around my shoulder as we head up the walkway toward the house. I look down. I'm walking where my father has walked nearly every day for years, I think. The blur returns.

For the second time in my forty-two years I'm about to see the man who helped to put me on this planet, whether he planned it or not.

My father's wife, Joyce, swings open the front door, and Greg, Jim Jr., and I enter the dimly lit living room, furnished in 1960s decor. Joyce takes my hand and covers it with hers. "Miriam, I'm so pleased to meet you." The large, round lenses of her glasses offer an unobstructed view of soft gray eyes.

I believe her—completely. Behind her, in the arched opening, stands the shadow from my dreams. Joyce motions him in. He shuffles into the room. At seventy-six he's still the towering man I remember from our last meeting, when I was thirteen. This time, however, his eyes do not connect with mine.

Jim's hand on my back nudges me forward. "This is Miriam, your daughter," my brother says in a mellifluous drawl. My father's expression remains blank.

God, why did he have to have a stroke?

"Miriam—Betsy's daughter," Jim says, emphasizing my mother's name.

As though the correct key had entered the lock, his eyes—*sky-blue like mine*—open wide with a light of recognition. His hand moves toward me and I wrap my arms around him—*my father*. He strokes my head and an ache rises in my throat.

Joyce rubs my back. "Come. Let's sit here." She gestures toward the dining-room table. Sunbeams streaming through the window bring the flowered tablecloth to life.

Jim Sr. lowers himself into the chair at the head of the table. His huge hand lies flat on the cloth, rubbing it back and forth. I want to take his hand, kiss it, and say, "It's all right; I'm not angry anymore."

He stares at me, and I strain to read his thoughts but find no clue. The stroke robbed him of his ability not only to talk or write, but even to understand . . . though he did respond to Mamy's name.

If only I'd contacted him when I became an adult. If only I could have known him. If only I could have asked, "Why didn't you come back for Mamy and me?"

"Hey, Mom. Are you daydreaming?" Cal asked, tapping my arm. "I brought *Liar, Liar* with Jim Carrey. Let's go watch it."

We moved to the family room. As we watched the comedy, Cal and I howled with laughter; Mike and Beth laughed like polite guests. By early evening they had all left.

Later, when Afshin returned, I dragged him into the living room and playfully pushed him into the loveseat.

"With everything going on with us, I forgot to tell you about my niece's wedding next month. My brother called today, and now that he knows we're married, he's invited you too."

Afshin gave me a look that said, "Do you think that's a good idea?"

"You're five years too late to meet my father, but I'd love for you to meet my brother and sisters. They're the closest relatives I have in the U.S."

He nodded but looked ill at ease.

"You'll also get to see what the Deep South is like." What fun it would be to take a road trip with Afshin. "Hey! This could be our honeymoon!" I said, jumping up and down on the cushion like an excited child. "What do you think?"

He looked at me with amusement. "Yes, let's go." An instant later he added, "But will I have to wear a suit?"

"That's what people usually wear to weddings."

"I hate suits." His fist slammed the sofa's thick arm and I jumped. "My mother tried to have me wear one, but I never did. She said it's to show respect, but I disagree. Suits come from the West."

"Oh, I see your point." I paused. "But this *is* the West, and going to this wedding without a suit would offend people. You may be the first Iranian they meet. I want them to like you. Just this once, would you wear one? I'll never ask again."

"Let me think about it."

On Friday, Afshin and I headed out to see my friends, Rachel and Gene. They'd invited us to share Thanksgiving leftovers and to hear more about my new status. Afshin drove, one hand on the steering wheel and the other holding mine. I settled contentedly into the seat. How many years had it been since I'd been part of an official couple? I felt completely secure in Afshin's love. I hadn't felt this way since David died.

From the first time I met Rachel at the hospital, I was drawn to her. She spoke with genuine caring for the patients we discussed at team meetings. One day we had lunch together and I found more reasons to like her. She was smart, frugal, and unpretentious; she enjoyed the simple pleasures of life, especially gardening and cooking.

We arrived at the ranch house and walked around to the back door. It opened and Rachel pounced on me with a hearty hug. Then she pumped Afshin's hand. "Congratulations, you two." She wore a huge grin and looked back and forth, from Afshin to me. Gene came up behind her. He stood an inch taller, and they shared similar stocky frames. His beard tickled my cheek as he kissed me.

"We love Miriam," Gene said as he turned to Afshin and shook his hand. "She's always doing something unusual, though I've got to say, she's never surprised us like this before." Shaking his head, he peered at me over his glasses as though inspecting some strange specimen.

I glanced at Afshin. Though he was smiling, he stood at attention, arms down in front of his body with one hand covering the other.

"Why don't we go sit down? Everything's ready," Rachel said, leading us toward the Early American dining room lined with knotty-pine paneling. After we were seated, she passed a platter of turkey and a bowl of mashed potatoes. Afshin helped himself. As he handed me a dish, a smile came and went like a passing hummingbird.

"We're curious about your marriage," said Gene. "Would you tell us more about it?"

Afshin made no move to answer. He looked at me as if to say, "It's all yours."

"Temporary marriages are nothing new," I said. "They were allowed by the Prophet at certain times. After the Revolution of '79 President Rafsanjani encouraged people to have temporary marriages. He saw it as a solution to the frustration of young people who couldn't get married because it was difficult for men to come up with the required dowry. It's definitely legal. Children born from a temporary marriage have the same rights as children born from long-term marriages." Afshin made no sign that he had anything more to add, so I ended with, "Afshin and I decided on six months because he'll be going back to Iran after that."

Rachel put her fork down. "I could never do that." She shook her head as though even the thought of it scared her. "I want the old fashioned 'till death do us part' kind of marriage." She reached for Gene's hand. "Yet if you two can handle it—good for you."

"We can handle it," I said, and as I turned to Afshin, his face shone with pride.

For a short time we went back to enjoying the food. Then Gene said, "Iran's in the news again. Your president seems like a good man."

Afshin took a deep breath and shifted in his seat. "Yes, he does."

"A majority of the people are with him, especially the students and women," Gene continued. "It's too bad the real power lies with Ayatollah Khamenei."

I was impressed that Gene knew about Iran's current Supreme Leader and didn't confuse his name with that of his predecessor, Khomeini, the ayatollah hated by many Americans during the hostage crisis.

"President Khatami is having a hard time making the changes Iranians want," Gene mused. "It sounds as though the women would like the dress code relaxed."

"*Some* women," Afshin said.

"Yes, of course, of course."

I hoped Gene wasn't assuming that Afshin would like to see Iran become Westernized. Afshin would resent that, and I wanted him to like Rachel and Gene, and vice versa.

"I visited Iran in 1978 when I traveled around the world," said Gene. "There was already unrest, but I found the people extremely hospitable."

Afshin smiled at Gene. "You're the first American I've met who knows this much about my country. The only thing most people know about Iran is the taking of the American embassy and hostages by students in 1979. Yet they have no understanding of why the students did it."

"Why did they?" Rachel looked at Afshin quizzically.

"People were furious that Carter allowed the Shah into the United States when he left Iran. He also let him put money in American banks. It was *our* money he took out of the country."

"I can see why you'd be upset." A moment of silence followed. Gene's eyes shifted between Afshin and me. "Tell me, what would it be like if Miriam went back to Iran with you?"

Afshin gazed at me. "A dream."

I thrilled to hear him say that. But . . . did he mean as his wife or as an English teacher?

"Would your family accept her?" Rachel asked.

"Yes, but it might be hard for others." He glanced at me, and then his eyes shifted from one item on the table to another, as though something there might afford him an escape route.

As Afshin came from a culture where privacy is the norm, I imagined these personal questions were unsettling.

"Because she's older or because she's an American?" Gene's eyes showed concern.

My jaw tightened. I hated being reminded of our differences.

"Both," Afshin responded.

"How about dessert?" Rachel asked, reading my mind. I gathered some dishes and followed her into the kitchen.

"I like him," she whispered to me.

At the end of the evening, as we headed for the car, I restrained myself from shouting at the top of my lungs, "I love Afshin! I love my husband!"

During the ride home, I sang, "*Oh, what a beautiful morn*—oops, *evening. Oh, what a beautiful day. I've got a wonderful feeling, everything's going my way.*"

"My impression of Americans is changing," Afshin said, keeping his eyes on the country road. "Your friends have good morals. They don't drink, and they have a happy marriage. Before I came to this country I believed that most Americans divorced at least once."

I hesitated. "Gene has been divorced."

"Nooo . . . he seems like such a good man."

"He *is* a good man. Sometimes people just aren't suited for each other."

"They should know that *before* getting married."

I didn't like his stern tone and reminded myself how young and inexperienced he was. "That would be nice." But how could we know in advance how two chemicals would react when poured together? The mix could prove disastrous or delightful.

As soon as we got home, we prepared for bed. Afshin said he wanted to tell me a story. I curled up on my side, and he started to tell me how Prometheus, a hero of Greek mythology, brought fire to human beings. I listened like a contented child hearing a bedtime story. I couldn't remember ever having had that experience before.

In the morning, even though the sky was cloudless, I grabbed my extra large umbrella from the closet on our way out. I was happy Afshin had asked me if he could pay his respects at David's grave. A half-hour after leaving the house, we pulled in to a cemetery lane that ran between a field of rotten pumpkins and a yard full of gravestones. After parking near David's grave, I snatched the umbrella from the back seat, led the way toward the headstone, and stuck the umbrella in front of David's birth date. I didn't want Afshin to figure out my age by seeing David's.

Afshin stared at the rest of the inscription. He didn't say a word for a while as we stood, hand in hand, six feet above the bones that had once supported the body of my first husband. *How strange life is*, I mused.

I reached for David's old wedding ring in my pocket and held it tightly. I recalled the words of my father-in-law, who had married us thirty-two years earlier: "As this ring is eternal in its circle, without beginning or end, pure love is also eternal. Let your love be as pure as the gold in this ring." I had appreciated my father-in-law's words, but for me, the key ring on my watchband also signified pure love, even though its structure *did* have a beginning and an end—just like our temporary marriage.

"This may seem like a strange place to give you this," I said, taking Afshin's hand and sliding the ring on his finger. "It was David's, and I'm sure he'd be happy for you to wear it. If he can see us right now, I'll bet he's smiling."

Afshin stared at it and nodded his acceptance. "I love her, David." He reached down and caressed the headstone.

He rose and we held each other. Like a blessing at the end of a marriage ceremony, our time at David's grave seemed like a blessing on the commitment

Afshin and I had made. Only when Afshin reached our car, eight feet away, did I retrieve the umbrella. He shook his head as though saying, "You silly woman. Don't you trust me yet?"

On the way home we decided to drop in on Ana.

When she opened the door, she stood for a second with her mouth agape and then exclaimed, "The newlyweds! Come on in."

We sat down in her living room, which was decorated with art she had collected during her world travels. "So, when's the wedding party?" she asked. "You can't get married and not let your friends celebrate with you." She crossed her arms and shook her head in mock reprimand.

Afshin and I had not considered a wedding party, but we agreed to give it some thought.

We didn't stay long. On the way home I asked Afshin how he felt about having a party.

"I'm worried that your friends will judge our marriage as inferior," he said.

"I think they'll understand, but if they don't, does it matter? I feel good about it."

"Do you know how beautiful you are?" he asked.

The now familiar question made me smile. It didn't seem as much connected to my appearance as to what I did the moment before he asked it. How lovely to be seen that way.

As we made our way through the weekend traffic downtown, we decided to hold a party for about twenty friends. I was thrilled when Afshin asked if he could invite his friend, Milad.

In the afternoon, I called Rachel and Gene to thank them for dinner and the warm welcome they'd given Afshin.

Gene answered and we chatted for a few minutes.

"Afshin seemed shy last night," he said, "but when he talked, I liked what he had to say." He paused for an instant. "However, don't even think of going over there with him. It's too dangerous for an American. When I traveled through Iran in '78, the oppression I felt made me want to cut my visit short. It's much worse now, and I'll do everything I can to stop you from going. Believe me." He said this with an intensity I'd never heard in his voice.

After hanging up, I felt shaken by Gene's warning. Over tea that evening I told Afshin about the conversation.

"He's overreacting," he said. "It's true, the fundamentalists and the *komiteh*, the social police, could give you problems, but not if you act and dress modest. Most Iranians like Americans. Why are you afraid of us? We're the ones who have reason to be afraid. You come to our country and tell us how . . ."

"Wait a minute! Don't include me in there."

"Of course not. But the West—especially the British and the Americans—all tell us how we should live, and when *we* get angry, they call *us* uncivilized. We were civilized long before you."

Hearing the word "you" again, I was about to take it personally, but realized he just wanted acknowledgment that his culture had produced physicians, poets, and scientists when much of Europe was still barbaric in comparison. Afshin had already described to me some of the great works of men such as Avicenna, Rumi, and Ferdowsi. I was only one American, but I was impressed.

Chapter 10

Sunday afternoon Afshin and I swung wide bamboo rakes through the decaying leaves that covered the lawn. We piled the leaves onto a tarp, which we dragged to the street, and then dumped the contents along the curb. By dusk the curb was lined with a mound that was three feet deep and almost as long as the house. After putting the rakes back in the garage, I followed Afshin to the kitchen. As he handed me a glass of water, I noticed his sad expression.

"What's the matter?"

He crossed his arms, leaned against the counter, and looked down. "Sometimes I feel spiritually empty, like a newborn infant. I can't fly at your height, and it bothers me."

Like grain rushing from a silo, happiness left me. I stood, immobile, and closed my eyes for a second.

"You fly more at my height than any man I've known, except David. And he flew pretty high," I said, hoping to reassure him.

"I don't feel that way. I'm happy now, but there are things I miss about the way we were before our marriage."

My eyes filled with tears. He didn't *look* happy. Only a week into our marriage, and he missed our former relationship? Would he want to return to it? A clamp clutched my belly.

He bolted over to me. "Please, please, don't cry. I'm sorry for what I said."

"Don't think you're hurting me," I said, pulling back to look at him. Tears pooled in his eyes. "Please don't think that. I just hate to hear that you feel we're at different places."

He pressed my head to his chest. As my fear subsided, I was able to imagine why he felt like an infant: I had twenty-five extra years of life experience. During those years I had developed a spiritual life—a way of giving meaning to life. No wonder it had been easier for him to relate to me as a landlady, or even a mother.

An idea came to me. I braced my hands at his waist and stepped back, forcing his arms to drop to his side.

"If you miss how we related before our marriage, why don't we pick a day and pretend we're not married? It could be fun. Let's do it tomorrow. All right?"

His face brightened. "You're so good."

I didn't like the idealized view he had of me. "Listen, I've done things I regret. I'd rather not tell you what, but I've shared them with friends. It helps to talk things over, and when they hear my stories, they feel freer to tell me theirs."

A fresh frown emerged, but instead of concern, it conveyed judgment. "In Islam people don't confess their sins to each other. Only God forgives sins. We should not expose them to others. It might give them the idea to do the same." A troubled look passed his eyes. "There's something I want to tell you." He led me downstairs to the sofa.

"I said you were like a mother to me before . . ."

Oh, God, don't bring that up, I thought.

He rubbed his thumb back and forth over my fingers as he stared at them. I waited, but he didn't finish his sentence.

"I've done things I'm not proud of, and I'll be judged someday." He gnawed his lip for a moment. "If you ever learn of these, please remember—I'm not the same person anymore. It was someone with the same name, but he's gone now."

He sounded so serious, but then his standards about right and wrong were much stricter than mine. My curiosity kept tugging, but after what he'd said about not confessing sins to others, I was reluctant to ask him to reveal his sin and thereby violate his belief. Did I really care what he'd done? Whatever it was, he must have had a good reason.

"No matter what you've done, I love you."

His chest expanded and froze for an instant before releasing a whoosh of air. He held me again. I was grateful that he had shared that he carried a secret, even if I might never be privy to it.

"Can you forgive yourself for what you did?"

"I have to wait for the Judgment Day to see if God, in his mercy, will forgive me," he said, with quiet resolve.

"I prefer the Christian way. It teaches that if we're truly sorry for something, God forgives us instantly."

"What an easy religion. But I can't believe it."

In his warm embrace, another thought emerged: Had he married me partly as a good deed to pay for sins—something like a mitzvah in Judaism?

Afshin let me go and relaxed onto the sofa cushion. He lifted my hand and pressed a kiss onto it. "If I have another wife someday," he said softly, "I will be as compassionate and loving with her as you are with me, even if she's a foolish young woman."

I rested two fingers over his lips. Though glad that my compassion might increase his own for his next wife, I didn't want to hear more about her now.

When I entered the house after work the next evening, Afshin came trotting down the stairs to greet me.

I held up my hand like a traffic cop.

"How are you?" I asked in a formal tone.

He did a double take, but the next instant he let out a half-laugh. "Fine, thank you, and you?" he asked, adopting a formal air.

"Glad to be home," I said on the way to my room.

Did he have to restrain himself from following me, or was he happy to replay our earlier relationship?

After changing my clothes, I headed downstairs and passed him on my way to the kitchen. It felt odd when he didn't reach for my arm and pull me onto his lap. Instead, he looked up and gave me a polite nod.

Would we share supper? No, we hadn't done so before our marriage. I decided to have an egg and onion sandwich.

"How was your work today?" he asked, as he brought out the previous night's leftovers from the refrigerator.

"A little hectic," I said, breaking an egg into a pan. "I have a patient, a young girl, who has multiple personalities. One of them is allergic to peanuts, yet the other two aren't. It's very strange."

Afshin's brow arched. "Do you really believe this? She must be trying to fool people."

"Oh, no. Her throat closes up, and she can't breathe. You can't fake that."

He shook his head in disbelief.

Did he think multiple-personality disorder was just an odd American behavior? Iranians excelled in rug design, poetry, and math, but when it came to psychology, I believed Americans had the lead.

Over supper we managed to use phrases and mannerisms that we'd used before our marriage, but like old clothes, they no longer fit.

I picked up my empty plate and was heading for the kitchen when Afshin seized my hand. "I can't do it. I want to hold you and kiss you."

"What! How dare you speak to me that way?" I stared at him in feigned shock. Then I pounced.

"It's not a game I want to play anymore," he pleaded, before smothering my face with kisses.

With our intimate connection reestablished, Afshin left for Milad's apartment to discuss a point from his thesis. He hadn't been gone long when the phone rang.

"Hi, Miriam. It's Mark. How've you been?"

"Great!" I said, before putting the brakes on my enthusiasm. I couldn't tell Mark about Afshin over the phone. I declined his invitation to a dance and invited him, instead, to meet for a talk. He hesitated but then accepted.

We agreed to meet at a pizzeria the next evening. After I hung up, I wondered how Afshin would react to my meeting with Mark. In Iran, being seen alone with a man who wasn't my husband would provoke more than raised eyebrows; it could mean a public flogging if the eyes seeing me belonged to a member of the *komiteh*.

Around ten-thirty, as I was sealing the last of the five Christmas cards I had just written to my Belgian cousins, Afshin entered the bedroom. He stopped behind my chair as though he were about to help me stand up. Once I stood, he put his face three inches from mine and, wearing an impish grin, nudged me toward the bed.

"The lion is awake," he said, casting a downward glance.

I backed away and happily fell back on the bed, ready to be devoured.

Later I watched Afshin heading down the hall toward the bathroom to wash away the "animal part." Couldn't he let that wait? I liked *all* his parts—animal as well as spiritual. Sighing, I glanced at the clock. How did an hour pass so quickly?

He returned a few minutes later, slipped between the sheets, and fit his body to the length of mine. He drew me close.

"*Bokhoramet*," he growled softly, gently nibbling at my neck.

I pulled away. "What are you saying?"

"At home, when we see cute children, we tell them we want to eat them up. That's what it means—I want to eat you up."

"We say it, too." I imagined that the desire to take someone into us when we find them strongly appealing is universal. I offered my neck for more nibbles.

In the quiet that followed, I hesitated to bring up the conversation with Mark, but there would be no other chance. "Mark called earlier tonight." Afshin didn't respond so I continued, "I'm going to meet him tomorrow to explain why I'm not available anymore—for dances or anything else. Do you mind?"

"No, but I don't like him." Afshin's disgust permeated each word. "He must be stupid not to have realized how special you are. He doesn't deserve you. Please don't ever settle for a man who is not worthy of you. I will pray that when I leave, God will send you a good man. And God always answers my prayers."

I nearly clamped my hand over his mouth. Ah, but maybe I needed the reminder now and then. With the concern in his voice still reverberating through me, I said, "I'll pray that you will find a good wife, too."

The following evening I headed for the pizzeria to meet Mark. I opened the door and caught sight of his back spanning half a booth in the rear. When I slid onto the bench across from him, he smiled nervously.

We exchanged the usual small talk, and the server brought our tea.

I took a deep breath. "I wanted to tell you what's been going on with me." He lost his smile.

"You've met Afshin, right? Well, over the past three months we've developed a friendship, and we recently became involved." I hated describing my relationship with Afshin with that vague phrase, but I couldn't bring myself to tell him that I was married. Maybe later, I thought, after he's gotten used to the idea that I'm no longer available.

He leaned away, against the wall. I couldn't read any emotion on his face. Then, as if pulled by puppet strings, a smile reappeared. "Uh . . . well, good for you," he said. Barely catching his breath, he added, "I've been dancing a lot lately. I got the phone numbers of three women at the last dance. Not bad, huh?"

I was stunned. There he goes, I thought, right back to talking about himself.

"No, not bad." Was he trying to save face with himself? He continued talking about his social life and I found myself playing with my used teabag. The loose ends with Mark were tied. I hankered for Afshin's solid presence.

Saturday I lay in bed with the midmorning sun filling the room. I gazed at Afshin, still sleeping, his lips parted. My finger drew the length of his smile line, a premature set of parentheses framing his mouth. He squinted, stretched, and let out a long moan before snuggling into me. I was happy that I'd converted him to sleeping nude.

By the time we got up, a distant church bell was chiming noon.

As I watched pancake batter bubbling in a frying pan, I reflected on how Afshin's childhood had been dominated by the Iran-Iraq War.

We sat down to breakfast, and I poured a spiral of maple syrup over the pancakes.

"You've told me a little about Iran's war with Iraq, but you haven't told me how it was for you to live with war," I said, before taking a bite.

He stared outside as though observing a vision in the distance.

"I remember the first bomb in our town," he said softly. "I was standing near the top of a ladder outside my house and, for a minute, I couldn't move. But the bombing continued for weeks, and the fear finally left me."

"But you never had to fight, right?"

"When I was fourteen, I wanted to. All my friends went to fight the Iraqis, but my parents refused to sign the papers giving their permission."

I let out a low whistle. "Am I glad."

"I'm glad too—now, but then, I was angry." His fingertips hammered the table. "Many of my friends died—and my uncle."

"The father of your cousins?"

"Yes. And it happened *just* before the war ended." The "just" exploded through his teeth. His lips quivered. Without warning, he struck the table, and I shot back in my chair as though propelled by the blow. Recovering my composure, I lay my hand on his. His eyes glistened. I wanted to say, "Cry, dear one, cry," but his teeth gripped his lower lip. He needed to hold his tears inside.

I wondered if he thought his uncle had died in vain, but I kept that question to myself. My questions had already stirred enough emotions inside him.

For a while we sat in silence.

"I hate war," I said. "It hurts everybody, even the so-called winners."

He didn't respond, but stared ahead through half-closed eyes.

"By the fifth year, it was no longer a holy war." Afshin spoke with a sharp edge on each word. "Khomeini allowed Iranian soldiers to go fight on Iraqi soil." I must have looked confused, because he added, "A war is holy as long as you fight against people who attack you in your homeland, as long as you are just defending it."

"And does that mean Allah would help you win?"

"Yes, but no one won *that* war," he said in a low monotone. "Can we talk about something else?"

I regretted having brought up the topic. Though I hungered to understand more about the events that formed this man I'd come to love, I hadn't realized how many painful memories he carried.

We ate our cold pancakes in silence. How frightening it must have been for him to experience war for eight years. And was he taught, even as a child living through a war, that fear was a sin?

"Let's go for a walk in the woods," I said, stroking his forearm. "All right?"

He nodded.

I ran upstairs and changed into jeans, a turtleneck, and a wool sweater. As we stepped outside, icy air shot up my nostrils. The sun had fooled me.

When we reached the park, we followed a trail to the top of a grassy hill with a lake at its feet. I hesitated for a second, but then I lay down, held my arms tightly to my sides and pushed off toward the lake. Afshin followed my lead. We stopped just short of splashing into the water. Laughing, we got up and picked clumps of dried grass from our clothes.

I pointed to another trail and Afshin dashed toward it. I followed, but couldn't keep up. He saw me struggling, came back, and ran beside me in slow motion, lifting his knees waist high with each step.

"Go on," I said, flinging my arm ahead. "Let loose."

He hesitated, then took off like a horse released from its pen. I wished for his energy and endurance. I tried running again but, after a few strides, was stopped by a stitch in my side.

Two minutes later he raced back. Wrapping his arms under mine, he lifted my feet off the ground and swung me around in a circle. I liked the way we'd just dealt with the difference in our respective levels of physical endurance and hoped we would always find ways to surmount such barriers between us as they arose.

As we strolled hand in hand, I turned to Afshin. "Guess what? Ana's going on a date with an Iranian."

"What happened to Ben?" he scowled.

"She broke up with him. They didn't have enough in common."

He came to a halt. "Why did she go out with him then?"

"She's lonely and wants a partner. I think she wanted to give him a chance, even though she had doubts from the beginning."

"That's wrong. People should know what kind of person they want to marry and wait for the right one." He resumed walking. "I hate this casual dating people do here, or 'shopping around' as some call it. Love is not a business."

"I agree that people need to take more time when choosing a spouse, but at least she didn't stay with him after she realized he wasn't right for her. A while back, she had a boyfriend for three years, but she was always torn about whether or not he was the man to marry."

"He didn't love her?"

"Oh, yes. He loved her, but she didn't have the same feelings for him."

"Feelings! Love is more than feelings—it's action. She should have stayed." He looked at me, puzzled. "Why do you keep friends who cannot make commitments?"

"But they weren't married," I said, shaken by what I heard as a reprimand.

"Three years? They *were* married if they were together that long. If one of my friends left his wife, I would stop being his friend."

I gaped at him. I couldn't give up a friend simply because she left a relationship, even if it were a marriage. I was ready to argue with Afshin, to tell him that I would be more concerned if a friend stayed in a marriage that suffocated her than if she escaped it by getting divorced. But I doubted he would listen to my reasoning.

He valued commitments. I liked that, but not when taken to this extreme. The training that had taught Afshin to label everything either good or bad ran as deeply in him as in any child indoctrinated in a strict Catholic school. How could I convince him—in less than six months—to view life in another way? Why spoil the afternoon even trying? So I just said, "I couldn't give up a friend for that reason."

A few minutes later, we reached a section of the woods where the branches of hundreds of tall pines overlapped, and only spikes of sunlight poked through. Pine needles cushioned our steps, and I inhaled their scent.

About fifty feet ahead I saw a tree supporting a set of seven-foot long branches that had been propped around its circumference. A teepee!

"Look! Let's go see what's inside." I pulled Afshin toward the teepee. Finding an opening, I dropped to my hands and knees and crawled in. Afshin followed. Once inside, we rolled on our backs. I sighed at the bright blue sky, visible through the gathered branches above. Afshin kissed my ear, and the kisses that followed left me feeling like a teenager, making out in a hideaway.

He propped himself up on his forearm and smiled. "Five hundred years ago an Indian man and woman made love here, but they had no idea that someday a woman from Belgium and a man from Iran would lie on the same spot."

The trill of a winter bird rang out above us.

Chapter 11

I told Afshin that I would love him to get a taste of a Christian church service. I assumed that since he'd already attended a Baha'i lecture, which was probably prohibited in Iran, going to church would seem easy by comparison. After all, Jesus is a prophet to Muslims. Afshin agreed to go, though probably only to please me. I doubted that he'd enjoy either the Quaker or Unitarian services I usually attended. A traditional Christian church would better represent my religious background.

My old friend, Diane, worshipped in a Presbyterian Church, and she'd said the minister gave interesting sermons. I told Afshin about her recommendation, and a couple of hours later the two of us crossed the threshold of the church. An usher greeted us and led us to our seats. The oak pews reminded me of the church David and I had attended. Just before the service started, I spotted Diane across the sanctuary. I'd told her that Afshin and I were involved, but not that we were married. I wanted to deliver that news in person.

The choir director announced the hymn: "Nothing but the Blood." We started singing, "What can wash away my sin?" and I sang the rest of the song by heart. Afshin struggled with an occasional phrase, but then he was quiet. "Nothing but the blood of Jesus," was the answer to the song's question—but this was not Islam's path to washing away sins. Afshin had to wait until Judgment Day to discover what punishment awaited him.

"Please open your Bibles to Genesis, Chapter Twenty," the minister said.

When I found the passage about Abraham and Isaac, I smiled. The story would be familiar to Afshin. After all, besides having the same God, Muslims, Jews, and Christians shared the same religious foundation. However, hearing again the story of Isaac, who nearly lost his life at the hands of his father, Abraham, I cringed, realizing that this story of the unthinkable—a parent willing to sacrifice his own child—was common to so many people in the world.

"The Qu'ran has the same story," Afshin whispered.

I nodded, but now wished the sermon was about Jesus's message of love and forgiveness. It wouldn't be familiar to Afshin, but it was the part of Christianity that I'd hoped he would hear.

During the next twenty minutes, I noticed Afshin's impatience barometer rise a couple of times as his knee vibrated up and down. The service ended, and we made our way into the aisle and toward Diane. Though an inch shorter than I, her mahogany ringlets made her easy to spot in the crowd.

"What a surprise to see you here." She tilted her head, waiting to catch an explanation.

Just then, I heard my name. I turned, and there stood a woman with whom I'd worked two years earlier. Paula had left to have a baby and hadn't returned after maternity leave.

"How've you been?" she asked. Motherhood suited her. Glowing skin surrounded her warm smile. "Is this your husband?"

"Uh, yes, but what made you think so? I wasn't married the last time I saw you."

I glanced at Diane, whose eyes widened.

"You always used to talk about going dancing. I assumed it was with your husband."

She extended a hand to Afshin and, after a slight hesitation, he shook it. I wondered how he felt, shaking the hand of an attractive young woman. And was he surprised that she'd guessed our relationship?

Diane grabbed my arm as soon as Paula left. "What's this all about? When did it happen?"

I gave her the short version, and she turned to Afshin. "Well, congratulations! Though I have to admit I'm in shock."

As we left her and walked to the car, I noticed Afshin's furrowed brow.

"What's the matter?" I asked.

"I see that rich people don't need religion. I felt no passion in that church." With hands in his pockets and eyes down, he continued walking. "People need the rules of religion. The poor understand that."

"We need rules until we can hear the spirit within—the God in each of us," I said, touching my heart.

He gave me a look that conveyed, "You must be kidding," but then simply said, "I disagree."

How could I give him a crash course in something that took me years to discover?

"So you weren't upset because that woman assumed we were married?" I asked as I unlocked the car.

"No. That was funny." He chuckled.

Strange funny, for sure.

In the afternoon Afshin drove off to pick up Cal for an informal game of soccer at the university. Both of them loved soccer. I hoped that playing together would form the basis for a friendship.

I picked up the phone and used the time alone to catch up with friends.

In the dimness of dusk, a set of headlights swept the house. A moment later, Afshin bounced in.

"Cal is so friendly." He shook his head as though surprised at this discovery. "He said he'd be here for supper around six."

After Beth's reaction to the news of our marriage, I supposed he expected Cal to be even more upset. What Afshin didn't know was how analytical Cal could be in his reaction to events. Sometimes I wished he showed more emotion.

As we prepared dinner, Afshin said, "I wonder how Calvin feels about his mother being married again."

Hmm. Is that why he was surprised at Cal's friendliness?

"I suppose it's strange for him to see me with someone his age."

He stopped stirring the chicken in the pan and turned to me. His serious stare sent a pang to my chest.

"Listen," he said, taking hold of my upper arms. "It doesn't matter to me, but why don't we get it out of the way? I'll guess your age, and you can decide whether or not to tell me."

He kept an intense gaze on me and my resolve to keep my age a secret weakened.

"Are you fifty?" He leaned forward and brought his eyes level with mine.

He guessed so close. If he already thinks I'm fifty, and he loves me, I suppose it's safe to admit it. I nodded.

"Don't worry," he said, smiling, "you don't look fifty. I figured it out because of the age of your children and some things you said."

"I do worry. I've seen too many older women left for younger ones."

"I'm different." He shook me gently, as though to wake me from sleep. "I've told you that your age doesn't matter to me, but *you* keep talking about it." He looked up and let out an exasperated sigh. "What is age? Why is it important?"

I wanted to believe him. Oh, how I wanted to believe him. But I couldn't.

"I'll try not to talk about our age difference anymore," I said.

His tight embrace said 'thank you.'

Later, at the dinner table, I asked Cal, "Would you tell Afshin about a memory you have of Dad? He'd like to know more about him."

Cal's eyes narrowed as he stared at the ceiling. Then his face brightened, and he said, "Whenever he came home he'd call out, 'Home, babe!'"

The two words flowed sweetly into my ears as they had hundreds of times. I never cared that feminists found the term 'babe' demeaning. I felt the love in David's words; they'd signaled his return and his caring.

During the rest of dinner, and while Afshin and Cal washed the dishes, I searched for signs of a budding friendship, but none appeared. A barrier stood between them, and I was sure Cal had raised it. If only they could become friends, then Afshin would feel included in the family—and be with us forever.

After Cal left, I handed Afshin a short story by Tolstoy: "What Men Live By."

"This is one of my favorite books. Would you like to read it?"

He took it to his room, and I didn't see him for the rest of the evening.

When he came down around eleven, he pulled me from my chair and led me to my bedroom. My body ached—I couldn't believe I was menstruating after a five-month break. And now, for the first time in our marriage of four weeks, I wasn't in the mood for lovemaking.

I hesitated. "I'm not feeling well. I have what women get every month. You know . . ."

"Oh, yes," he said, with no hint of embarrassment. "Let's just lie down together a while, and then I'll go sleep in my bed. In Islam, a man shouldn't touch a woman with desire during this time."

We cuddled under the flannel sheets and Afshin kissed me. Then he propped himself up. He gazed into my eyes and shook his head. Finally, looking up, he let out an extended "Wow."

Some moments passed. "You know, I finished reading your book," he said. "That story is amazing. I love it. Maybe the reason I'm with you is to learn the third lesson the angel had to learn: people live by the love they give to each other."

"If so, you've learned it well."

His lips pursed to the side, but then he kissed my temple and said he was going to sleep in his bed. He got up, but after he took a step, he turned and held me again.

"How will I ever leave for Iran when leaving your bed is this difficult?"

A vice gripped my chest. I breathed to relieve its hold and told myself to stop fearing the future. Afshin was here now.

After working out at the gym the next day, I met Ana for dinner. We slid into our usual booth at a Mexican restaurant. It felt just like old times. Between bites of corn chips and salsa, I told her about life with Afshin.

"It feels wonderful to love someone who loves me the way he does. Since David died, I haven't felt that kind of love." Ana's grin told me she shared in my joy. "I feel safe in this relationship, not as though he has one foot out the door like most of the men I've been involved with these past eleven years. At least I know *when* he'll leave, but for now, he's fully here."

She stopped chewing and leaned forward with concern in her eyes. "That's one way to look at it. Are you thinking of going to Iran with him?"

I stared at the ring on my watchband for a second. This key ring with a beginning and an end.

"I love him enough to go, but also enough not to. If we agreed to stay married, I'd be afraid that one day our age difference would really matter. I couldn't stand it if he lost interest in me as a woman, and what if that happened in Iran a few years from now? I'd have to leave."

"Even without your age difference, can you see yourself in a chador? Never again feeling the wind through your hair or the sun on your skin? I couldn't stand it." She grimaced.

"I wouldn't have to wear a chador," I said, eager to share what I'd recently learned from Afshin. "Things have loosened up over there. I could get away with wearing a scarf and a long coat called a *manteau*. I pushed the basket of chips toward Ana. "But, you're right, even that wouldn't be fun."

"No, but I can understand why you'd go." She rested her chin on her palm. "It's so rare to find the kind of love you two share. And if anyone could pull this off, you could."

The Bird and The Fish

Tears filled my eyes. She understood.

The server brought our meals and we took a break from our conversation.

If Afshin asked me to live in Iran, would I do it? Could I deal with the restrictions the clerics imposed on people? No make-up and no alcohol wouldn't crimp my style, but I wouldn't be allowed to ride my bike, play the flute, or have friendships with men who weren't family. And I would feel isolated as a foreigner. Even if Afshin and I could survive economically, could our relationship survive the challenges his society would present to us?

Anyway, he hadn't asked me to go live with him, so there was no use dissecting this scenario.

Life in America was comfortable and interesting for me. Sure, there were things I didn't like. In comparison to Europe, we barely received any international news. Work seemed to take precedence over relationships. People moved constantly for their jobs and accepted a mere two weeks of vacation a year.

Yet I loved the richness we enjoyed: the various ethnic foods, music, philosophies, and skin colors. And in what other country could I, as a middle-aged woman, go to college? Most of all, I appreciated the freedom to choose how to live life. I was part of this great experiment, this huge mishmash of people, each bringing swatches of cultures from other lands. This was home—a place where I could be true to myself.

To survive in Iran I'd have to hide anything that screamed "Westerner" and, even then, I'd always be an outsider in such a homogeneous society. Learning the language like a native wouldn't make me Persian or Muslim, either. But I'd be with Afshin.

Ana stopped eating. "Listen," she said, "I want a written promise from him that if you end up going to Iran, he'll protect you."

"It feels good to hear your concern, but don't worry. I'm sure Afshin would take good care of me. His protection genes are dominant ones," I said, hoping to bring a smile to Ana's lips.

"Good. And I'd come visit you. I just wouldn't tell people I'm Jewish."

"I doubt that would be a problem. Afshin says many Jews live in his neighborhood, and they get along fine."

"Then why have so many emigrated?"

"My guess is that they're still second-class citizens. After all, it is the *Islamic* Republic of Iran. Afshin has never walked in their shoes, so he doesn't realize what it's like to be a minority."

"You're probably right. Anyway, I'd feel more comfortable keeping my heritage to myself. You never know when you're going to run across some fanatics who'd love to get their hands on an American Jew. Nooo thanks."

Her fear surprised me. I rarely thought of her as Jewish. When did she last attend a synagogue or observe a holiday? If anything, she worshipped nature and beauty.

"Before we worry about that, let's wait and see if I go," I said. "But enough about me. This time with Afshin is consuming me. I'm sorry. What's been going on with you?"

She told me about her unsuccessful date with the Iranian—no chemistry—and her worry about her recently hospitalized grandmother. Then we decided what kind of cake she would make for my wedding party a couple of weeks later.

"Let's have dinner like this more often," I said. She smiled and nodded. I'd make time somehow.

∽⊘∽

When I walked in the door, Afshin darted from his chair and wrapped his arms around me. He growled and playfully bit my neck. "*Bokhoramet.*"

"I could eat you up, too," I said, nudging my way into the softness of his neck and nibbling at it. "Let's go upstairs," I whispered.

"Are all women as sweet as you?" he asked, as we lay side by side a while later.

I almost said, "No, so you'd better stick with me," but I didn't want to force myself on him—even in jest.

"I was like a barren desert before you were in my life, and now I feel like a blossoming garden," he said.

"You sound like a poet."

"You make me a poet," he said, running his finger down my nose. "My mother used to read poetry to me. For a while I wrote poems, but I never showed them to anyone." He took a deep breath and was quiet for a minute. "You are so clean."

Puzzled, I stared at him for a second. "What do you mean?"

"It may sound like a strange way to say it, but that's how I feel about you. I know your body is clean, but I'm talking about your spirit."

"I told you I've made mistakes in my life," I insisted, fearing someday he'd discover things about me that he'd consider unclean.

"Yes, but I know your heart."

I reached around the nape of his neck and embraced him. Finally, a man who appreciates my heart—what more could I ever want?

My nose circled the crown of his head as I inhaled his scent. After a while, he sat up, looked over his shoulder at me, and laughed—a joy-filled laugh.

"Why are you laughing?"

"For happiness. I want to be with you until I'm sixty-five."

He wanted me forever. In Iran sixty-five was considered old. Were we dreaming?

After a minute I turned around. "Afshin, could you stay here one more year?" I braced myself for a "No."

His face turned serious. "I don't think I should. If I stay, it will be extremely difficult to leave." He paused. "But tell me, what would be easier for you?"

"Easier? I might not choose what's easier. I want what's richer."

In the quiet that followed I realized that over and over, I'd chosen the deep end of the pool. Though scary at first, I'd found satisfaction in those waters.

"Let's pray," Afshin said. "How can *we* decide what is best?"

We joined hands and asked for guidance. I hoped God had time for this one.

After the "Amen," Afshin said, "You are like a mountain, and I feel that I am climbing the mountain and learning many things. In Iran we say that mountains are the nails of the earth."

If he meant that I was solid and stable, and that through me he was discovering landscapes he'd never seen before—good. But I wanted more. I wanted to be his paradise.

Chapter 12

One evening soon after that, a dozen people from my Spanish group gathered around my extended dining-room table for a potluck dinner. I liked taking a turn to host the bi-monthly *tertulia*, a social event that gave me a chance to use my Spanish.

After dinner, Beatrice's petite frame darted between the dining room and kitchen as the two of us cleared the table. Ever since spending two weeks together at a language school in Cuernavaca, Mexico, we'd shared news from our lives whenever we ran into each other at Spanish group meetings.

She set a stack of plates on the counter and stared at me for a second. "You say you're happy with Afshin, but it seems crazy to me. How can you be happy in a relationship you know will end?"

"Don't they all? And how can I *not* be happy? If it's crazy, it's a wonderful crazy. What *if* I had only six months to live? It would mean I'd be spending the rest of my life with this man I love." I filled the teakettle and noticed my defensive tone.

She rolled her eyes. "Sure, but you'll probably live a lot longer."

"True, but I'll find a way to savor what comes next. I want my headstone to read: 'She lived life to the fullest.'"

"But you better not move to Iran. Do you know that many American women who've married Iranians are unable to come back to the U.S.? You remember that book, *Not Without My Daughter?*" she asked, sliding the last plate into the dishwasher.

"Oh, please. That man had problems. But you're right—it is ridiculous that women still have to get permission from their husbands to leave the country. Yet I've also heard about American women living in Iran who are free to travel and are quite happy with their Iranian husbands."

"Maybe so, but I hope you'll never risk going."

"It wouldn't be a risk. Afshin isn't a controlling husband."

"I hope you're right," she said, her eyebrows arching.

"Besides, the plan isn't for me to go."

"You know . . ." A long pause followed. "I have a hard time imagining a relationship with someone so young."

"You consider yourself a feminist, right?"

"Of course."

"Well, look at all the men who are with younger women."

"I have trouble with that, too."

"I used to, but now I see every relationship as unique. It all depends on the people and circumstances. When I'm with Afshin, I don't feel that I'm with someone that much younger."

She hunched her shoulders and held her hands up like a shield. "Being with a man younger than my son is inconceivable."

"I know, I know. I never imagined I'd be in this position, either."

Beatrice shook her head as we joined the others in the living room. A smile lingered on my lips at Beatrice's last statement. In the short term, I loved being with my younger man: the beauty of his firm body, his lively thinking, his hopeful dreams. It was sweet when friends showed acceptance, but Beatrice's revulsion didn't bother me. I understood her concern and didn't deny the possibility of getting stuck in Iran if I went. In the end, however, whether or not to take that risk would be my choice.

By ten o'clock everyone had left.

"I'm starving," Afshin said, heading straight for the refrigerator as soon as he got home. "I had a sandwich with Milad, but I'm hungry again. I told him that I'm always hungry now that I'm married. It takes energy, and I need more protein." He threw me an impish smile as he brought out a quart of plain yogurt. "Milad told me not to talk to him about such things until he's also married."

Ah, yes. He and Milad never discussed sex.

He finished eating and stared at the wedding ring I'd given him. He slid it from his finger and placed it in my palm. "I thank you very much, but this ring is too rich for me. Would you give me a key ring like that one, instead?" He pointed to the ring on my watchband.

"Sure, why not? Then we'll match." His discomfort with objects he considered luxurious was understandable.

I ran upstairs and searched through a box of old keys until I found a ring and a long leather boot lace. I slipped the ring onto it.

"Look, you can wear this as a pendant," I said to Afshin, who stood in the doorway.

"I like this. It's more natural." He kissed the ring before knotting the lace behind his neck.

The next afternoon, with no one home, I stuck my hand between the mattress and box spring and pulled out my journal. Over a month of the marriage was already history.

I placed a pillow against the headboard and leaned back on it. My pen flew across the page as I recorded thoughts, feelings, and experiences related to Afshin. Someday I could read the contents and relive the sweet and bitter moments. Two pages brimmed with words when I heard Afshin come into the house. I stuck the pen in the spiral notebook and slapped it shut, but before I had a chance to stow it away, he came in. His lips pressed mine for a long moment.

"It's so neat that you write things down." He'd noticed the journal stuck in my hand along the side of the mattress. "I think it makes your thinking clear."

"I do it because my grandchildren or great-grandchildren may want to know about their grandmother, and because I don't trust my memory." I lifted the notebook to my lap. "With this I can go back and read what happened. You probably can't understand that with the incredible memory you have."

"Don't worry about your memory," he said, tapping my forehead. "The Indians have a saying, 'The river has no memory,' yet they revere the river."

Like sparkling champagne, joy bubbled through me. With the kind of memory he had, I was sure he'd be impatient with mine, but instead, he had offered me a way to be at peace with what I had.

"I want to know you better," he said. "Would you read your journal to me?"

I bolted upright. "I'll have to think about that!"

My face flushed as I imagined reading to him about the way I'd desired him weeks before we were married. That, I would rather keep to myself.

At dinner that evening I'd eaten only half my food, when Afshin finished his plate and spun back into the kitchen for more.

"I used to worry because you ate so little. Now look at you!" I said, amused at the change in him. I stared at the pile of spaghetti threatening to overflow his plate.

"It's what I was used to. At home, we had to eat small portions." He took a mouthful, barely chewed it, and swallowed. "One time my mother served us soup, and my grandmother found a piece of meat in her bowl. She passed it to my father. He passed it to my mother, and then she passed it to me, but I quickly gave it back to her." His lips curled in a nostalgic smile. "Iranians put up with a lot of suffering. Even if they're starving, they believe that it's all in God's hands. They say, 'He who gave you the teeth, will give you the food.'"

His plate was empty within a few minutes. "*Chai mi-khai?*" he asked.

"Yes, I'd love some tea," I said, warmed by the comfort of our daily ritual.

As we sipped tea and crunched butter cookies, I caught him gazing at me.

"You talk like a woman, walk like a woman, and feel like a woman. There is a softness about you that many women here don't have. You are both feminine and strong."

I stared at my amber tea. "I wish I were twenty-five." *Oops, I mentioned age again.*

"Why? I'm 25, and we are one." He paused. "Would . . . would you come to Iran if you were twenty-five?"

"Yes!" exploded from my lips.

"Damn! Why were we born at different times?"

⁂

"What would you like to do today?" Afshin asked one Saturday morning.

"It's not exciting, but I'd like to get the walls in the family room ready for painting."

"OK, we'll do it. And later would you like to watch *The Message?* It's a movie about our prophet, Mohammed."

"I'd love to."

We changed into old T-shirts and jeans and started work on the project in the family room.

I rubbed the sanding block over rough spots. "I'll think of you whenever I sand a wall from now on."

He lowered his spackling tool, stared at the floor, and then concentrated his gaze on me with uncommon seriousness. "Maybe it's easier if you don't remember me."

"What!" My arm went limp. "That's impossible. You said you would never forget me—I have the same right!"

"Men have big chests. They can hold a lot in here." His knuckles rapped his sternum. "I don't want you to be sad."

Quiet moments passed before I spoke again. "Let's not think ahead."

"I try, but I think of it at least ten times a day."

"I do, too."

A shoebox on the bookshelf near Afshin caught my eye. I reached for it and knelt on the Afghan rug as I opened the box of old pictures.

"This is me with Greg, right after he was born," I said, handing Afshin a picture. "David was still in the Marine Corps, but we lived off base in this mobile home."

"You never told me that David was a soldier," he said, frowning.

"Oh yes—four years. He enlisted the summer after high school, even though he'd already been accepted to college. He was with a friend who was enlisting, and the recruiter persuaded him to join, too. I still can't believe it. The Vietnam War was on, but I doubt he thought about it in that moment."

Afshin's eyes widened. "Did he go to Vietnam?"

"No. Thank God."

I handed Afshin another picture.

"This was taken the year after David died."

In the Olan Mills portrait, sixteen-year-old Greg and I are standing in front of a painted woodland backdrop, Calvin and Beth directly in front of us.

"This picture reminds me of my aunt," Afshin said. "She was left alone with six children when my uncle was killed in the war."

"Did she ever remarry?"

"Oh, no. She wouldn't do that. It would hurt my cousins. She did the right thing. Children don't want to see their mother with another man."

A surge of guilt zapped me. What would he think if he knew how many times my children had seen me with another man? Had it hurt them? Did Afshin think it still hurt them, even though they were now adults? Given his response to Beth's first reaction to our marriage, it was likely. Or, maybe he was uncomfortable with the judgments they might have about him. I'd let him grapple with his guilt on this one, though from what he'd just said, he seemed blind to the fact that his words contradicted his own actions. I gathered he wasn't feeling any guilt at all.

"But your aunt needed someone to help her, didn't she?"

"My mom helped a lot," he said, still looking at the portrait. "We were always at their house."

I handed him a few more pictures that I'd picked out and, while he looked at them, tucked others into the back of the box. I wasn't about to show him photos of me with men I'd dated.

"You look like my mother here, but something about you is unique. It appeals to me tremendously," he said, eyes held by the photo taken at my brother's house when I was forty-two. "May I keep this?"

"Sure." I was pleased that he wanted it. "Shall we get back to work?"

A couple of hours later, we finished the last of the sanding.

In the evening we cuddled on the sofa, watching *The Message*. Afshin paused the video a few times to provide details about the story.

"The Qur'an was inspired by Allah, through an angel. The language is so exceptionally poetic that Mohammed himself could not have written it."

"Christians say the Bible is inspired, too."

During my days in the Baptist Church, I'd heard how God inspired men to write the books of the Bible. And if the Bible *was* the word of God, who could argue with it? But Muslims believed the same thing about the Qur'an. Hmm . . .

"So tell me, what does it take for a person to be a Muslim?"

His eyebrows shot up, and he took a moment to answer. "You must believe in the existence of God and His uniqueness, that Mohammed was the messenger of God, and that a day of judgment is coming when people will be sent to heaven or hell."

His recitation reminded me of catechism.

He drew me closer. "Thank you for watching this. I hope it's not boring for you."

"Boring? Not at all. I'm interested in learning about religions. Especially *yours*."

Sunday, Afshin was downstairs writing letters home, and I was in my room, catching up on some overdue bills, when I heard a smooth, melancholic female voice coming from the stereo in the living room. I recognized the Iranian singer, Googoosh, from a tape Afshin had once played for me. What a shame to ban such gorgeous music. Fortunately, Iranians found ways to listen to her after the Revolution. Clandestine tapes moved underground like subway trains at rush hour.

As I walked past Afshin on my way to get a drink, he grasped my hand and pulled me to his lips. The urgency of his kiss surprised me, and I noticed tears spill from his eyes. Had the music made him homesick? He looked down. I tried lifting his chin, but he resisted.

"Afshin, you're an emotional being. Why hide your tears? Do you believe I'll think you're weak? I know better. Please tell me. Why are you sad?"

He blew through his lips. "Writing to my sister. She's getting married soon, and I won't be there to celebrate with her." He swallowed hard. "I wrote to her fiancé and told him, 'Be careful, Saravan, you're leading my heart.'"

The phrase's romantic connotation startled me. "What does that mean?"

"Years ago, when caravans transported people and precious goods, the leader was called the saravan." He paused for a second, and I pulled a chair up beside his. "There's a story of a boy who had a deep love for a girl. Her family didn't want her to marry him. They decided to send her far away to marry someone else. As she was leaving with the caravan, the boy ran to the leader. 'Be careful, Saravan,' he said. 'You're leading my heart.' So it became a saying we use to mean, 'Take care of her—she's precious to me.'"

"You love your sister very much, don't you?"

"Yes. In Iran, brothers and sisters are close." He paused as though he'd just had an insight. "Do you see how I'm opening up?" he asked softly. "I can even cry in front of you. I always heard about how sin darkens the heart, but not about how love makes it shine like a bright light."

Finally, the day of our wedding party arrived.

After we returned home from a run to the grocery store, I found a phone message from Tom, an old admirer. He stayed in touch even though I'd told him I wasn't interested in a romantic relationship.

After listening to the message, I hurried to the kitchen to find Afshin, but he wasn't there. I found him downstairs, staring outside at the garden. He turned toward me with a creased brow.

"That was Tom, someone I met last year at a Baha'i dinner," I said. "He wanted to date me, but he wasn't my type."

"You didn't like him?"

"I admired what he did—he worked for peace—but I just couldn't get interested in him beyond that. He was too old."

A smirk played on Afshin's lips, but he didn't comment. Whoops, what was I saying? I paused for a second. No, that wasn't the real reason. Even if he'd been younger I wouldn't have been attracted to him. He had no fire.

"I loved you the first moment I saw you," Afshin said, as he wrapped his arms around my waist. After gazing at me lovingly, he shifted his gaze outside at the day fading into dusk. "I still remember when you opened the door," he continued. "You wore your blue shirt and those long shorts. Your eyes and your smile penetrated my heart. My love was pure—it had no lust." His smile grew. "I felt we were of one blood. Usually, I avoided being close to people who were just passing in my life, but I told God I wanted a significant relationship with you."

And you got that, I thought, smiling inwardly.

"As I came to know you, I loved you more, but when you told me you wanted a husband, not a son . . . that was hard to hear. Yet I wanted to make you happy." He smiled at me.

How had he gone from loving me as a mother to loving me as a wife? Living with the enigma wasn't easy.

"I used to talk about you to Milad all the time," he said. He stopped and laughed softly to himself. "He said to me once, 'Why don't you marry her if you like her so much?'"

"Really?" My body grew lighter hearing that even his friend had noticed something romantic about the way Afshin talked about me.

"After I decided to marry you, I came to love you as my wife, and now, I'm very happy," he said, pulling me into a tight embrace.

Tears stung my eyes. He'd done it for *me*—he'd given me what I wanted even though it wasn't his original desire. Strange. I felt satisfied with a love that didn't spring from a passionate place.

But wait . . . I leaned back and searched his eyes. "Are you saying I should have married Tom to make him happy?"

"Oh, no, not if your heart didn't lead you to do that," he said, his brow furrowing. "My heart led me to marry you. At first, it was hard. I wanted to be at your level, but you had years of experience. I couldn't catch up." He was silent for a moment. "I no longer feel that difference. I don't know why." He gazed outside again, and a burst of amusement lit his face. "Maybe it's because you don't have to tell me what to do in bed anymore."

I laughed. Yes, he'd learned quickly. How many twenty-five-year-old men in America could say they'd recently had sex for the first time? Yet I had no trouble believing it of Afshin—sex outside of marriage was a serious offense in Islam. No wonder someone came up with the idea of a short-term marriage.

"And," he continued, "for me the most important part of our marriage is my devotion to you and seeing you happy."

Devotion? It sounded old-fashioned, yet it gave me what I wanted—somebody whose love I could count on.

"But what do *you* want?" I asked.

"I told you—to be devoted to you." He could tell I wanted more and added, "The only thing I do for myself is soccer."

"What about math? Don't you love math?"

"Even math is for others." His voice dropped.

It lacked the vibrancy I'd noticed before when he'd talked about math. Was he kidding himself? What about his enthusiasm when he taught it to me, and his awe when he spoke of its mysteries?

Again, I felt perplexed. I wanted to understand Afshin better, but he refused to discuss other reasons for which he might have decided to marry me. He must have needed affection, warmth, and caring after three years without his mother, sister, or grandmother. Sex was a bonus. But, since he'd been taught that devotion to God and others was the highest good, perhaps it was easier on his pride to think that only those ideals prompted his actions toward me. His love felt real and so did the connection between us, whatever name he gave that love.

"People will start arriving soon." I took his hand and moved toward the staircase. Once upstairs, we headed for our own bedrooms.

My favorite outfit, a green and black Ikat-patterned skirt and matching vest, hung ready on the closet door. I'd bought it in Guatemala City while there on vacation with Cal and Beth. The outfit carried that special memory. I wanted it to carry this one, too.

I dabbed a hint of Je Reviens behind each ear and on my palm. Mamy's perfume—a way for her to share this evening with me. I could bring her ashes from my closet, I thought mischievously, but no, Afshin or some of the guests might be appalled.

Afshin came into the room wearing jeans with a gray and maroon sweater. The key ring dangled from the leather strap hanging over the turtleneck. I smiled at his casual attire.

"You must know that my friends don't need formal dress to prove an occasion is important."

Soon friends started arriving, one after another. Each placed an appetizing hors d'oeuvre, salad, or entrée on the dining-room table. My gratitude overflowed for the feast on display and the caring that had gone into its preparation.

Afshin greeted people at the door as he took their coats. I was glad he'd met most of them before, especially since Milad wasn't coming. Afshin hadn't told me why, and I didn't ask. Now Afshin was the only person present from his generation.

Ana wouldn't be coming either. I couldn't blame her. The grandmother she adored had just died. "You know how much I'd love to be there," she'd said, "but I can't even bring myself to bake the cake I promised."

From the stereo playing in the background, Kate Wolf sang *Give Yourself to Love*.

> Kind friends all gathered 'round, there's something I would say:
> That what brings us together here has blessed us all today.
> Love has made a circle that holds us all inside;
> Where strangers are as family, loneliness can't hide.
>
> You must give yourself to love if love is what you're after;
> Open up your hearts to the tears and laughter,
> And give yourself to love, give yourself to love.

Her lyrics fit the day perfectly and especially the way I felt.

"Hey, Miriam. Are we eating soon?" Rachel asked, from across the room. "This spread looks outrageous."

Down-to-earth Rachel. Speaking right from the heart—or stomach—without pretension. I loved her for it.

Everyone converged on the dining room. I turned to Afshin. "Do you mind if I first say a few words?"

He looked down. "Please don't," he whispered.

His answer caught me by surprise. Was he embarrassed? I had hoped to share my joy with these friends who'd come to share the celebration. With pleading eyes, I tilted my head and whispered. "It's really important to me." For an instant, I felt like a child pleading with a parent: "Please! Please! Can't I go play with my friends?" Strange how he brought that out in me.

"OK, but please keep it short," he said, sounding nervous.

Arms around each other's waists, we stood next to the table. My friends clustered in a tight half-circle around the other side. The psalmist's words, "My cup runneth over," described my mood.

"Once, I made a list of the characteristics I looked for in a man. I thought that if I found someone with half of them, I'd consider myself fortunate." I gazed at Afshin. "This man has all of them. As you know, a month ago we exchanged vows and rings because we wanted a fully committed relationship, even if only for six months. Many people won't understand, but I hope you will."

Clapping erupted. I was thrilled to have friends who could celebrate with us even though our marriage wasn't based on the usual "'til death do us part" agreement.

Rachel motioned for Afshin and me to start the line at one end of the table. We served ourselves and sat in the living room, where we'd set up folding chairs to ensure that everyone got a seat.

Henry, a former boyfriend, came over. "You're a unique person," he said, giving my back a gentle rub. "You're teaching us all something with this relationship." He then seated himself next to Afshin and engaged him in conversation. Would Afshin be as friendly to Henry if he knew I'd dated him?

I scanned the room. In pairs or small clusters, people chatted. I glanced often at Afshin, and our eyes drew smiles from each other.

Later, after we'd sliced the cake and given everyone a piece, Afshin made his way from one person or couple to another, chatting a little with each one. I imagined he was playing the part of the host as he'd learned from family events in Iran. Each time he passed by me, he rubbed my arm or squeezed my waist. Did that mean that he felt more at ease? I hoped so because I had a splinter of guilt about insisting on making my pronouncement at the table.

Cal and Beth arrived after ten. Cal had left his shift early at the restaurant, and Beth had probably synchronized her arrival with his. Though late, at least they had come.

Cal shook Afshin's hand. "I hope you'll be happy together."

Just then Rachel came by with a camera. "Look here." She motioned for us to stand together.

The flash went off, and as quickly, the evening ended.

Rachel was the last to leave. "You guys are beaming, and we're all thrilled to see you so happy." She hugged me and whispered, "Afshin's special. He's ageless and sincere."

I beamed more brightly at her affirmation.

Chapter 13

Afshin's eyelids creased and fluttered before he peeked at the new day. I'd already been gazing at my more "official" husband for a few minutes. I wove my fingertips through the black curls on his chest and traveled down his side to where the skin dipped before it rose again toward his thigh. I lingered there, delighting in the velvet softness.

Afshin reached for my elbow and pulled me over his chest. "*Dooset daaram,*" he said, barely opening his morning mouth.

"I love you, too," I whispered in his ear.

"How did you and David make love?"

His question surprised me. "You don't want details, do you?"

He shook his head no.

"I can tell you that it was about twice a week—and that was in a good week."

He raised his eyebrows.

"I know. It's hard to believe." For the past month we'd made love at least seven times a week. "Remember, David and I were married when I was nineteen. I think that after moving a dozen times and spending my teen years in a boarding school, I was looking for a home more than a husband."

Afshin pressed my head to his chest and kissed my hair.

"Don't get me wrong—I loved David . . ." I sighed and Afshin stroked my head. I looked up at him. "But why do you want to know about David and me?"

"I'm a curious man," he said with a mischievous smile.

I had a feeling that wasn't the only reason; he probably needed reassurance that I was satisfied with him.

His face became serious. "I love you as much as David did."

How could he know? He sounded boyish, but I didn't care. I believed him.

Afshin needed new shoes for my niece's wedding, so after breakfast we headed for the stores at the mall. With only four days until Christmas, the shops bulged with customers. People carried bags filled with presents, but many faces didn't manifest the spirit of joyful giving. Since Christmas wasn't part of Afshin's culture, I wondered what he might be thinking.

"Let's hurry," he said. "I don't like watching all this silly buying. Do people need all those things?"

He picked out a pair of black shoes and tried them on. After strutting rapidly up and down the aisle once, he said, "I like these. Let's go."

"Let me buy them for you for Christmas," I said. He didn't earn much, and after all, they were needed only for *my* niece's wedding.

We reached the cashier, and he pushed my hand away when I brought out my wallet. "I have the money. I can pay."

To lighten his financial load, I wanted to share from my abundance, but he had yet to let me pay for anything. His salary for teaching two classes at the university covered living expenses, but little else. He'd once told me that after he left home he refused money from his parents, except for the plane fare to come to the United States, and he'd paid that back within a year. I'd asked if his parents expected him to live in poverty to repay them. They didn't have much, he replied, and the necessary scrimping didn't hurt him. He hadn't said it boastfully, just as a matter of fact.

We pulled out of our parking space and passed a woman pushing a stroller.

"What if we had a baby?" he asked, smiling. "Would you like a boy or a girl?"

"Either one," I said. "I wish I could have a child with you. She would be amazing." I recognized my wish as a fantasy, even with a mind saturated with new love. "It's still possible for me to get pregnant. What would you do if that happened?"

"If we had a child, I would stay," he said firmly.

Even if possible, I couldn't hold him that way, and told him so.

Back at home, we gobbled leftovers and rushed to the playhouse for *A Christmas Carol*. I wanted Afshin to experience another activity enjoyed by Americans—one that allowed our creativity to shine and that made me proud.

As we pressed through one of the many doors into the theater, I heard chattering and laughter from children and adults. The contrast to the shopping crowd of the afternoon struck me. Maybe these theater-goers already knew the ending to this well-known story. The spirit of giving and loving that heals Scrooge had brought smiles before—and tears.

Afshin had never heard of *A Christmas Carol*. In fact, he'd never attended a play, at least not a Western one. The revolutionaries had banned all forms of Western entertainment. As the play unfolded, his eyes never left the stage. The Spirits of Christmas Past, Present, and Future each appeared on stage with dazzling special effects.

At the end, Scrooge carried Tiny Tim on his shoulders, the curtains closed, and we all sprung up and clapped—even Afshin, who was forbidden to clap in the Islamic Republic of Iran.

"This was *so* good," said Afshin, shaking his head and dropping back in his seat. "People here don't know how much they have."

I agreed, and I wished the whole world could be this lucky.

We stayed seated until the theater was nearly empty. Then we went home and danced.

On Christmas Eve, I left work early and drove home with the radio blasting "Jingle Bells." I sang along. I was excited about the evening ahead with my family, including its newest member. I wondered though—how would Afshin's presence affect the mix?

No one was home when I stepped into the house fifteen minutes later. Beth had told me she'd have customers until five because they wanted their hair styled at the last minute for the holidays.

I dropped my briefcase near the staircase and rushed through the family room to the closet where my tree stood, all year long, waiting in full Christmas dress. In the living room, I set the tree on the antique oak dresser. Afshin materialized as I was arranging fluffy white material around its base.

"Guess what happened?" he asked, as I stood up to greet him. "I got an e-mail from Kamran, my friend in Boston. He wanted to know why I had left the Thanksgiving party early, and then he asked, 'Are you married or something?' I typed back 'yes.' He thought I was joking at first, but with Milad's help, I finally convinced him." Amusement played on Afshin's face.

"What did you tell him about me?"

"That you're my landlady." He straightened his back as he made the pronouncement.

I buried my face in my hands, laughing, and heard Afshin's laughter echo mine.

Pouncing on him, I scrunched his lips with mine. "Oh, shucks. I better get things ready for this evening," I said, straightening up and heading toward the kitchen.

I got out the crepe batter from the refrigerator and started preparing our traditional Christmas dinner of crepes with a variety of fillings. Just after six, Cal and Diane—my children's "Aunt Di"—toted in two huge shopping bags of presents. Afshin dashed over to take Diane's bags.

After Beth arrived, I suggested we sit down to dinner.

"The Little Drummer Boy" played softly from the stereo as everyone found their seats. I set two bowls—one with Shrimp Newburg, another with spinach and mushrooms in cheese sauce—beside a plate of crepes on the red and green plaid tablecloth. We joined hands and expressed our gratitude for family, friends, and food.

No one said a word for a couple of minutes after the food was served. Then, like the crank on a Model-T Ford, Diane started the conversation going.

As usual, Beth listened more than she talked. Cal said to her, "Remember when you were little and someone asked you what you wanted to be when you grew up?"

She nodded, with a knowing smile.

"You said you wanted to be a cash register, but you meant a cashier," he said, looking at her with the bond of shared history.

More family stories and laughter followed. Although Afshin said little, he looked relaxed. I hoped he'd enjoy his first Christmas with a Christian family.

After we finished our dessert of strawberry crepes, Afshin said, "This was delicious. Thank you."

"Let's open our gifts," said Beth, as she left the table and headed for the pile in front of the tree. "Mom, when are you going to get a new tree? I remember when you bought this at my school yard sale. That was at least *twelve years* ago!"

I made a face of mock embarrassment, but I was proud of the way I'd stretched the life of many household items.

We filed into the living room. I wished I'd found more gifts that would excite each person. It had been easy to buy for Afshin—there were so many things he needed.

Cal donned the Santa hat and distributed the gifts. Afshin's eyes grew wide as Cal placed a box on his lap for the fourth time.

I leaned closer to Afshin. "I guess Santa Claus decided that even a Muslim would like some Christmas gifts."

He smiled, but I noted discomfort in his demeanor. Maybe I'd made a mistake by telling him he shouldn't buy us gifts. I'd forgotten his pride when I tried being considerate of his religion and his finances.

"Go ahead, Beth. You start," said Cal.

She opened a box. Seeing the flannel sheets with a floral print that I'd bought for her, she exclaimed, "Wow! I can sure use these." Even with two blankets and a comforter on her bed, she complained of being cold.

"And if that doesn't do it, I'll get you a hot water bottle next year."

She laughed. I loved her laughter. I'd heard it so rarely since she reached her teens.

After she opened the next few boxes, each containing clothes, Cal took his turn.

He seemed pleased with the clothing he received, but his face lit up at the latest John Grisham book that came from me.

Did Afshin think us materialistic because we exchanged such a large number of gifts? If only he knew that in many American families, each person received three times as many!

Afshin carefully unwrapped his gift from Diane, a navy blue and green travel bag. "How did you know I needed this?" He looked genuinely pleased.

The card on the other three boxes he received bore Santa's signature. In them Afshin found a belt, then a shirt, and, finally, a pair of jeans. He looked to the ceiling and said, "Thank you Santa, you even knew my size." He sent me a knowing glance and whispered, "You don't have this much money."

But what a joy to spend it on you, I thought. "Hmm. Looks like Santa knew what you needed, too," I said. I thought of Afshin's outdated wardrobe: he didn't seem to mind it, as long as it was functional, but I wanted to see him totally gorgeous, at least now and then.

"I've never received so many gifts at once. We have a holiday, at the end of Ramadan, when children receive small gifts. But all other gifts, such as a little money or food, are for the poor."

"I like that," I said. I was about to ask the others if they'd like to do that for our next Christmas, but I stopped myself. Our style of gift exchange was the tradition they'd known and loved. They might resent a change, especially if it came from Afshin.

After Diane and I finished opening our gifts, Cal and Afshin got up, simultaneously, and cleared the dining-room table together.

"We need to hurry if we want to make it to the candlelight service," I reminded them.

Beth came up from her room with an overnight bag slung over her shoulder. Since Afshin and I were leaving early in the morning for my niece's wedding in Mississippi, I was grateful Beth would spend Christmas Day with Mike's family. She offered her cheek for a kiss. "I want to get to Mike's before it's late. I'll see you next week. Mississippi's so far. Please, drive carefully." Ever since David's accident, 15 years before, she had regularly given me that warning.

Diane, Cal, Afshin, and I didn't arrive at the Unitarian Church until ten after nine. We slipped into the last row. I had a feeling Afshin was relieved to get there after everybody else was seated. He didn't see the point of being introduced to people he would not see again.

Near the end of the service, Afshin whispered, "This is a strange religion. I haven't heard them mention God."

My impulse was to explain why it wasn't necessary, but if he was used to hearing Allah's name constantly at the mosque, the omission of God's name would indeed leave a strange vacuum. I'd been surprised, too, at my first Unitarian service. But soon I found that simply gathering with others whose values resonated with mine was satisfying. For me, loving one another in actions, not only in words—*that* was the essence of God.

Chapter 14

From the shower, Afshin's Persian voice danced up and down the musical scale. I closed my eyes and inhaled the passion in the air. But no, we had to get going. I stuck a yogurt container and some cheese into a red-and-white cooler and tossed bread, almonds, and a few other items into a canvas bag. Mississippi, here we come!

A half hour later, we drove out of Girton.

"Would you teach me a song in Persian?" I asked.

Afshin pressed his lips together, put a finger to his chin, and looked away for a few seconds. "OK, I'll sing it once, and then I'll teach you the words."

Dooset daaram miduni
Kaeeyn kaareh deleh
Gonah-e man nist
Taghsireh dele

I caught the first two words—"I love you"—and although the rest of the words meant nothing to me, Afshin's deep, mellifluous voice, full of emotion, once again travelled to my body's cells and sent them into a whirling Sufi dance.

I parroted Afshin's Persian, singing one line at a time, after him. Then I sang the song alone. Afshin laughed. "*Go noooowiman nist*," he mimicked my pronunciation. "How I love your voice," he said in a gentle tone. "Will you teach me a French song now?"

"Yes, but first, what does your song mean?"

"I'll try. It's something like this: I love you. Do you know it? And because this is the business of the heart, it's not our fault—or sin. It's because of the heart."

"Oh, yes. The heart has so much power. It reminds me of a simple romantic tune from *The Land of Smiles*, an opera in which my mother danced."

Mon amour et ton amour sont nés le même jour.

> *D'un regard très court mais qui nous charme pour toujours.*
> *Mon amour et ton amour se disent tour a tour:*
> *Je t'aime bien, tu m'aimes bien,*
> *Et le reste n'est plus rien.*

"What does it mean?" he asked.

"It means 'My love and your love were born on the same day. We exchanged a short glance and were charmed forever. My love and your love take turns saying, *I love you so, you love me so* . . . and nothing else matters.' It's a perfect song for us, isn't it?"

After teaching each other the lyrics, we sang the songs a dozen times. Six hours into the trip, I put the seat back and dozed off for a couple of hours.

When I woke up, Afshin said, "How I wish you could come to Iran."

"You'll want a young wife, especially so you can have children."

"But maybe we could adopt," he said. "I don't need to have a child of my own."

My heart expanded with warmth and I lay my hand on his thigh. He sounded sincere, but I thought he was dreaming—just as I often was. "Let's see what our future brings."

Silence followed, offering us a place to dream. But, after a while, our hunger brought us back to reality. We pulled into the next roadside picnic area. Unhampered by clouds, the sun's rays warmed us as we spread our food on a table. We straddled a picnic bench, facing each other, and in no time, I finished a bowl of plain yogurt and put my spoon away.

"That's all you're eating?" he asked. "If you can be satisfied with only yogurt for a meal, maybe you *could* survive in Iran."

My face lit up. He was imagining me in Iran. I squeezed his knee.

His comment also made me consider the tough living conditions of the Iranian people. If his salary as a professor were so low that even *he* wouldn't be able to afford certain foods, how could less educated people survive?

We were about an hour away from that night's destination when Afshin said, "When we first started touching, I got scared, but you seemed to have complete confidence. That gave me strength to make the decision to marry you. If you had hesitated, my guilt would have forced me to move out."

"Really?" I was amazed that my confidence had played a key role in his decision.

"Yes, but don't worry," he said, chuckling at my reaction, "we're married now." He reached for my hand and kissed my palm.

As we drove on, I looked forward to our first night together in a different bedroom.

We arrived at a motel near Athens, Tennessee. As soon as we closed the door to our room, I undressed to take a shower. "Will you join me?" I asked.

"No, you go ahead," he said, averting his eyes. I smiled at his re-emerging modesty.

Later, as we lay in an embrace, he pulled back and looked at me seriously for a moment. "Promise me that you will never settle for someone who does not love you completely."

I heard his concern, and it stirred the pond of sadness in my soul.

I laced my fingers between his. "I promise, and it's an easy promise to make now that I've tasted your love. How could I be happy with less?"

"Choose a man worthy of you; otherwise it's better to be alone," he added, as though he spoke from experience.

He'd given me that advice before, and though I appreciated it, I also wondered how he could talk about someone else loving me this way. I wanted to keep the curtain closed on the future without him.

"You're a wonderful lover," I said, hoping to return to the present.

"I had a good teacher." He put his hand on my cheek and slowly moved it down my side.

"Yes, but the way you touch me and take your time, never hurrying—that comes from you, not from a well learned lesson."

Moments later he kissed me goodnight. "Am I a good husband?"

I pursed my lips, and looked at the ceiling for a few long seconds. "Excellent!"

He glowed. You'd have thought I'd just given him the best gift in the world.

Around five-thirty we pulled up to a motel outside Jackson where other family members were staying. After Afshin and I settled into our room, I left him to say his evening prayer and went to find my sister Rona's room. A few minutes later, Rona ran across the parking lot toward me, looking upset. "I wish I'd seen you out here. I knocked at your door and opened it, and there he was, prostrated in prayer. I feel so embarrassed."

I gave her a tight hug. "Don't worry. I'm sure he's not bothered by that. As long as he can pray, he'll be happy."

A few other family members joined us because we were soon to leave for a restaurant. Afshin came out of our room, and I introduced him to everyone. Each one gave him a warm welcome before we headed for Crawley's, a restaurant where my father had often taken his family.

A couple of hours later we were back at the motel, sitting around in Rona's room, our bellies full of hush puppies, fried shrimp, and soft-shell crabs. My other sister, Kathy, and her boyfriend, Jay, were there as well.

"How about a game of penny poker?" asked Jay.

Afshin sprung up from his chair. "Yes, I would like that."

His enthusiasm surprised me. When Afshin's turn to shuffle came, I gasped to see him zip through the cards like a Las Vegas pro.

"Where did you learn that?" I asked.

He looked at me proudly. "At the university. We weren't supposed to play cards, because those games are considered sinful, but poker was my favorite."

"That's funny. My Baptist boarding school also frowned on card-playing," I said.

As we played for the next two hours, I heard more laughter than I'd heard all evening. One by one, we dropped out from fatigue, but Afshin showed no sign of quitting. He and Jay played on until, at the end of a round, Jay said, "That's it. I can't think straight anymore."

The next afternoon, I listened to the familiar words of the ceremony. Lisa and Sam, flanked by four bridesmaids and four ushers, provided the usual wedding scene—another piece of America for Afshin to experience. Little by little, he would gain a broad view of the many squares forming the quilt of our society. Our square, the one we'd formed only six weeks earlier, as we exchanged private marriage vows, would call attention to itself by its uniqueness. Nevertheless, it was part of the quilt called America, where anything goes.

That night, after an informal get-together at Jim and Emily's home, I lay in bed reviewing the day's events. Right after the marriage ceremony, Afshin and I had stood like spectators during the reception in the country club's banquet hall. What had I expected? An introduction to the other guests? It would have been one thing for the family to introduce a half-sister who had appeared late in their lives, but I must've been in fantasy land if I'd thought they'd introduce her 25-year-old Iranian husband. I could just imagine all the questions, spoken and unspoken, that would be stimulated by that introduction.

In my excitement at having Afshin meet the family and showing him the Deep South, I hadn't considered the possible effect of our presence on the reception. Just because I was madly in love and ready to try an unconventioanl relationship didn't mean others had to feel at ease with my choice.

Lying in the darkness, I realized I'd been the dandelion in the well-manicured garden. I smiled.

In the afternoon of the following day, Afshin and I left Jackson with plans to see the mountains of North Carolina and caves of Virginia on the way home. Unfortunately, a heavy snowstorm prevented us from taking those side excursions.

"What would you do with your life and decision if you were me?" Afshin asked, as I watched the windshield wipers struggle to clear the snow.

By "decision" I assumed he meant whether or not to stay married. Like a nighttime mosquito, that topic kept buzzing around us.

"First, I'd let our love be an example. I want people to see that a man and woman from two very different religious and cultural backgrounds can still be happy together."

"Yes, but would people believe that our love was real if I went back to my country?"

"I don't know, but if you're sure that your mission is to teach in Iran, you should go." I knew better than to discourage him from following his dream.

"Would you go to Belgium with me?" he asked.

"Sure," I said, thinking he was talking about visiting my homeland on his way back to Iran.

"Are you sure?" he asked, sounding surprised. "I wonder if they have a need for my specialty there. I cannot imagine ever leaving you."

Move to Belgium? And forego his dream?

"Clouds cover Belgium eighty percent of the time, and it rains a lot," I said, testing his seriousness.

"My love for you keeps growing." A quiet moment passed. "I still can't understand why you didn't meet someone to marry sooner."

"I don't know." I was tired of trying to explain.

"You *have* to know the reason you turn someone away. It helps you know yourself."

There were plenty of reasons I hadn't married sooner, but the main one was that I'd had no lasting desire to take that step with anyone thus far.

"I don't love this way easily," he said. "I usually find something in a woman that I would not want in a wife."

"Hmm," I replied. What did that tell him about himself? Too picky maybe? But wait... he could say the same thing about me. Was he seriously thinking about staying with me by living in Belgium? An electrical current zapped my belly. Could I leave my life here?

The following evening, around nine p.m., Afshin pulled in to our driveway. Once inside, I sorted through a stack of mail, and we headed for our respective bedrooms. I fell asleep quickly.

In my next moment of consciousness, I heard the door squeak. In dawn light I watched Afshin tiptoe toward me. He slipped into bed and said, "I've gotten used to sleeping with you. I didn't sleep well alone." Our bodies molded to each other.

⁂

Later, when I woke up for the second time, my throat felt as though a squadron of viruses had spent the night scrubbing it with bristle brushes. I called my supervisor and left a message. Sometimes sickness comes at the perfect time.

From the kitchen, I heard the teakettle whistle. I knew Afshin hadn't left the house yet, but I didn't feel like getting up, even to join him.

A few minutes later he carried in a breakfast tray and set it on the floor beside my bed. As he sat on the edge of the mattress, he nudged my hip with his to make room for himself.

"You need to stay in bed. I'll be back in a few hours."

He leaned forward to kiss me, but I clamped his shoulders and held his face away from mine. "No! You'll catch this cold."

"If it's from your germs, I'll love it." Without hesitation, he pulled my hands aside and kissed me.

I loved his devil-may-care attitude when it came to love.

After placing the tray on my lap, he left for the university. Between mouthfuls of steaming tea, I munched on bread and jam. When I finished, I turned toward the books on the shelf of the headboard. *Gift from the Sea* by Anne Lindbergh caught my eye. I propped two pillows behind me and began reading. A third of the way into it, Anne Lindbergh compares the first phase of a marriage to a double-sunrise shell: ". . . two flawless halves bound together with a single hinge, meeting each other at every point, the dawn of a new day. . ." I re-read the words and something stirred in me. She continues: "Because it is not lasting, let us not fall into the cynic's trap and call it an illusion. Duration is not a test of true or false. The day of the dragon-fly or the night of the Saturnid moth is not invalid simply because that phase in its life cycle is brief. Validity need have no relation to time, to duration, to continuity. It is on another plane, judged by other standards."

I closed my eyes and inhaled the passage. Our marriage *did* have validity beyond the confines of time and had as much raison d'être as the marriage that says, "Till death us do part." I gazed outside at the naked trees, and smiled at them as though they were witnesses to my celebration.

Closing the book, I slid under the covers and savored my new companion—Anne Lindbergh.

A few minutes later, I heard a timid knock at the door before it opened an inch. "Mom, are you awake?"

I motioned for Beth to come in.

"I saw your car was here. Are you sick?"

"Yes." I signaled for her not to come closer. "Let's say hello from here for now. You catch colds too easily."

She nodded and plunked herself down at the foot of the bed.

"What's the matter?" I asked, seeing her sad face.

"I broke up with Mike last night," she answered in a monotone.

"Oh, no! What happened?" I stretched forward and touched her arm.

She didn't answer. Her mouth and brow twitched, and I waited expectantly, but she shook her head and said, "I don't feel like talking about it." She raised her head, and our eyes met. "Don't worry. I'll be all right," she added softly.

I was used to her private ways, so the little that she shared helped me feel connected to her.

"How was your trip?" she asked, trying to sound perkier.

"Fine." I didn't elaborate. "Mind if I tell you more another time? My throat really hurts when I talk."

She got up, looked at me with concern, and gave me a brief wave, her hand at waist level.

Before shutting the door, she looked back. "Did they like Afshin?"

I nodded, and smiled to myself. She cared. She really did care.

Chapter 15

Ramadan. For thirty days Afshin would neither eat nor drink from sunrise to sunset. To keep him company, I considered fasting, too. Not eating during daylight seemed possible; not drinking did not.

"Will you please drink at least two quarts of water during the evening? You could get dehydrated otherwise," I said, handing Afshin a tall glass of water as he came down the stairs from his evening shower.

He downed the water in a few long gulps. "Don't worry, Muslims do this every year, and they stay healthy. At least Ramadan is in the winter this time."

"Did Mohammed ever explain why fasting this way is required?" I asked. "It seems physically harmful. Why would God want us to hurt ourselves?" I balked at such a God.

"Miriam *junam*—my dearest," he said, brushing my cheek with his fingertips. "Don't try to figure out God's ways. The Prophet said that fasting would teach us to control our appetites and also help us have sympathy for the poor." He hesitated and his eyebrows arched. "And don't forget . . ." He grinned broadly. "Sex is also prohibited during daylight hours."

I slapped his butt.

The alarm jarred me awake thirty minutes before sunrise. My legs slid over the edge of the bed, and I rushed into my robe. In the cold darkness, I tiptoed to the kitchen and prepared the same breakfast tray Afshin had made for me the previous day.

Slowly, I opened Afshin's bedroom door and glimpsed his form in the pre-dawn light. He was lying on his stomach on the futon he used for a bed. I approached and knelt by the futon, balancing the tray on one knee. His parted lips puffed rhythmically. After a slight hesitation, I tapped his shoulder. His breathing stopped for an instant, and he squinted at the tray looming above him.

He cupped a hand over his mouth to shield me from his morning breath. "Thank you. Thank you very much," he said.

I kissed his forehead and turned to go, but he reached for my hand and touched it to his lips.

The third morning when I carried the tray to his bed and woke him, he looked up with a pleading expression.

"*Azisterinam*—my dearest." His hand rested on my knee. "I love your devotion, but sleep is more important than food for me."

"You're married to a nutritionist," I reminded him in jest. "It's hard for me to watch you fast all day. I want you healthy . . . but, all right."

I carried the tray to the kitchen and scurried back to the warmth of my bed. I'd hoped to make his month easier, not harder. Maybe sleep *was* more important, I thought, as I snuggled under the blankets to recover my own.

The winter sun disappeared by five o'clock, so Ramadan didn't affect our dinner hour. On Friday, however, Afshin joined other Muslims for a Sabbath fast-breaking meal at the university's Muslim Center. At first, I was disappointed that I couldn't share such a special time with him. But then I realized I'd been packing so much "Afshin time" into my schedule that I was at the point of sweet suffocation. I missed a sense of spaciousness in my life.

When he came home, he joined me at the dining-room table. I told him about an author I was reading who stressed the need to make happiness a daily priority.

"You say that happiness should be a priority," Afshin said, "but our prophet said the most important thing is devotion to God and others."

"But Afshin, if I'm happy, then I'll naturally be concerned about others. Happy people can't be selfish. They love to give, because their own cups are full."

"I don't agree. I think unselfish devotion must come first. Then happiness may follow. But it's not guaranteed."

"If devotion comes from a sense of duty, I'm afraid resentment will follow."

"We should never resent serving God," he said as though even such a thought were a sin. "He knows what is best for us." He got up and went to the kitchen. "Would you like tea?" he asked as he filled the kettle.

I nodded.

Devotion. Afshin had often said that he was devoted to me. I'd accepted that, and even liked the idea, but I wanted that devotion to come from love, separate from a sense of duty. Whatever he was doing felt like love. He'd said that his heart had led him to marry me.

He returned carrying two glass mugs and, tucked under his arm, a box of German biscuits. He motioned for me to follow him to the living room, and we sat, thigh-to-thigh, on the sofa.

"Oh, I almost forgot. Let me give you the rent for this month," he said, pulling out his wallet. His driver's license fell to the floor and I picked it up. His picture on it reminded me of a Persian prince—chest out and chin tilted up.

"Will you give me this license when you leave?"

His expression turned serious. "It expires in May."

My gut quavered. May—the month our marriage would end.

"Our marriage will end, but our love won't," Afshin said, his eyes pleading for me to agree. "It will just be different. I hope we can be mother and son as I first thought we could be."

"Mother and son?" I fell back against the cushion and tried to find my bearings, but, like a bird who has just flown into a closed window, I was too stunned to make sense of Afshin's idea.

His eyes held me, but he stayed silent. A second later, a thought startled me. Could it be that part of him was still seeing me as a mother figure? I shuddered. No! That was impossible, given the way he loved me. Coming home from Mississippi, just two weeks before, he'd said that he couldn't imagine leaving me. What had changed?

"You hope we can be . . ." I forced myself to say the rest, "mother and son?"

He nodded.

"Why mother and son? Can't we just be friends?"

"We can't 'just' be friends. I want you in my life in a more significant way. Nothing is closer than a mother. Also, if you are a friend and not a relative, then I'm forbidden to touch you. I couldn't *stand* that." He paused.

I relaxed a little, hearing the strength of his assertion.

"Please understand. If you become my mother, I can still kiss you, hold your hand, hug you, and dance with you."

A tear spilled onto my cheek.

He turned abruptly and balanced on the edge of the loveseat. "How are you different from other women if you cry this way?"

There was no reproach in his tone. I heard: *I know how strong you are. You can do this.* My logical brain could understand the reason for his manipulation, but not how he could offer his plan without expressing distaste for going from husband to son. Unless he felt distaste, but kept it to himself because *he* had to be strong.

It took a moment before I could speak. "Yes, I am strong. You know that, and time will prove it."

Over and over people had told me how strong I was—when Mamy died, when David died, when boyfriends said goodbye. I believed in moving on, but first I needed to cry. Crying was my release valve. If only Afshin could see tears as healers.

He shifted back onto the cushion and laid a hand on my back.

"Yes, you *are* strong. And remember—just because I won't be with you is not a reason to be sad. We'll be in touch often. As your son, I will ask for advice about the woman I should marry," he said as though adding an extra bonus.

My jaw dropped. What planet had he come from? *Calm down, calm down,* I told myself. *Take a deep breath.* I felt like screaming that he was the most insensitive man I'd ever known, but I held back. What would screaming accomplish?

Afshin had no intention of causing me pain. Of that, I was sure. Yet I wished I could understand how he could even talk about a future wife only two months into our marriage.

How could he jump back and forth in his imagination, so easily, between the roles of husband and son? How could he think I would possibly be interested in helping him pick a wife?

My body suddenly shivered. I realized that Afshin had no idea how much pain he had just stirred in me. All I could think was that there must be a malfunctioning connector between his heart and brain.

I leaned toward him and my eyes bored into his, trying to bring him into my reality. "Maybe it's easy for you to say these things because you'll go on, get married, and have children, but how will I ever find someone else? I haven't met anyone like you since David died."

He held my hands. "It's not because I can look forward to another wife that I'm not sad. It's because our love will not end."

"You tell me I shouldn't be sad because you'll always love me. That doesn't satisfy me." The edge in my voice grew sharper. "How can I *not* feel sad when I realize you'll suddenly be gone and I won't be able to hold you or share my days with you?" My voice cracked.

"But I'll *always* be there for you," he insisted, his brow folded in puzzlement.

"It won't be the same!" I yelled in frustration.

He jumped back, as though I'd pushed him.

After a moment, he said, "No—but we can still make it good."

He sounded so sure. He tenderly folded me in his arms, and I didn't resist. He kissed my eyes and sipped the falling tears. No one ever had ever done that before—it felt loving, but my heart continued to weep.

"Don't be disappointed. God has given us something good. Let us be thankful. If you have a good desire, God will give you what you need. If you are ever lonely, you can come live with me in Iran."

I believed he meant it and seized this promise like a security blanket.

As he held me, stroking my hair, I couldn't say another word. After all, I'd been the one to say that six months with him would be worth it. We hadn't discussed what would follow, and I'd assumed we'd return to being friends. He'd assumed something I couldn't have imagined. Yet now, unless I insisted on just being friends—without *any* expressions of physical affection—I didn't see another option.

Later that evening we went upstairs and began our nighttime routines. While I washed my face, I pictured Afshin on his prayer rug.

"Mother and son." I enunciated the words and groaned. The face reflected in the mirror looked like it had just smelled a skunk. *God, I thought, how am I going to manage that one?*

I slid the dish of stuffed shells I'd prepared the night before into the oven and started washing lettuce for a tossed salad. Even though I'd left work early, I felt rushed in getting dinner ready in time for Rachel and Gene, who were arriving at six. Unable to find a weekend evening that was free for all of us, we'd settled for a mid-week dinner.

Ten after five. Strange. Afshin had said he'd be home by five to set the table. Might as well do it myself, I thought.

At five fifty-five everything was ready. I stood in the middle of the dining room, lips pressed together and arms crossed.

As expected, Rachel and Gene arrived on time. Gene handed me a loaf of his homemade whole-wheat bread. I couldn't wait to taste its nutty sweetness.

"Afshin's not here," I said, as I hung up their coats. "He said he'd be home at five and I'm worried. This isn't like him."

"He's probably engrossed in his studies," Rachel said.

"But he knew you were coming at six."

"Maybe he doesn't want to hang out with a couple of Baha'is," she said lightly, but I wondered if she was actually concerned. After all, the Baha'is in Iran had reason to fear Muslims, some of whom had jailed Baha'is, or even killed them.

"No, no. He likes you," I said, as we sat down in the living room. I didn't want to tell her that Afshin thought Baha'u'llah was a false prophet. I heard a car door slam and I met Afshin in the foyer. While he removed his shoes, I fantasized about giving him a couple of quick karate chops. But no, that wouldn't do, I thought, almost laughing aloud at the idea.

"What happened?" I asked, in a cool tone. "You said you'd be home at five."

"I thought they were coming at six-thirty," he said, looking uncomfortable. I gave him a private growl, but kept my anger under control.

"Hello. I'm so sorry I'm late," Afshin said, as he shook Rachel's hand and bowed in polite acknowledgement. It reminded me of the formality of men in bygone times. Afshin turned to Gene with an outstretched hand, and Gene took it between both of his own, shaking it heartily.

"Dinner's ready." I motioned for them to sit down.

The four of us held hands and I gave thanks for the food and the company of friends. When the food was passed around, Afshin put one stuffed shell on his plate and a mere cupful of salad in his wooden salad bowl.

"Aren't you hungry?" I asked.

He squirmed. "I went to Milad's house and he was having a fast-breaking dinner. I was so hungry. I couldn't resist his great cooking. I ate—a lot."

"But you knew you were having dinner here. I'm *mad*." I hoped he realized I was more upset than I felt like expressing just then.

I looked at Gene and Rachel and wondered what they were thinking. Her brow and shoulders rose slightly. Gene buttered his bread with exceptional care. Thank goodness I didn't have to pretend around them. Yet the fact that I didn't need to put on a happy face didn't mean I wanted to stay angry.

"I guess you lose control when you fast all day," I said, trying to understand what had kept him from coming home at five. He reached for my hand and squeezed it.

We ate quietly for a few moments.

"How did you enjoy your trip to Mississippi?" Rachel asked, between bites.

"We didn't get much time with my family, but it went well," I said. "I'm glad Afshin had a chance to meet my brothers and sisters and see some of the South."

"This country is amazingly beautiful," Afshin said. "You have such huge forests, and rivers, and lakes everywhere. It's so different from Iran. We have mostly deserts. It can be hard to find a tree for shade."

"I found the landscape majestic," said Gene referring to the trip he'd taken to Iran the year before the Revolution.

"Yes, but the desert can be harsh. We have to ration water," said Afshin.

Rachel tapped Gene's arm. "Would you pass me the salad?"

"How have you enjoyed your first six months of retirement?" I asked Gene.

"I wish I'd done it years ago. I'm having a ball." What a luxury it must seem to Afshin to retire at fifty—even Rachel and I were envious. Working for the state as a social worker had paid off for Gene, but then, constantly being around children who'd been beaten or sexually molested had taken a toll on him. He'd needed to stop before depression engulfed him.

"Gene has become involved with the Cancer Society," Rachel said. "He drives people to their doctor appointments."

I was relieved that she'd added that information. Afshin would admire that activity, especially because he'd said that he rarely saw people helping others in our country.

"Miriam told me that you'll be teaching at a university when you go back home. How will that feel after teaching here? Aren't there many restrictions on what you can do?" Rachel asked.

"Not with math. I will enjoy teaching. In Iran, students are starving for knowledge." He shook his head and closed his eyes as he said those last words.

"Most of our students have lost that hunger. They have too many distractions," Gene said.

Later, over dessert, Rachel asked, "How will you two ever stand living apart? I see how happy you are together." Her eyes welled up with tears.

Gene added, "Yes, your relationship—"

"Our *marriage*," Afshin corrected.

"Afshin doesn't like the word 'relationship' applied to our marriage. He thinks the word is used too lightly. Many people don't seem truly committed in relationships, whether friends, parents and children, or husbands and wives—at least not in the way Afshin has experienced," I explained. I thought of the ease with which Afshin and his friends loaned or gave money, and felt free to drop in on each other any time of day or night.

"It will be difficult to live apart, but we're strong," Afshin said, answering Rachel's question. "We both have work to do in our own countries, and that's something we can't ignore."

Afshin's foot met mine under the table and lingered there, stroking my instep as we continued talking. How could we make others understand something that we wavered over constantly? One day we lived with the hope of staying together and the next day we knew it was unrealistic.

"I can appreciate that," said Rachel, "but I could never do what you're doing." Her sad expression stirred the sadness sitting in me.

Afshin and I exchanged a glance of understanding. We knew we could do it.

"Life in Iran is very hard," he said. "The war with Iraq killed thousands of boys. Then the Ayatollah Khomeini encouraged people to have many children. Now people work from morning until night just to give their family the things they need." He paused. "When we go outside the house, we have to be careful what we do. The *komiteh* can arrest us for things you do here every day—dress the way you want, or show affection in the street." He stopped for a moment, his eyes pensive, as though the magnitude of the difficulties he described weighed on him. "Perhaps this is why we learn to accept hard times." He looked at me with a sad smile. "It would be too hard there for Miriam."

"Then why would *you* want to go back to Iran?" Gene asked.

"Because when I was hungry to learn, there were few good teachers left. I want to be there for other students like me."

This was why I loved Afshin. He cared about others. He didn't care about making a name for himself or making lots of money. David was like that, too. Were men like this rare? The attractive ones were. And, if you could find them, they were usually married.

Later, after Rachel and Gene had left, I confronted Afshin about his failure to come home in time for our guests. Although I could sympathize about his being hungry, I was upset because he'd broken an agreement with me and hadn't called to explain. He expressed sufficient remorse to allow the rest of my irritation to dissolve.

"Let's dance," he said when we finished the conversation. He rolled up the rug in the dining room, creating a dance floor, and then dropped a compact disc in the player. I heard the first notes of an Irish waltz I'd taught him. We waltzed from the living room to the dining room, gazing at each other.

"In Persia, the moth and the candle signify a great love. I feel that way with you," he said quietly. "You are the best woman in the world."

Chapter 16

While I pedaled the exercise bike at the gym the next evening, I thought about how much of my mind was occupied by Afshin. I needed to regain some balance in my life and decided to go to the French group after my workout.

I opened the door to Jeanne's house and all heads turned in my direction, their faces lit up. "Miriam! *Ca fait longtemps qu'on ne t'a plus vu,*" Jeanne said.

Yes, it had been a long time. The group's welcome made me feel like someone returning from a long trip. By the time I left, I felt reconnected to my Belgian soul.

But when I arrived home, around nine-thirty, I was brought back to the U.S. with a jolt. Beth, making a sandwich at the kitchen counter, was wearing a black, see-through blouse that provided a good view of her lacy black bra. Afshin stood nearby, at the sink. I almost screamed. What was Beth thinking, dressing like that? Did she have any idea of the effect her outfit might have on a man? Especially Afshin.

She glanced up from the sandwich she was making. "Hi, Mom," she said, in her muffled tone.

I only nodded in response.

Afshin turned and bowed his head toward me. I hated his polite hello; it made him a momentary stranger. Though I understood his discomfort at showing affection in front of others, I'd never adjust to the public Afshin.

"I need to do some reading," he said, slipping the last plate into the dish drainer.

After working all day? I doubted it. He was probably giving Beth and me time alone. On his way out of the kitchen, he kept his eyes down. Was he embarrassed? Or protecting himself from sinful thoughts? I wanted to throw my sweater around Beth.

She carried her sandwich to the table and sat down. I hesitated. Here was an opportunity to try connecting with her, but I felt annoyed. I stood with my hands on the back of a chair, and the image of the little girl with long black pigtails flashed in my mind's eye. She meant no harm. I pulled out the chair across from her and asked about her day.

Since her breakup with Mike, she'd been spending more time at home. But I doubted she'd exchanged more than a few words with Afshin before I'd come home, even though they'd been standing within five feet of each other.

After some small talk, her phone rang downstairs. She charged past me as though someone had screamed, "Fire!" I heard animation in her voice after she picked up the receiver, and I sighed.

Afshin must have heard Beth on the phone, too, because he joined me a minute later. By now he knew that once she answered her phone, she'd be busy talking for at least a half hour. With arms crossed, he stood at the end of the table for several seconds without saying anything. Something was brewing behind those eyes.

"I don't understand. How can you two be so uninvolved with each other? In Iran, mothers and daughters are close friends."

Close friends with Beth? That wasn't my goal and I doubted that Beth wanted to be my "close friend," either. Each of us had friends our own age. Once again I recognized a big gap in Afshin's knowledge of American culture. How many American twenty-somethings wanted "Mom" to be a close friend?

"Our interests are so different," I said, hoping my explanation would answer his question. "I have little to talk about with her."

"Find something!" he said emphatically. He sat on the chair beside mine. "Even if you have to talk about things that don't interest you, at least you would communicate."

"Wouldn't that be insincere on my part?"

"Nooo." He seemed surprised. "The important thing is to show that you love her enough to enter *her* world. Spend an hour with her each day." His eyes lit up. "When I was about sixteen, I didn't feel close to my brother or father. My mother knew it, and she worked hard to stay close to me. She would even get up early so that she could go running with me before leaving for work. I never saw another mother do this. At first, I didn't like it. She couldn't run fast. But when I realized she did it to keep me from feeling separate, my love for her grew." He stared into the night for a moment, past his reflection in the window, and then turned to me. "Maybe you could get closer to Beth by becoming more like her. You could get your hair styled like hers and wear the kind of clothes she likes."

"Are you kidding?"

"No. You could also get to know her friends. This will convince her that you love her."

"But that's not me!" My gut tensed. "Can you see me getting my hair streaked, going out to clubs, getting artificial nails? She and I have completely different kinds of taste."

"What's more important?" he asked in a soft tone. "Your taste? Or the two of you being close? If you get close, maybe she'll be willing to accept some of the good things you can teach her—like how to be a good wife and mother."

"But if she didn't learn those lessons during her childhood, do you really think there's hope that she'd change at this point?" I wanted to say, *And besides, she may not want to be a wife or mother*, but that would sound too strange to him.

"It's never too late when there's love, but maybe for her, the love has to be shown strongly before she will trust it."

"I understand what you're saying, but I'm not convinced that I need to act like her to prove that I love her. I'm sure she knows that I do." A doubt flew by like a bat at dusk. "Why can't you accept that we care about each other even though we have different interests?"

"Because love makes an effort."

My hand reached for his cheek and rested there an instant. His words had a ring of truth.

Throughout the next day at the hospital, when I wasn't busy with patients, I pondered the previous night's conversation with Afshin. Motherhood. I wished I'd been better prepared for the role, but considering my own upbringing and David's sudden disappearance, I thought I'd done a decent job. Yet I had my regrets. Maybe Afshin's concern had merit; maybe I could do more to show Beth my love.

As I found myself yielding to his point of view, I decided that I needed to consult someone more objective. When it came to Afshin, I had more blood flowing to my heart than to my brain. Rachel could help. She'd spent time with Iranians, through the Baha'i community, and could tell me about the role of Iranian mothers.

As soon as I got home, I flung my coat on a chair and called Rachel. When her cheerful hello sang over the line, it lifted my spirits, and I poured out my concern.

She explained that the Persian mothers she knew did everything for their children. Mothers washed their sons' clothes and cleaned their rooms even beyond adolescence. She reminded me, however, that I was an American, with American views about child rearing. I'd done a good job and didn't need to feel guilty. Hearing those reminders helped me relax, though I decided to put more care into my relationships with my children.

Saturday afternoon, I noticed Afshin examining the books on a shelf in the living room. When he pulled one out, I crossed the room and stood next to him as he leafed through it. The book, *Sex in History*, contained material that I was sure would shock him. I wanted to snatch it from his hands. He stopped at a cartoon showing a man seated with a woman kneeling in front of him, about to remove his boots. The caption read, "Oh woman, masterpiece of creation, queen of humanity, mother of the human race . . . take off my boots."

"That's the attitude of men in Iran, isn't it?" I asked, expecting him to agree.

Afshin's eyes flashed at me. "Not at all! In fact, of all the poetry I've read from many countries, the one that speaks with the most love for a woman is the Persian. My father loves my mother and would never talk to her like this stupid man," he said, slapping the cartoon with the back of his fingers.

"But I've heard this view of Arab men for so long that it's the impression I have of them," I said, trying to explain myself.

"Arab men are not Persian! We are different—*very* different. You *know* we treat women with respect."

"I think you're an exception." I wrapped my arm around him as we headed for the dining room. "That book also explains how common it was in times past for men in many cultures to have multiple wives."

As we sat down, I noticed Afshin's lips tighten, and he shook his head. "I told you before—that kind of marriage is no longer well regarded in Iran.

And in times past we were not the only ones to have many wives. It happened in Europe, too."

An idea flashed in my mind. "I was just thinking of an *advantage* to that custom. You could have an American wife *and* an Iranian one." I paused. "Although, to be fair, I'd have to have an American husband, too."

He glared at me and then looked down.

I clutched his forearm. "I was only kidding."

He leaned back. "I don't like kidding about that. Do you enjoy trivializing something so serious?"

"Not really."

But I wondered—had I been kidding? Wouldn't that solve our problem? We could then still share our days and occasional nights. If all parties agreed—why not?

Afshin's eyes bore into me. Finally, he spoke. "Our marriage may be different because it's only six months long, but I consider it real. I hate to hear you talk about marriage like that."

I was shaken by his tone, but I loved hearing how seriously he took marriage—this marriage. I got up and stood next to him for a few seconds. Before he knew what was happening, I straddled his lap, facing him, and kissed his forehead, cheeks, and lips. Slowly, the corners of his mouth lifted. He kissed me once carefully; a cascade of kisses followed.

"You're wonderful!" he said. "How did David ever get his work done?"

"I'm relieved you don't stay angry."

"How can I—toward you?" he said, his hands cradling my cheeks. "I wish we could go off somewhere, like an island, and live together—alone."

Two months of our marriage had passed; four more lay ahead. I savored each day the way Beth used to savor a rare piece of cake—one tiny bite at a time. She thought she could make it last forever.

Chapter 17

Henry and Judy were expecting Afshin and me for dinner at seven o'clock. I leaned back in my office chair at work and stared at the familiar apple tree outside the window. What if Afshin knew that Henry and I had been romantically involved? Should I tell him? No, he didn't need to know, and surely Henry wouldn't tell him. I guessed it would be hard for an Iranian to understand. Even some of my American friends couldn't understand how I managed to stay in close touch with former lovers.

When I arrived home, I found Afshin in front of the bathroom mirror with a long black scarf wrapped around his neck and covering his mouth. I pulled it down and screamed—his mustache was gone.

"Why did you shave it off?"

"I cut too much while trimming it, so I had to," he said, raising his shoulders and cocking his head while an embarrassed smile spread over his naked face.

The fullness of his exposed lips made them irresistible. My lips pressed his. Their softness made me test them again before stepping back to examine his face. Not only had he shaved off his mustache, but five years from his appearance, as well.

"Are you going to let it grow back?" I asked, noticing I sounded worried.

"Oh, yes. I've always had a mustache."

"Born with it, eh?"

"I got it when I was twelve." He ran his fingertips back and forth over the denuded skin.

"Twelve! You had an early burst of testosterone." I grabbed him in a playful hug.

During the fifty-minute ride to Henry's, I turned the radio on for music, but was diverted by an interview with a woman on National Public Radio. She described the restrictions under which women had been living in Afghanistan since the Taliban took over.

"Isn't it disgusting?" I said, hearing that girls could no longer attend school.

"Yes, but do you know that the U.S. helped the Taliban get in power?"

"Come on. I can't believe that; the Taliban are extremists," I said, thinking that Afshin had heard this story from the government in Iran, which wanted to make America look bad.

"It's true. You can look it up," he insisted. "The U.S. gave millions of dollars to the Taliban to help them beat the Russians. You can guess why. Democracy is nice, but oil is better, and Afghanistan is needed for oil pipelines to reach the Arabian Sea."

He sounded so sure. "All right, I'll look it up," I said, intending to show him it wasn't true. "Enough news for today. Let's relax and have a pleasant evening."

I found Spanish music on the radio and turned the volume down.

Afshin had agreed more easily to Henry's dinner invitation than to those we'd received from other people.

"Henry and I have been friends for over ten years," I explained. "You know what I like about him? He's as honest as they come, and he gets pleasure from the simple things in life."

Afshin brought my hand to his lips and kissed it. "Of all the people who attended our wedding dinner, I got along with Henry the best—for the same reason you like him."

We arrived at Henry's townhouse complex, and I maneuvered rights and lefts until I found my friend's house at the end, where the woods began.

Henry opened the door. "Hi. I'm sure glad you didn't arrive five minutes earlier. Judy might have answered the door naked." He looked half embarrassed and half amused.

Afshin didn't laugh. If Henry hoped to put Afshin at ease, he'd chosen the wrong tactic. We followed Henry into the kitchen where Judy stood at the sink, shaking a colander of linguine.

"Please excuse Henry," she said, smiling at us, her elfin face draped in long dark hair, parted in the middle, in a style reminiscent of the sixties. "He often puts his foot in his mouth with the best intentions."

Afshin and I stood with our backs to the refrigerator, watching while Henry and Judy finished the meal preparations. They'd been a couple for three years—a record for Henry—and they seemed perfect together in numerous ways, from their mutual love of bird-watching to their phlegmatic natures.

When I was dating Henry, his unflappable nature got on my nerves so much that one cool November day, as we were strolling past a shallow lake, I'd pushed him in—simply to see whether I could get him to express some emotion. I smiled whenever I recalled the shock on his face as he screamed, "Why did you do that?" Did Judy accept his placid exterior? It probably balanced the emotional turmoil she heard, five days a week, in her sessions as a therapist.

"Is there anything we can do?" I asked.

"No, thanks. We're ready," said Henry. He arranged French bread in a basket and wiped breadcrumbs from the chopping board with his usual thoroughness.

I marveled at his appearance at fifty-two. His smooth skin and curly black hair, without any traces of gray, made him appear ten years younger. This impression was reinforced by his childlike naiveté.

We moved to the adjoining dining room, and I sat down to Afshin's right, across from Henry. My mouth watered at the aroma of chicken and ginger.

"Would you like some wine?" Henry asked, holding the bottle toward me.

"No, thanks." I would have liked some, but it was more important to be Afshin's wife—a wife who doesn't drink alcohol. Henry held the bottle toward Afshin, who shook his head. Like pork, alcohol had never touched his lips.

I noticed Judy staring at Afshin. Was she curious about our relationship or about him as an Iranian? She'd lived her entire life within fifty miles of Trenton, New Jersey, and I imagined that she rarely had a chance to interact with a person from a culture so different from her own. "How are your kids taking this marriage?" Judy asked.

"Greg and Cal have accepted it. Beth said she'd accept it for my sake, but she hardly talks to Afshin. Of course, that's nothing new. She usually ignores men who aren't her friends. Maybe she's uncomfortable because they tend to go gaga around her."

"No wonder. She's gorgeous," said Judy.

"Yes, she is." A twinge pinched my heart as I remembered feeling jealous when Afshin reacted to Beth's tears over our marriage.

We ate quietly for a few moments. "Afshin doesn't understand why Beth and I aren't best friends. I've tried to explain that to be friends we need common interests," I said, looking to Henry for agreement. When he looked down thoughtfully, I turned to Afshin and saw a disapproving look. *Whoops. Maybe he'd prefer I keep those conversations between us.*

"Yes, you and Beth are different, but I can see the two of you becoming friends—in the future, that is. First, she has more growing up to do," said Henry.

"Hmm . . . you're probably right," I said.

The subject of the conversation shifted to food for a while, and then I thought about a topic that was more interesting to me.

"Afshin and I were discussing censorship a few weeks ago," I said. "He knows Americans are proud of having freedom of speech, but he thinks some material, especially in magazines and television, should be banned. What do you think?"

Henry put his fork down and leaned back, stroking his chin. "I think we need to be careful of the material that reaches children, but for adults, I don't believe in censorship."

"But pornography is not good for adults either, so wouldn't it be better not to allow it?" Afshin asked, appearing confident Henry would agree with that argument.

"I don't choose it for myself," Henry said, in his quiet way, "but how can I tell others what to do?"

Afshin's back straightened. "Why not, if it will protect them?"

"I'd rather let them make their own decisions," Henry said.

"That's how I see it," Judy added.

Afshin must have been disappointed. He lowered his eyes to his plate and returned to eating. It was obvious to me that he was trying to avoid showing his disappointment.

Another conversation change was needed. Quickly. What innocuous topic could I bring up?

"How was your trip to California last week?" I asked Henry. "You went birding, didn't you?"

"Yes, and it was great," he said, with a fresh smile and enthusiasm reserved for his hobby. "I saw magpies and acorn woodpeckers. I'd never seen them before."

"I loved California, especially the redwood trees," I said.

"Was that when you and Henry were together?" Judy asked.

A spasm struck my gut. I glanced at Afshin. His face had turned into a pale mask.

"Yes, but I haven't told Afshin about that," I said, hoping she'd sense her faux pas.

"I'm sorry," said Judy to Afshin. "I thought you'd know."

He looked at her for half an instant and then stared at his empty plate.

She must have no idea that men from his part of the world find it offensive, to say the least, to hear of their wives' previous love interests. I wished I'd warned Henry and Judy not to bring up my old romances. Before we were married, I'd told Afshin about one of my romantic relationships. His disapproval showed as his face had turned expressionless. He didn't have to say anything. I didn't want a repeat of that.

We finished eating, and I glanced at Afshin. In an effort to be polite, he'd pulled his features into a neutral expression, but I sensed discomfort. The conversation, in general, seemed off-putting for him. On top of that, he'd just discovered that Henry was an old boyfriend. By now he probably felt like an alien. I yearned to hold him, with nothing coming between us.

For the rest of the evening he kept quiet except when addressed directly. I listened to Henry and Judy describe their desire to build a miniature Stonehenge where people could come for earth-based rituals and meditation. As soon as they finished their description, Afshin gave me the "Let's leave" signal—a quiet *"Berim."*

As we drove off, neither of us spoke.

After a while, I said, "You seemed uncomfortable."

"I was tired," he said, looking straight ahead. "Maybe I ate too much."

"Is that all?"

"Maybe." He pressed the gas pedal.

"Can I guess why you were uncomfortable?" I asked, with hesitation. "You didn't like hearing that I dated Henry, and you didn't like the talk about censorship."

"Let me think about it and get things clear before I tell you."

We held hands, but didn't speak for the rest of the trip.

In the center of the dark country road, the white dashes zipped by and reminded me of each passing moment with Afshin. I cherished just sitting near him. On Sunday, Cal and I were leaving for Florida. I'd looked forward to visiting Greg and Jacob since Cal and I bought our plane tickets three months earlier. Though I understood Afshin's desire to stay home to concentrate on his thesis, I felt a pang at the thought of six days without him.

When we got home, I took off my long, cocoa-brown wool coat. After I hung it up, Afshin took me in his arms. He held me, not saying a word, but I sensed deep emotions in the strength of his embrace.

"Is it because you're with older people so much, these days, that you're uncomfortable?"

He stepped back and stared at me. "I hope you don't include yourself in that."

"Why shouldn't I?"

"Because you're different."

I laid my hand on his cheek and, as our eyes met, I stepped into a place that felt like home.

"Let's go to bed," he said.

He lit the candle on the nightstand, but its glow and warm jasmine scent didn't dispel our low spirits.

As we lay in an embrace, Afshin said, "Henry and Judy are nice people, but I don't share their values." He paused, took a deep breath, and released it in a groan. "I'd like to ask you one thing. Can we stop visiting so many of your friends? Everyone asks me the same questions everywhere we go, and I'm tired of these conversations. I just want to be with *you*."

My friends . . . my treasures.

His fingertips touched my cheek. "Yet, if you want, I will go with you again."

"I wouldn't feel right asking you, if you're doing it just to please me. You may start to resent it."

He turned my head and looked into my eyes. "A devoted husband never resents pleasing his wife."

How I loved him. I loved my friends, too, and wished Afshin could enjoy their company. But why should he? He hadn't chosen them. I'd wanted to give him an opportunity to experience our society on a personal level. I'd also wanted my friends to know Afshin. But I was imposing my wishes on him. Not a good idea, or a respectful one.

"I can spend less time with my friends—for now, at least," I said.

"Thank you. And yes, I was shocked that you were with Henry. It's hard for me to digest. How serious were . . ."

I pressed my fingers to his lips. "Don't ask more. There's no purpose to it, is there?"

"No. You're right. I just wish there never was anyone else."

"I'm completely with you now, Afshin *junam*."

Chapter 18

As I drove toward the Math Department, I spotted Afshin's lone figure on the street corner, trotting in place to keep warm.

"I'm so sorry I'm late. My watch stopped," I said, as he hopped into the car with his nose red from the cold. "I feel terrible that you waited out there so long."

"Forty minutes," he said as he cupped his hands toward the hot air flowing from the dashboard vent. "Now do you believe I'm a patient man?" He raised his eyebrows at me.

"You pass the test with flying colors." I reached over and rubbed the back of my fingers on his ice-cold cheek. "Do you still want to walk along the canal?"

"Of course. What do you think? I'm not fragile," he said, a lilt in his voice.

I parked near the bridge. From there we crossed over the canal and proceeded down the towpath that ran along the canal built in the 1800s for barges transporting coal. It reminded me of the canals in Belgium, although those were lined with orderly rows of tall willow trees rather than the haphazard mix of trees and shrubs along these banks.

Hand in hand, Afshin and I walked briskly, the sand crunching under our shoes. After we'd gone about a mile, a blue heron skimmed the surface of the canal and flew away. Moments later, he returned, gliding a few inches above the water.

"A bird in love with a fish—it reminds me of another love." Afshin looked at me sideways and I saw him suppress a smile.

"You mean ours?" I stopped.

He nodded.

"Our age difference doesn't make us as different as a bird and a fish," I said, annoyed at the comparison. We had lots in common.

"Our age *and* our backgrounds," he said, in a serious tone.

"No. It *is* our age that separates us most." I yanked my hand from his. "People from different backgrounds marry all the time."

"How can I tell you?" He looked hurt. "It *doesn't* matter to me."

I strode ahead. If he meant that age didn't matter *during* our short marriage, all right. But I wanted years with him—not just months—so for me, it mattered a lot.

After a minute, I slowed down. He passed me and did a one-hundred-eighty-degree turn, landing eighteen inches in front of me. I crossed my arms and stared at him for a few seconds. He'd never done a thing to make me feel old. I was the one for whom the slightest whiff of an age-related comment set off an alarm. How I wished we weren't at the mercy of society's norms.

"All right," I said. "You've convinced me by your actions."

Looking down, he shook his head and let out an exasperated exhalation. "Convincing is a logical process. It's not with logic that I'll convince you."

No wonder I love this man, I thought. He knows the heart doesn't deal in logic, though at times he forgets that, too.

Overhead, gray clouds congregated, and the wind rustled the leaves left on the pin oaks. Afshin rested a hand on my shoulder, but my arms stuck to my sides. Finally, here was a man I wanted to be with—but those stupid differences stood in our way. Afshin didn't move or press me to walk on. I hated to admit it, but I had to keep in mind the reasons why a long-term marriage with Afshin wouldn't work. And here I was again, trying to be logical. Afshin was right—convincing is an exercise of logic and no amount of convincing would move my heart. I wanted to share life with Afshin forever, and I wanted him to be as illogical as I was.

Miriam, an inner voice whispered, *enjoy him while you can.* My arm lifted and encircled Afshin's waist.

We trudged back to the car in frozen silence. A bird and a fish. Who was I? The fish? Like the water that the fish can't leave, my age prevented me from being with Afshin for life. But wasn't he even more restricted? He couldn't travel freely, cry freely, or choose a permanent wife without his parent's blessing. He'd once said that he couldn't fly at my height. Perhaps I was the bird after all—a bird free to try its wings in skies of many colors.

That evening, we watched a favorite film of Afshin's: *The Power of One.* When it ended, tears coursed down my cheeks, as well as Afshin's. Afshin and I—*we* were one.

Suddenly, I remembered an unusual species: the flying fish. In my mind, I could blend the bird and the fish—Afshin and me. The thought comforted me.

A few seconds passed, and Afshin said, "Come, let's go upstairs."

I sat down on the edge of the bed, and he knelt between my thighs. His fingers fumbled with the buttons of my blouse. My desire ignited. The blouse slid off my shoulders, and he kissed each breast tenderly.

"You are a beauty," he said, and arching back, he murmured, "Oh, God!"

Moments later, our bodies joined. I took in each "I love you" like a plant drawing in a vital nutrient.

He propped himself on his elbow and gazed at me. "Making love . . . it's all up here," he said, tapping his temple. "Some people think of their own pleasure, or the image they are making on their wife. For me, it's the way to get tied up and know you in the deepest way. When I make love to you, it's a spiritual experience, and it melts the frozen corners of my heart."

Get tied up . . . I liked the expression. It symbolized a strong connection.

"Before you go to sleep, I have a story for you," he said, and I rested my head on his arm.

"I hope it has a happier ending than the last story you told me—the one about Rostam and Sohrab. I still can't get Rostam's mistake out of my mind. The idea of killing your own son on the battlefield—what a nightmare!"

"You will like this ending." He patted my arm. "A long time ago, the birds of the land wished to meet God, who they called *Simorgh*. And so, with the bird Hoopoe as their leader, a thousand of them started out on the long journey to Simorgh's home. They faced huge difficulties on the way, and many birds dropped out."

My eyes closed, and I listened to Afshin describe the hardships the birds faced. Finally, they arrived in the land of *Simorgh*, but only thirty birds were left. "They searched all over for *Simorgh*, but all they could see was each other and their reflections in the lake. They then realized that *Simorgh* means "*Si morgh*," or "thirty birds." God was just the total of who they were."

"I *do* love the ending," I said, now wide awake. "I believe the same thing about people—each of us has the spirit of God in here." I placed my hand on Afshin's heart.

"You sound like a Sufi," he said.

"Quakers believe this also."

"We don't respect the Sufis."

"That's too bad. I think that if we believed that God lived in each of us, we'd treat each other better."

"*Bekhob.* Go to sleep," he said, and I remembered his impatience with philosophy.

Cal and I spent the following week in Florida, visiting Greg and his son, Jacob. Unfortunately, we went without Beth, who had no vacation time, and Afshin, who had to work on his thesis. I enjoyed multiple aspects of the trip. Besides connecting with my dear ones who lived so far away, I also, finally, had time for serious reading. I finished *The Iranians* by Sandra Mackey.

When Cal and I flew back to Newark, I spotted Afshin at the arrival gate in his olive-green army jacket and day-old beard. He looked every bit the revolutionary I'd just been reading about in *The Iranians*. As I approached him, he reached for my hand, and touched it to his lips. My hand hung in mid-air for a second, but I recalled his reserve around others.

As we followed Afshin to the parking lot, I realized that it wasn't just the week apart and his greeting that left me feeling distant. The last three chapters of *The Iranians*, which I'd just read on the plane, stirred a stew of emotions in me. Especially upsetting were the accounts of how some revolutionaries killed thousands of their fellow Iranians after the 1979 Revolution.

We passed under a lamppost, and I looked at Afshin, walking briskly two steps ahead, my bags in hand. Young men like him had been executed by their peers. Why? Just for belonging to an organization that had threatened the power of the Ayatollah Khomeini. Khomeini had actually told parents to turn in their "wayward" sons and daughters if they belonged to the *Mujahedin*. An icy chill shook me. Did those mothers and fathers think they were doing the right thing, in Allah's eyes, by denouncing their own children?

The ride home didn't help. Afshin swerved from one lane to the next. I breathed a sigh of relief when we finally dropped Calvin off at his apartment. I hoped I'd soon reconnect with the Afshin I knew.

Five minutes later we pulled in to our driveway. As soon as we walked into the house, Afshin dropped my bags and wrapped his arms around me.

"I missed you when you were gone, but I miss you more now," he whispered in my ear. "Let's go upstairs."

Without witnesses, Afshin gave me a warm welcome home.

"I never knew I could love a woman this much. How will I ever find another woman like you? I wish you and I could go off somewhere, like Africa, and live together—alone."

The joy of being loved and the pain of the envisioned end swirled through me. This was our recurrent theme. Sometimes we dealt with it through denial; sometimes, through dreams.

Chapter 19

I was in the family room, looking through the latest issue of *Nutrition Action*, when Beth came home. She plopped down next to me on the sofa, and gave me a peck on the cheek.

Then, abruptly, she said, "Some of these Girton people are so snooty. A customer came in today in her fancy outfit and, right away, I could tell she'd be trouble. You wouldn't believe the way she talked to me." She rolled her eyes and groaned. "Like she's better than me!"

I hadn't seen Beth in a week, and her leap into her day's experience after the briefest hello made me smile.

"Oooh . . . that must hurt," I said.

She was quiet for a while, but the way she fidgeted with her arms and looked toward the far window told me she was about to say something that didn't come easily.

"I slept at my friend's house while you were away. I was uncomfortable staying here with Afshin."

"Why? He'd never bother you. He's not at all like some of the men you know."

"I believe you, but I still felt uncomfortable." She stared at the television as though it were on.

"Why won't you talk to Afshin?" I asked, slipping into the space she'd given me to understand her.

"I don't want to," she said, sweeping that possibility aside. "I never talk to people who rent here. You know that."

True. I couldn't recall a time when she'd said more than a few words to a tenant. She said that she had nothing to say to them and that she didn't like strangers in the house.

"I can understand you don't like sharing our space, but with Afshin it's different. He's special to me, and . . . he thinks of you as a sister," I added, hoping to alleviate her discomfort, but suddenly realizing I'd told her what he'd asked me *not* to tell her.

"That's not the problem." Her head snapped forward and she turned to me, her eyes glaring. "How can he even *think* of leaving you?"

My heart jumped. So that was it. She feared seeing me go through another loss.

"He wants to teach in Iran. They need him there," I said. "It's more important to him than anything. He feels it's his duty. Can you understand that?"

Her head shook like a rattlesnake's tail.

"How will you stand it when he leaves?" she asked, her eyes pleading for an answer. "You seem so happy with him."

She'd noticed. I reached for her hand but seeing the depth of her concern, I couldn't tell her that I wondered, too.

"I *am* happy. Very happy," I said, steadying my voice with difficulty. "And I want to enjoy this while I can. I don't want to think of 'later.'"

She stared at me for a moment and slowly shook her head.

"Don't worry. I promise. I'll be able to handle it." I shouldn't have let her see me cry when others left—especially David. But no, that wouldn't have been real.

"I'm glad you think so, but *how*?" She leaned forward and almost screamed the last word.

So, behind her often quiet demeanor, she cared.

"I wish it could be longer, but the length of our time together isn't as important as its depth and richness," I said, hearing Anne Lindbergh's words.

"I don't understand you."

"I don't understand you either, so we're even," I teased. She flashed a smile at me. "And you're not alone. It's hard for my friends to understand, too—especially Ana." I stared at Beth's hand for an instant before giving it a squeeze. "I love you."

Her face brightened. "I love you, too."

We stayed silent for a minute, and then she rose, still holding my hand. I leaned forward to get up, and she gave me a pull.

"'Night, Mom. I'm tired." We hugged. She went to her room and closed the door.

Funny. Same door closing, but this time I don't feel that she's shutting me out.

"Thank you, God." I had a feeling that the love Beth and I had for each other would eventually express itself outwardly more often.

A few days later, I heard the answering machine in my room beeping as soon as I entered the house. I pressed the button, and a woman's voice said, "Afshin . . . " I couldn't understand the rest, but guessed that the caller was Afshin's mother.

Fifteen minutes later, Afshin came back from his soccer game and zoomed upstairs toward the shower. He still didn't believe that I *liked* the aroma of earth and sweat he exuded after a game.

"Wait a minute," I called. "Come hear this message."

With his chest already bare, he came into my room. I pressed the playback button.

A moment later he said, "Play it again." His eyes glistened.

He then trotted downstairs and made a call from the kitchen phone. I heard him say, "Mama," but the rest of his conversation was unintelligible. "*Boodi.*" "*Bozorg.*" "*Deerooz.*" These words stood out for me like the ones in a word scramble game. Someday they would make sense. Someday, once I was teaching English in Iran, *I'd* be able to rattle them off.

After a few minutes, I whispered, "May I say hello to her?"

He nodded, and I ran back upstairs to the bedroom to get the cordless phone.

"*Che to ree?*" I asked, in the best accent I could muster.

"Fine, thank you," she said, her voice warm and soothing as a summer breeze.

That's as far as my vocabulary allowed me to go, so Afshin translated the rest of my short conversation with his mother. I ended with "*Khoda hafez,*" and Afshin spoke with her a little longer. Finally, he kissed into the phone three times and hung up.

"My mom said, 'You'll have to bring your landlady to Iran someday.'" A hint of a smile appeared. "I want to tell her about you, but to explain this over the phone would be difficult. Expensive, too, at a dollar a minute. I'm afraid she would start to worry."

"And I'm afraid she'll think I seduced you. Then I won't feel free to visit you in Iran."

"Don't worry." A twinkle lit his eyes. "When the time comes, I'll tell her, and she will know that it was *I* who picked *you*."

My heart swelled with joy.

Just then I heard a click at the front door. Afshin flung his arms across his bare chest and dashed into the corner of the kitchen. Beth said hello to me and headed downstairs. I peered into the kitchen. There stood Afshin, wearing my bright green bib-apron.

I started to laugh, and he pulled me to him. "Your laugh is so warm." He held me for a moment, and then snuggled his face into my hair. "You are my heart, my breath . . ."

When I stepped back a minute later, I noticed the empty space around his neck. "Why aren't you wearing your ring?" I asked.

"I don't wear it in New York because my friends there don't know we're married."

"Even before you went to New York, I noticed you weren't wearing it." I undid my watchband and pulled off the ring. "Then I won't wear mine, either." I slammed it on the dining-room table.

He looked stunned. "You know I love you, even if I'm not wearing the ring, don't you?"

I thought for a moment, and relaxed.

He wrapped his arms around me firmly. I didn't resist. "Put it back on," he ordered.

Like a child hearing the voice of a loving parent, I reached for the ring lying, lonely, on the tablecloth. How many times had he kissed his ring as he took it off before bed? An eerie realization flooded me. In that moment, Afshin felt like a father, someone with wisdom greater than mine. I'd felt it before when he'd admonished me to spend more time with my children. Now I smiled: how complex our relationships become from time to time. Satisfied for the moment, I nestled, secure, in his embrace.

"Your face is always before me, no matter what I'm doing," he said. "You're in my breath and in my blood. Sometimes a marriage has spice in it. Ten years from now, you'll think of tonight and smile."

Yes, I liked the spice. A bland marriage wouldn't satisfy me.

That evening, in Spanish class, we pulled our desks into a circle and took turns reporting a current event. A gray-haired man, his back curved with age, had a glint in his eye as he told us about three aging male celebrities who had married much younger women.

The teacher agreed that men could get away with doing that—especially famous men. I couldn't let her comment pass, and I told them of my relationship with Afshin.

Jaws dropped, and the women expressed envy.

When I got home, I told Afshin what had happened.

"You and your adventures," he said, as he ruffled my hair. "If this gets out, all the women in Girton will be renting out rooms."

He started toward the stairs and stopped. "Oh, my friend, Yamin, called tonight. He's getting married next month and wants me to come to the wedding. He also invited Milad."

My eyes stayed on Afshin while waiting to hear, "I want you to come, too."

"I wish you could go with us, but Yamin doesn't know we're married. Can you understand?"

"I do." He could tell only trusted friends about our marriage. If news of it got back to people he knew in Iran, he'd have to deal with their judgments. Most young women are looking for a virgin groom. A temporary marriage, especially to an American woman, might make Afshin a less desirable candidate for marriage. "But that doesn't mean I like being kept a secret," I added.

Mid-February. We parked two blocks from the coffee shop and held hands as we hurried along a side street. When we reached the main street, however, Afshin let go of my hand. I understood that he didn't want his university acquaintances to see us, but I still felt sad.

On a bench in front of the coffee shop, two boys in baggy jeans sat smoking. Their cigarettes looked as out of place as baby bottles in men's mouths.

We entered the shop, filled with the cacophony of conversations, bought our drinks, and found seats at a tiny round table. I hugged a tall glass mug and sipped my café latté. Afshin ran his fingers up and down my arm. I was puzzled but imagined that he'd scanned the customers and decided he was safe from familiar eyes.

"When we see people doing something wrong, do you think we should tell them about it?" he asked.

I assumed the young boys' smoking prompted his question.

"I think it depends on how we say it—with concern or judgment. It's so easy to become self-righteous."

"I agree. I usually tell people when I see them doing something wrong because they need a reminder. Yet, I have not heard people do this in America." He blew on his steaming tea. "Once, when my mother and I were walking home, we saw a woman beating her son. We went over to tell her the punishment was too harsh."

"You're kidding! People here might call the Child Protection Agency, but they wouldn't talk directly to the parents. They'd be told to mind their own business."

"But if we care, are we not all each other's business?"

"*I* believe that, but how do you sell that idea to people who'd think you were intruding on their privacy?"

"Just start doing it with the right attitude," he said, as though his response were the only logical answer.

That sounded right. Yet, with strangers, I usually followed the norms of privacy rather than the impulse to help, even though when I *had* followed that impulse, I'd almost always been thanked. There was an exception once when a friend responded, "Mind your own business!" I wanted to reply, "What do you mean? You *are* my business."

Afshin dipped his teabag repeatedly in his glass mug. "You know what Milad told me? He wants a wife who shares his interests in the Qu'ran, religion, and discussing ideas. I don't. For me, the most important thing in a marriage is to make a loving environment at home—a safe place." He sipped his tea. "People have come to expect too many things from the person they marry."

"I agree, a spouse can't be everything to their partner."

Later that night, we lay side by side before going to sleep. "I need to sleep alone," he said after a few minutes. "I'm afraid I'll move around too much tonight."

It took me some seconds before I blurted, "I wanted to make love. You don't?"

"The love we have for each other is the most important thing. Sex is secondary."

Another time, I would have been delighted to hear that, but since we usually made love at least once a day and hadn't had sex at all that day, I wondered what he actually felt.

He proceeded to satisfy my physical desire, but then left right away. The bed spread out like a desert around me.

In the morning, I heard the shower running. Longing to feel reconnected with Afshin, I decided to join him. In the bathroom, I dropped my robe and opened the shower door. Steam billowed out and I stepped in.

Afshin frowned. "Beth might hear us," he said.

Beth? Was that *really* what concerned him? I felt I'd overstepped a new boundary. What had created it?

We exchanged few words during breakfast, but as he stood to carry his dishes into the kitchen, he said, "I have to go study, but we could have lunch at the hoagie shop." His eyes focused on the tabletop as though he could see right through it, and his face brightened. "I'm in the middle of solving the second 'gap' in my thesis. I hardly slept last night. This math is so exciting!"

My chest expanded and relaxed. Ah, yes. He'd told me recently that I was his beauty but that another beauty was competing with me. I'd felt a pang of jealousy until he'd quickly added, "Her name is Math." So now *she* was the one keeping Afshin occupied.

At lunchtime, I smiled to myself as Afshin ordered two hoagies. As a nutritionist, and a picky one at that, I didn't indulge in the kind of food sold there, but since Afshin had introduced me to the grilled chicken-breast hoagie, I'd become a convert.

The day was unseasonably warm for winter, so we decided to eat outdoors. Stone steps at the foot of a narrow alleyway nearby provided seating. We unwrapped our food, and the fragrant blend of fresh-baked bread, chicken, onions, and vinegar aroused my appetite. I bit into my sandwich with relish.

Looking up, I reveled in the hydrangea-blue sky of this last Sunday in February. Couples walked by, hand-in-hand. Mothers and fathers strolled with their children. The *plat du jour* featured togetherness, but Afshin wasn't interested in that menu item—he had math on his plate.

He ate in silence. Though his body sat next to mine, he could have been a mannequin.

A moment later, he said, "I'm sorry I'm not much fun today."

"Sometimes I'd like to hate this mistress of yours, but then I remember that if it wasn't for her, you'd never have come to the United States."

I still had half of my hoagie left when Afshin popped the last chunk of his into his mouth. Like the "All aboard!" announcement of a train conductor, Afshin's leg jack-hammered at full throttle, signaling his imminent departure for his cave in the university library. I told myself not to rush as I finished my sandwich.

"I won't be home until late," he said.

I watched him walk away without the usual spring in his step and fretted that he'd get sick. Yet, no talk about health would convince him to get to sleep earlier. His young body served him well, except for the backaches that had started soon after we married.

I trudged the long eight blocks toward home. One self-pitying thought after another lined up for attention, and, when I reached the house, I hurried to the phone to rid myself of each of them by talking to a friend.

A few hours later, I was heating soup for supper when Afshin appeared.

"I have to sleep," he said, "and I'm not going out again."

"Until tomorrow?"

"Yes."

"You mean I won't see you for the rest of the evening?" My upturned palms begged an answer.

Without answering, he gave me a quick hug and left for his room. I followed, but the door shut in front of me.

I froze. Was it really Afshin who'd just come home?

I stood for several seconds before retreating to my room and dropping into the velvet armchair. An ache gnawed at my heart. I'd gotten quite used to being treated as a princess. Now I pouted at my lost position, even though I realized Afshin needed to complete his thesis.

Later that night, soft lips on my cheek woke me from a shallow sleep. I opened my eyes and saw Afshin's face, lit by the moonlight. He reminded me of an anxious father checking on his sick child.

He caressed my head a few times. "*Bekhob*, sweet Miriam. Sleep."

I must have gone back to sleep right away because the next sound I heard was music from the clock radio. After the comforting effect of Afshin's kiss, I woke up in a good mood and ready for work.

At the end of the day, I whistled as I walked up to the house. Afshin met me at the door, and we held each other for a moment. He stepped back and stared at me.

"I haven't been a good husband, have I?" He gestured toward the loveseat. "Come. Sit with me."

On the way, he turned on the CD player and guitar music floated into the room.

I sat a few inches from him, but he reached around and pulled me close.

"I was thinking about you last night," he said. "You don't have your mother or father, your children are busy, and so are Ana and Rachel. And now I'm busy with math. I feel bad."

"I know your thesis is important, but I miss you."

"*You're* important to me."

"Yes, but you need more time to yourself."

"You *are* my self!"

My soul did cartwheels.

A month passed. Afshin and his other love spent days, evenings, and nights together at the campus library. He followed a new schedule: he came home to eat dinner with me around six o'clock, returned to the library for a long night of study, and finally got home to sleep at three or four in the morning.

One evening, while washing the supper dishes, I thought about our birthdays, which fell within a week of each other. If we ended our marriage on its six-month anniversary date, we'd no longer be married when our birthdays arrived a week later.

Just then, Afshin came up behind me, wrapped his arms under my breasts, and kissed my hair. "I'm going back to work for a few hours. Don't wait for me."

I turned. "Before you go . . . when we have our birthdays, how would you like to celebrate?"

His lips parted, but a moment passed before he said, "There's a math conference that week at Yale." He cocked his head and scrunched up one side of his face. "Can we celebrate early?"

My arms dropped to my side.

"Our birthdays come right after our marriage ends, a few days before you move to New York. I'd hoped we could spend extra time together then."

"I don't see it that way. You see the end—I see a change. We can still spend time together." He looked over my shoulder, out the kitchen window. Suddenly his eyebrows arched. "We could take this coming weekend and make it a special one for us. I won't study."

I didn't respond, and he added, "Anyway, don't we spend time together almost every day?"

"But that's now. We're talking about the last week that we'll still be living together. I don't want 'life as usual' right after our marriage ends," I said, struggling not to cry.

He grabbed me in his arms. "That's it! I'm not going to the conference."

I squirmed out of his embrace. "Don't change your plans. I want you to be with me because you *want* to be, not to stop my crying." *Or to assuage your guilt*, I thought.

"I want to be a good husband because that's what God wants."

"Not for me?" I tried to read his face and noticed his eyes glossed with tears.

"God is the one who deserves our devotion."

So he loved me out of devotion to God. And that was why he was upset—he was afraid God would punish him because he'd "made" me cry.

Stop it, Miriam. There you go again, trying to sort things neatly into boxes. Life isn't that simple. Afshin and I are made up of many feelings and beliefs. No wonder we're not always consistent.

"It's not easy to be a good husband." Afshin said.

He made his role sound like a chore. I pushed that thought away; I would let nothing ruin our marriage.

"As you said, let's make the coming weekend a special one," I said, unclear as to whether or not the weekend was a substitute for the last week together that I wanted in May.

Saturday afternoon, Afshin tossed a soccer ball into the back seat of the car. After a short ride, we arrived at Deerfield Park, a huge expanse of lawn under a cloudless sky. Afshin punted the ball onto the field and ran after it. He tapped it toward me, and we kicked it back and forth. My technique was improving.

Afshin pointed to two boys a couple of hundred feet away. "Let's see if they want to play with us."

A man and woman stood near them, and I was reluctant to ask strangers to join us. It didn't matter—Afshin was already heading their way. He tapped the ball to the older boy, who appeared to be about eleven. The boy kicked it back, and the other boy joined us. They seemed to enjoy themselves, but after ten minutes their parents called them to leave.

"In Iran, people on the streets or in the parks talk to strangers easily," Afshin said, "and games like this happen all the time. I thought that we Iranians didn't reach out to strangers, but I see that in some ways Americans are more reserved than we are."

I agreed, and after a few more passes of the ball, I led Afshin to the woods and trails behind the open field. As we walked, arm in arm, our footsteps hushed by the thick layer of damp leaves, I noticed Afshin gazing off into space, as he'd done a few times that day.

"Are you here or off with math?"

"With my mind I love math, and with my heart I love you." He paused and added, "I love you with the purest part of my heart that has never loved a woman this way before."

If I'd had wings, I would have taken off and flown in circles and loops over the woods.

A moment later, he said, "I still don't understand why you did not marry again, so many years after David."

"I was afraid," I said. "I told you that during my marriage to David our lovemaking wasn't very passionate—at least not on my part. At times he was disappointed, but he loved me and accepted my lack of enthusiasm. Yet, I never wanted to repeat that with another husband. I loved David, so I don't understand why it's different with you."

"There's something special about human beings making love when their souls are involved," he said.

I squeezed his waist. I felt that soul connection—but I'd had one with David too, though of a different flavor. And who knows? Maybe if I'd known my marriage to David would be so short, I would have felt more passionate.

Chapter 20

Tuesday evening, with some time alone, I studied the Spanish subjunctive. Other verb tenses had been easy. With this one, I was grateful to have uninterrupted time, so I wasn't entirely sorry that Afshin was staying overnight in New York City. His weekly stay in the city made it easier to do things that were harder to do with him in the house. The solitude also allowed me to pull out my other self, the one who didn't hide previous relationships, who thought divorce was necessary at times, and who wanted people to have the freedom to live openly in gay relationships.

While I mused on this, the front door opened and closed. I assumed Beth had come home, but then Afshin appeared.

"What are you doing here?" I asked as I rose to greet him.

He lowered his eyes, and I sensed something amiss.

I reached for the hand that hung limply at his side. "What's the matter?"

He said nothing, but tears pooled on the rims of his eyes.

A few seconds passed before he spoke. "My advisor told me that someone at Harvard has solved my thesis problem."

"Nooo! You were so close to finishing." I held him and felt his chest quiver against mine. Maybe he had to hold back, but I cried. It wasn't fair. He'd worked so hard.

"He said he was sorry," Afshin continued, steadying his voice. "He tried to tell me that I could get a doctorate on the work I've done so far, and that even though it wouldn't mean a gold medal, it would be worth a bronze."

"Are you considering doing that?"

"No. I want to complete a problem. I can't be satisfied with a partial solution, but this means . . . " He bit his lip. "I have to start all over with a new problem."

"What? Does that mean you can't go home this summer?" I wanted to cry—not only for him, but for his mother, his father, his grandmother, his brother, his sister and the others who'd missed his presence for four years. I forced the tears back.

He looked outside, into the darkness. "When I first heard the news, I was disappointed."

"Disappointed! Devastated, you mean."

He stopped for a second, without agreeing with my correction, and I remembered that for Afshin, disappointment was already a feeling of huge magnitude.

"I fought that feeling—it's the worst sin. God wants us to overcome obstacles. It would be weak to give up now—*camdel*. 'Chicken,' you say here."

"But it's natural to be disappointed. You've put so much time and effort into this project, and then, in the blink of an eye, it's gone."

"I can't question it. God has a reason. I have to trust Him." Afshin looked down. "I had more bad news. Iran is not renewing working visas. If I go home this summer, I can't come back." He paused. "There is a way around it: you can get a visa if you pay three hundred dollars. But I hate this corruption, especially in a religious government." His words burst forth, sharp with anger.

"Your poor mother. How will you tell her that you can't come home this summer?"

Tears streamed down his cheeks, and his hold on me tightened. After a moment, he said, "I'm so glad I have you. I came home tonight because I needed to be with you. I don't know how I would get through this alone."

How crushed he must feel to talk this way. What if, over the past few months, he hadn't spent so much time with me? Would he have solved his thesis problem earlier? I shuddered.

In the morning, I couldn't bring myself to leave Afshin—an atmosphere of mourning permeated the house. I called in sick without a hint of guilt. Around ten o'clock, I asked him to go for a walk at the nearby bird sanctuary. He didn't argue. We parked in the gravel lot, and I led the way to a boulder that protruded from a hill and overlooked a grove of bare trees, forty feet below. We lowered ourselves onto the edge of the flat granite and dangled our feet. I listened to Afshin speak about the next steps he'd take for his Ph.D. He sounded hopeful. Perhaps the Native American spirits who once held council on the boulder were encouraging my brave tribe mate.

After a while, we headed home. I thought Afshin might need time alone, so I went to the supermarket. But when I returned, Afshin came trotting down the steps.

"I couldn't wait for you to get home." He caught me in an embrace.

It wasn't like Afshin to cling. He might not want to dwell on his loss, but it was affecting him more than he'd admit. In the kitchen, he helped put the groceries away, and I noticed that he moved at half his usual speed—now matching my own.

"Come," I said, motioning for him to sit down. "I have a poem I'd like you to read." I handed him a poetry book opened to "If" by Rudyard Kipling.

I watched his eyes move across each line. He started nodding, and by the end of the poem he was smiling for the first time since the previous night.

"This is beautiful, especially this part:
> If you can make one heap of all your winnings
> And risk it on one turn of pitch-and-toss,
> And lose, and start again at your beginnings
> And never breathe a word about your loss . . .
> Yours is the Earth and everything that's in it,
> And—which is more—you'll be a Man, my son!"

He caressed my cheek. "Thank you for this. It will give me courage."

"You have the courage, *azizam*."

"I hope so. But right now I have to make plans to go to the Pakistani Embassy, as soon as possible, to see if Iran will renew my working visa."

"Why the Pakistani Embassy?"

He explained that since the United States stopped diplomatic relations with Iran after the hostage crisis in 1979, Iranian officials had had to maintain an office in the Pakistani Embassy so that Iranians in the U.S. could get their paperwork done. He then headed for the kitchen phone. "Milad also needs to renew his visa. I'm going to call him."

After a few minutes, he hung up. "We'll have to get to Washington the night before we apply. The line at the embassy forms early. Milad will stay at his friend's apartment for the night, but what will we do? I hate to spend money on a hotel." He paused. "Could we sleep in the car?"

Could *we* sleep in the car? I hadn't realized I'd be included in this trip. Yes! It wouldn't be comfortable, but an adventure with Afshin would be worth it. Besides, the idea of spending a hundred dollars for a room didn't appeal to me either. "OK. Why not?"

Sunday, the three of us drove off toward Washington, D.C. We hadn't gone more than a couple of miles when Milad started asking me questions about the meaning of life and how we should live. Knowing that he was a devout Muslim, I guessed his questions were based on teachings from the Qu'ran. He continued throwing out questions for most of the trip, and I enjoyed the chance to share some Belgo-American viewpoints while Afshin listened. I wasn't sure that Milad wanted answers. Was this questioning his way of teaching me concepts he thought were important? To instruct an elder directly would probably have been disrespectful.

"And do you think that choosing to do a good thing is as valuable as doing something good spontaneously?" he asked.

I heard a deep sigh coming from Afshin. Though he respected Milad, Afshin's patience was exhausted. I'd tried to discuss religion or philosophy with Afshin, but he'd always made it clear that he wasn't interested.

I glanced in the rearview mirror at Milad. "I think it's better if the motive springs from love, rather than from wanting to look good to others or God."

"But everything is for God!"

Now he sounded like Afshin. Milad would probably have liked to hear me say, "Both motives are good, as long as one acts in order to please God."

"In a way," I said, but decided not to explain that I thought loving others was equally important as loving God. Listening, especially to beliefs other than his own, wasn't one of Milad's strong points.

We arrived in the city and dropped Milad off on a corner, to meet a friend who'd be putting him up for the night.

Since Afshin and I had the afternoon to ourselves, we decided to visit the Museum of Natural History. In the first room, huge dinosaurs surrounded us; Afshin gaped at them with the amazed eyes of a child. We meandered through a dozen other rooms. Afshin examined the displays and read the descriptions. I was surprised. Somehow I hadn't thought of Afshin as the museum type. We entered a large room housing dioramas of early people. In one, a family of hunter-gatherers roasted a rabbit over an open fire. Afshin's face lit up as he read about them.

"They lived on the land that is now Iran," he said, gazing at the family for a long time, the barest smile on his lips and sadness in his eyes.

In that moment, I hated every border that kept families apart.

Around four-thirty, we left the museum, hand-in-hand, and headed toward the Vietnam Memorial by way of the National Mall. Now and then, we stopped for a hug and a kiss. No eyes to judge us here.

Twenty minutes later we reached the memorial and stared at the rows of names engraved in the 110-foot-long black granite wall. To think that David might have been one of them. My getting phlebitis when Greg was born had turned out to be a blessing. My inability to walk with an inflamed leg may have been the reason the Marines didn't send David to Vietnam. Baby Greg and I had no one else to take care of us.

"There are about fifty-eight thousand names here," I said. "It's so sad. When will we use a different way to make the world better for all of us?"

I turned to make eye contact with Afshin, but he was gazing above the wall. "That's nothing. We lost three hundred thousand in the war with Iraq."

Nothing! I wanted to remind him that every life has worth. But I'd be wasting my breath. He was probably too angry remembering the grief all around him—especially the deaths of his uncle and many school friends.

After a delicious meal at an Ethiopian restaurant, we strolled around Georgetown until bedtime. Then we headed for the car and began our search for the perfect "hotel" location. Slowly, we drove through streets illuminated by black iron streetlights, searching for a safe place to park and sleep. A half-hour later we found ourselves at Kalomara and 34th Street, a quiet neighborhood with large, stately houses, each displaying the flag of a different country. Embassy Row—how appropriate, I thought. I maneuvered my car into a tight space between two others. No traffic and not a soul in sight.

We reclined the seats and climbed into our sleeping bags. A few minutes passed as I told myself, repeatedly, that I *could* sleep in this unusual position. Before I could succeed in nodding off, however, a light slowly filled our sleeping quarters, growing brighter and brighter. I held my breath as I spied a police emblem on the side of the car crawling past us.

"Oh, no! What if they ask us what we're doing here?" I whispered. "With your three-day-old beard and army jacket you look the perfect picture of a terrorist."

He patted my shoulder as if to say, "You worry too much."

I released a big sigh of relief when the police car kept going, and we soon fell asleep.

Rain, pitter-pattering on the roof, woke me up. I glanced at the clock and gasped. It was after seven. I put my hand on Afshin's forehead and ran it back over his hair. "Let's go get in line. You said they're only taking fifty applicants today. I'm worried."

"Don't worry, we have time," he said in a groggy voice, as he pulled his sleeping bag over his head.

I yanked it down. "Let's not take a chance. I'm driving there right now," I said, glad to be in the driver's seat.

I shrieked when I saw the line at the Pakistani embassy. There seemed to be over fifty men there. Were we too late? Was Milad already in line?

Afshin sprang out and sprinted across the street to the end of the line. He called back to me, "I'm number 47. Meet me in that coffee shop later." He pointed to a building nearby.

I'd wanted to wait with Afshin, but he told me it was better not to do anything that might raise questions in the officials' minds. A pale-faced, middle-aged woman with an Iranian student might do just that, so I parked, grabbed my umbrella from the trunk, and strode down the avenue.

A couple of hours later, after walking for dozens of blocks, my feet were squishing in my shoes. I made my way toward the coffee shop where Afshin and I had agreed to meet. I ordered tea and sipped it while I read a book. I whispered another prayer that Afshin would get his visa without having to pay $300.

Two and a half hours later, Afshin and Milad burst into the coffee shop. Afshin's fist shot up. "We have our visas! We didn't have to pay."

I jumped up—almost into his arms. But then I remembered Milad. A public embrace in front of his friend would be embarassing for Afshin. I froze and let him take the lead; he reached over and kissed my temple.

As the three of us headed for the car, I started singing an old spiritual: "A-a-amen, A-a-amen, A-amen, Amen, Amen." On the second round, Afshin and Milad joined in. As we had only one umbrella, the driving rain soaked our clothes, but we didn't run. We didn't care about getting wet—our mission was successful.

We arrived back in Girton that evening. I looked forward to a real bed where I could snuggle with Afshin and sleep in comfort—if he didn't strip me of the blanket during the night.

"I need to go clear up my desk. The papers are piling up," I told Afshin, before marching upstairs.

He followed me and kissed my ear.

"Afshin! I really have to get these bills paid." I smiled crookedly at him and added, "The hungry lion will have to wait."

He left the room without a word. A minute later, I heard the television downstairs.

After sealing the last of five envelopes, I joined him. He patted my thigh without taking his eyes from the screen. What did I expect? He was engrossed in a program about the solar system. I found it interesting but had trouble keeping my eyes open. I kissed him and went to bed.

A little later, he joined me. I was on the edge of sleep, but his caresses drew me back. We made love in slow motion.

Afterwards, he said, "Don't worry, in June you can get enough sleep."

"I don't want to hear that! It's easy for you to say. You'll have no trouble finding someone else."

Afshin clasped my shoulder. "No one will ever take your place in my heart, but I will love you in a different way." He paused for an instant. "Doesn't a mother want the best for her son?"

"But I already have two sons!" I said, slapping the mattress.

"And you will have three and love them all," he replied. "You'll see. It won't be a step down to be my mother. You will have a place of honor."

I stared at the ceiling. *This is too strange*, I thought. I couldn't imagine transitioning to a mother-and-son relationship. How could he? I didn't want a place of honor in his heart. The word "honor" had a formal ring. Admiration and respect, yes. But honor?

I struggled with the words that finally spilled out. "Are you looking forward to the end of May?"

"What?" In the pale light, I saw his features twisted with pain. He looked down. "No, but what will follow will be no less special to me than what we have now. Love is love."

Sure, love was love—at its core. But I wanted him to agree that our love would be different, that it would be difficult to change the roles we played in each other's lives. Would it actually be *easy* for him?

Chapter 21

The day of Yamin's wedding arrived. Afshin was upstairs getting ready, and I lingered over my morning tea. The previous evening he'd taken me to the middle eastern restaurant to celebrate the Iranian New Year, *No Rooz*. I was surprised he'd turned down an invitation to a New Year's party with other Iranians. Perhaps he wanted to make me happy, especially since he was going to attend the wedding without me.

"Will you come with me to buy flowers and chocolates for Yamin and his wife?" Afshin asked, coming down the steps.

I agreed and we left immediately. As soon as we stepped into the flower shop, the lilies' perfume shouted their presence. I helped Afshin form a bouquet from purple anemones and white Stars of Bethlehem adorned with greens. We then walked to a nearby gourmet shop where we found the best Belgian chocolates in town. Afshin didn't comment on the price. He seemed happy to spend money for these gifts.

"One more stop," Afshin said. "I need to get money from the bank."

We pulled up to the drive-in window, and I watched him withdraw two hundred dollars.

"It's for Yamin and his wife," he said in response to my questioning look.

"But you can't afford that."

"He's my friend."

His tone told me that that explained it all. Yet Yamin wasn't one of Afshin's closest friends. Though I'd witnessed it often, his generosity amazed me.

Back at home, he rushed upstairs to finish getting dressed. A while later he returned wearing a dark suit and holding up a tie as though it were a dirty diaper. "Can you help?" he asked.

I fumbled with the blue-striped fabric, but failed to make a proper knot.

"Don't worry. Milad can help me," he said. "Let's have a dance before I go."

We danced the Colombian Cumbia, but it didn't cheer me as he'd probably hoped.

"I wish you could go," he said, as he kissed me goodbye.

I shut the door behind him, telling myself, "I'm all right," and went about my day. But by evening, I was worn out by the effort to believe my own story. I dropped into the armchair in my bedroom and let out a long sigh. I belonged with Afshin at that wedding party. Perhaps Ana was right when she said that I was too understanding. For a moment, I closed my eyes. But when a vision floated by of Afshin dancing with a young woman at the wedding party, I snapped them open again.

Around one in the morning, I heard the front door open and breathed a sigh of relief. His driving made me uneasy. Through squeaks and creaks, I followed his movements up the stairs: first to his room, then to the bathroom. Finally, the noises got closer to me. He lifted the blanket and slid into bed. I touched his foot and pressed my toes on it.

"How was it?" I mumbled.

"Not fun," he said, molding himself to me. "There was no dancing. Can you believe it?"

I believed it. I believed it. And, in the darkness, I smiled.

No hint of sunshine poked through the closed blinds when I opened my eyes in the morning. Lying on his belly, Afshin breathed long and deep. As I often did, I studied his face, memorizing lines, the texture of his skin, the length of his lashes, and the curve of his lips. An urge came over me to fling back the blanket and study every square inch of his body. Just then, he released a contented grunt as he snuggled close. I leaned back to see how awake he was, and he opened his eyes. Our skin met from head to toe as we extended our bodies, finding pleasure in each other. Afterwards, a tide of tears rose. Only two more months. I squeezed my eyes shut.

"What would you do about our marriage?" Afshin asked after a moment, as though he'd read my mind.

"I suppose it's easier for you if you're not married when you go to Iran this summer, but I'd rather end our marriage about two months before you leave permanently—whenever that is. That would give us more time together, and we'd still have a chance to get used to the change in those last two months."

"Let me tell you why that wouldn't work," Afshin said, taking my hand in his. "I have to put all my effort into finding a new thesis problem and then solving it. I need to work in New York, especially because I can no longer use the library here after Milad leaves in June. I will be *very* busy. I could not be a good husband to you anymore. For me, that's the only reason to end our marriage in May as we planned."

"Why not let me decide what a good husband is," I said, pulling myself up and leaning against the headboard, arms folded.

But did I really have a vote? He'd just given me sensible reasons to keep to our original date, but darn it, love wasn't sensible.

"If we were in a long-term marriage," he said, " it would be different: we could be separated for a while and then continue. But we've done it right in the short-term—let's do it right to the end." He nodded with those last words and waited for me to agree.

"All right," I said without conviction. But a second later, my heart blurted, "But why can't we stay married forever?"

"You know why," he said softly. "You belong here with your children, at least until they're married. And as I've told you, life in Iran would be too harsh for you. I would not ask you to live there."

"But shouldn't that be my decision? The hard life in Iran wouldn't stop me if you wanted me there. The only good reason I see for us to end our marriage is that you need a wife near your age so that you can have children."

"That's not my reason," he said. "When I decided to marry you, I knew it was a great responsibility because of the pain it could cause in the end. I would not have had the courage if you had not said that you would rather have a six-month marriage with me than thirty years in a boring marriage."

"Damn! I wish I were twenty and could marry you for life."

He caressed my head. "Don't cry, we have to be grateful to God for what we have. Few people experience this much love. We're putting a lifetime into six months."

I was packing in as much as possible, yet wished for a longer lifetime.

After breakfast, Afshin left for the library. I was standing at the kitchen sink, scrubbing hardened pancake batter from the frying pan, when the phone rang. It was Rachel. We chatted for a while, and then she told me that an Iranian man who'd seen me with Afshin at the Baha'i dinner in January had asked whether we were involved. She'd explained that we had a temporary marriage. I felt uneasy as I imagined that he might judge the marriage as inferior, even though it was legal for Shias.

That night Afshin and I sat on the edge of the bed talking about the events of the day. When I told him about the conversation with Rachel, his smile vanished.

"Are you upset?" I asked.

"I shouldn't have gone to that dinner the second time." His lips tightened.

I recalled with regret the way I'd persuaded him to go. "You said that people should prove their love. Coming with me to the dinner would prove your love for me." I'd hoped that another exposure to all those friendly Baha'is would make Afshin like them. It hadn't worked.

"There's a student I know who attends those dinners," Afshin continued. "If he finds out and tells an Iranian student that we're married, it may get back to my mother. News travels in strange ways. I don't want her to find out through someone else."

"Are you still concerned that a future fiancée or wife would find out about this marriage?"

He chewed his lip but didn't answer.

"I wish you hadn't made me go to that dinner," he said. "This may cost me a lot in Iran."

"I didn't make you go," I said, annoyed by his blame. But then, I realized I was playing with words. As far as he was concerned, I had made him go. "Anyway, you haven't done anything wrong."

"It doesn't matter," he said, snapping his head. "People don't have to do something wrong to be penalized."

Oh, that's right, Iranians were fined just for listening to western music or playing an instrument. Never mind the bigger offenses, such as being gay or writing the "wrong" viewpoint in the newspaper. People were stoned or jailed for those "sins" against Allah.

"Don't worry. I'll ask that man not to mention our marriage to anyone."

"No, no. Don't do that." He sat erect and his frown deepened. "He wouldn't listen, and then he would know I want to keep it a secret." He took a deep breath and kept rubbing his thumb over my hand. "There are people who disapprove of temporary marriages because they're sometimes used for . . . " he hesitated, "prostitution."

I must have looked surprised because he went on to explain.

"Some men marry for just one night, and for the women, it's a way to earn money." He paused. "I'm worried about how people will think of you."

"I'm not worried about that," I said, but as soon as the words left my lips, I realized that my reassurance wouldn't assuage him. He'd learned early that the judgments of others could have serious consequences. Afshin judged in black and white, and this was probably the public norm in Iran. Those who saw grays had to stay in the shadows.

Afshin looked at me, unsmiling. He kissed me lightly and left for his room. I slid between the cold sheets and hoped he'd quickly get over his worry. The next morning, his pat on my tush as he passed me on the stairs told me he had.

Later that evening, we lay side by side before going to sleep.

"Are you happy?" Afshin asked, in a tentative tone.

"Extremely."

"Learning to love a woman has been so sweet for me."

"And it's sweet for me to be with a man I can trust . . . fully, the way I trusted David." I thought for a moment. "That kind of trust makes lovemaking better, too. And it doesn't hurt that you're so sexy, either," I teased. I couldn't bring myself to say I felt more relaxed with him than with previous sexual partners because I knew that, unlike them, he couldn't compare me to other women. He couldn't recall sex with *any* other woman, let alone one who he found more exciting than me. Ah, yes, my insecurities still lurked.

Chapter 22

The ruckus of birds setting up house in the backyard trees woke me. Spring in full force. Go away. Afshin lay on his stomach with a pillow over his head. After breakfast, I'd kiss him goodbye, and he'd be off to a six-day math conference in Boston. I tiptoed downstairs and brewed a strong cup of English breakfast tea. I needed words of wisdom, something to carry me through the next few weeks. In the drawer of the credenza, I found *The Prophet*. Khalil Gibran's words had brought me comfort after David's death; they could help again. I turned to the chapter on joy and sorrow, my constant companions, and read,

"The deeper that sorrow carves into your being,

the more joy you can contain."

The upstairs floorboards creaked, and I whisked tears from my eyes.

Afshin trotted down the stairs and stopped after we made eye contact. Two seconds later, he pulled me from my chair and held me tightly. Suddenly, he stepped back. With a flourish, he unbuckled his belt and unzipped his pants. I had to laugh as I was reminded that he'd warned me, "If you cry again before the end of our marriage, I'll make love to you on the spot."

He bent his knees to meet me at eye level and tried to wear a serious expression. "Promise me you won't cry while I'm away this week."

"I can't do that," I said, dropping back into the chair.

He buckled his belt and shook his head as though he were dealing with an incorrigible child. I hated that he didn't understand my emotions.

A while later, we headed in separate directions. I sighed and decided to try focusing on the benefits of our short separation. I'd get a taste of what was coming.

The Bird and The Fish

I returned from visiting friends the next evening and stepped out of the car. The emptiness of Afshin's parking space next to mine jarred me. I gazed at the sky. *How will I ever bear the loss of Afshin's presence?* I asked the silvery lights in the darkness. *One moment at a time*, my heart replied. I walked up the bluestone path to the house and whispered that counsel to myself. Once inside, I made a straight line for my room and got ready for bed.

Over the next six days I read other passages from *The Prophet* and took long walks at dusk. Even simple acts, such as paying bills and sorting through flyers and ads, soothed me like the movement of a rocking chair. Friends fed me with food that tasted of love, and I knew that they'd dish out comfort in double portions after Afshin left.

Sunday arrived. I expected Afshin home around nine that evening; my heart trotted at the thought. Yet I was grateful for our week apart. It had given me a sense of the resources I had, inside and out, to navigate the separation ahead. Cal, Beth, and I met for brunch at The Merry Widow's and, after leaving Cal at his apartment, I walked home. Every now and then I skipped. I loved feeling like a carefree child.

Once home, I took out my Spanish workbook and started doing grammar exercises. A horn beeped. Afshin's car! I dashed outside, and he came running toward me. We collided in an embrace, and I burst into tears. I leaned back to take him in and noticed wet eyes. We gazed at each other until we broke out in laughter.

"The pigeon is back at the harem," he said.

I chuckled at Afshin's use of an old saying from his country, and though I liked learning sayings from Iran, I was glad to be the only woman welcoming my husband home. No harem for me, thank you.

"Before anything, I have to take a shower," he said, squeezing me again before dashing inside.

I watched him as he took the steps two at a time. I'd missed him, but not as much as I'd imagined I would, so the intensity of my present emotions surprised me. Had I used mind over heart all week?

Ten minutes later he flew down the steps and went straight to the stereo. He dropped a tape into it and I recognized ABBA's song *Money Money Money*. With head tilted forward and eyes gazing at me, he offered his outstretched hand. We erupted in a wild dance as we sang with the group about money and living in a rich man's world. One moment he spun like a top; the next, he slowed to half-time as his arm encircled my back and held me, while we moved as mirror images of each other. He released me and my feet pummeled the floor as my arms cheered his return. Afshin doubled up in laughter before stopping me with an embrace. Our bellies met in an exaggerated slow grind, and we attempted to maintain that contact as we danced our way up the stairs.

An hour later, we lay in a cuddle, and I asked, "So . . . what else did you do all week besides attend the conference?"

Afshin turned toward me. "There were five of us grad students, and we stayed at a friend's apartment. Every night we talked and played cards. Sometimes we watched TV or danced. And of course, we talked about girls." He flipped his hand up as though saying, "What else could I do?"

"One night we were playing cards when one of them asked, 'What's that ring you're wearing around your neck?'"

"Oh, no!"

"'I'm married,' I told him. Let's hope he thought I was joking."

"Oh, yes. You don't want that news getting back home." I felt happy that he'd shared this story. Like me, he may have said he was married in order to enjoy watching his friends' reactions, or to acknowledge our marriage, however casually.

He wrapped his arms around me. "Nothing is better than being with you."

I savored that moment's truth and our closeness.

Afshin met me outside with a soccer ball under his arm when I got home from work the following afternoon. He covered my face with kisses.

"Let's walk to town," he said.

"Yes!" I ran inside and changed in two minutes.

We headed for town, kicking the ball back and forth across the street. Once on the main street, we continued our game on the sidewalk, and I noticed people smiling at us. A few blocks further, we headed back home, hand-in-hand.

"A man without a love is like a man without a soul," Afshin said, looking ahead with pensive eyes and a determined look. "A man without a love is like a tree without leaves. A man without a love is like a sky without stars."

With a smile and a tear, I took a deep breath and kept my eyes on the far end of the street.

Later that night, I walked into the dining room, and Afshin motioned for me to sit down. "We have an important decision to make," he said, caressing my arm. "On what day to end our marriage."

My chest tightened. "Could we make it a little longer?" I blurted.

His face turned quizzical. "I'm confused. I thought you understood why May is best, but I think it would be even easier if we do it about ten to fifteen days before I move so that we can get used to it."

"No!" My heart pounded. "I want a full six months."

"Why?" he asked, with a look of surprise.

I stared at him and then closed my eyes for a moment. "Our marriage is already short. Six months seems like the least amount of time to still have it feel real. I don't want to make the change gradually. I want to keep our marriage the way it is until the very last day. That's it!" I strode to the calendar. "May 17th," I said and burst into tears.

He darted over and held me. Tears coursed down his cheeks; I immediately felt better in their company.

"All right," he said, looking down. "May 17th."

The next evening, after a special dinner with my Spanish class, I arrived home and found Afshin at the dining-room table looking dazed.

"My grandmother died today," he said, his voice faint.

I dropped to my knees and wrapped my arms around his waist.

"I wish I could hold my mother now," he said. "She sounded so sad."

I placed my palm over his heart.

After a while he rose and headed upstairs. I lay my cheek on the warmth of the seat he'd left. Only a month before, he'd learned that his grandmother had liver cancer and didn't have long to live. Because of his visa situation, he couldn't go see her. The steps creaked. I looked up and saw Afshin coming downstairs, gazing at a picture in his hands. His eyes stayed on it until he handed it to me like a holy object. "My grandma," he said, his voice cracking, "with me and my sister." He dropped back into a chair and I pulled mine close to his.

His grandmother stood with head uncovered, eyes squinting under the desert sun, and a contented smile gracing her round face. On each hip, a child rested: one who looked about three years old; the other, a toddler who didn't yet know that someday his mind would revel in abstract math and he'd marry his American landlady.

"My grandmother didn't deserve this cancer," he said through his teeth. "You cannot believe how religious she is. She is so good."

For a second, I expected the next sentence to be, "How could God allow it?" But no, he didn't have the freedom to ask. Silently, I asked.

"I hope I die alone. I couldn't stand to see tears in the eyes of those I love," he said.

"I hope you'll be there holding my hand when I die."

He sat up and gripped my hand. "No! Please don't say that! I would have to die with you."

His grasp hurt, but I didn't ask him to let go, or to explain what he meant. All I knew was that I was important to him; I didn't need to know anything else.

A long moment passed, and then he showed me another picture. "Here, she and my mother are holding the Qu'ran over my head just before I left for the U.S." Tears spilled onto his cheeks. "She had a hard life. A weaker woman would have bent under the load, but she turned to God and came out stronger." He paused. "She was the mountain of our family. I can't believe she's gone." His chin quivered.

He hadn't even had a chance to say goodbye. First, he'd missed his sister's wedding, and now this. What a price to pay for the education he wanted. When I looked up, Afshin handed me a two-by-three-inch piece of notepaper with Persian writing.

"My mother sent this for you last fall. I was too shy to give it to you then, because in it she said, 'Take care of Afshin, my jewel of a son.'"

"You are a jewel, but more precious," I said, stroking his back.

"I want to tell my mother of our marriage. She's my friend. It doesn't feel right to keep it from her." He shook his head. "But I don't think it would be good to tell a wife—especially if she's Iranian."

"You may be right."

In the past, I would have disagreed. I'd have told him that telling her about his relationship with me was important. It would create authentic intimacy because only as we know and accept each other fully can we relax into a relationship. But now I questioned the necessity of full disclosure. Maybe fewer facts meant fewer worries. There were relationships that I hadn't shared with Afshin, and yet I saw no evidence that his ignorance of them had negatively affected us. And besides, would a young Iranian woman want to know that "her man" had been someone else's?

I noticed that I'd put my own sadness aside at the thought of Afshin's future with another woman. In the face of his sadness, I just wanted his happiness.

"I'm going to pray," Afshin said, getting up and brushing the top of my head with a kiss before going to his room. I envisioned him standing on the two-by-three-foot Oriental rug that his grandmother had given him, and then prostrating himself toward Mecca. I hoped Allah would comfort my Afshin's heart.

A few days before April fifteenth, Afshin cleared the table after dinner and spread out the papers for his tax return.

"This is complicated," he said, puzzled by the forms. "In Iran we don't pay taxes like this."

"Then how do you run the country?" I asked, happy for any excuse to take a break from working on my own return.

"The government gets money from the oil it sells. They also take money out of paychecks, but that's only if you work for them. Business people are supposed to pay taxes, but you would not believe how they cheat. Otherwise, people don't have to fill out crazy forms like this," he said.

"Sounds great. I hate these forms," I said.

We both returned to our calculations, and a sigh of exasperation escaped one of us now and again.

"It bothers me that my taxes will be used to support Israel." The base of his pen struck the table a few times.

"And I'm not happy that so much goes for military spending instead of research into other ways to solve conflicts, but what—"

"But the Jews chased the Palestinians out of their homes! Now, they don't even have citizenship."

"Oh, I don't think that's true. When David and I visited there in eighty-one, the Palestinians were Israeli citizens."

"I don't understand. How can you have gone to that place as a tourist and never investigated what was going on while you were there?" His voice grew tense. "Do you know how badly the Jews have treated Palestinians? Going to Israel just to see the sights was wrong."

"Wait! David and I were interested in seeing where Jesus had lived—not in the politics of the country."

"That's wrong! How can you be a tourist when people are suffering?" He got up and grabbed his backpack. "I'm going to study."

The door slammed behind him. I sat immobile, but my blood sped through my heart as I watched him stride down the street. Why was he so angry about a trip I'd taken twenty years before? At the time of my trip to Israel, I'd been living in a bubble, ignoring news of the world. I'd done the best I could at the time. Allah—the Compassionate One—he'd understand. His compassion overflowed to all people, not just Palestinians. I wondered whether Afshin had ever learned the Jewish side of the story—their story of suffering, of properties confiscated, of loved ones killed. I doubted he'd even heard of Anne Frank. I stared outside at the invisible trail of his flight, took a deep breath, and blew it out through vibrating lips. No. I couldn't expect him to know. His teachers probably never told him the other side of the story. Maybe they didn't even know it themselves.

I called a couple of Jewish friends and asked what they knew about citizenship for Arabs born in Israel. One told me that Arabs are prospering as Israeli citizens; the other, that Arabs are citizens—but only second-class citizens. Knowing each person's political leanings, I wasn't surprised by the differences between their statements. We all find evidence for our own views.

I would tell Afshin what I'd found out from my friends. But could we even talk rationally about this topic? I wished he were open to hearing the Jewish side of the story, just as I wished more Jews were open to the stories of Palestinians.

Later, I climbed into bed, still stinging from Afshin's accusatory tone. I heard him come in, and within an instant he was sitting next to me, wearing a big smile. I had to struggle to keep a straight face. He nudged me over and stretched out. I closed my eyes and stuck my tongue out at him, but he gently touched my cheek.

"I thought you wanted me to tell you how I feel, even if it's unpleasant," he said.

"I do. I guess you think I'm ignorant, but when David and I were together, all that mattered to us was living a Christian life. We didn't watch the news or read newspapers." I paused. How oblivious I'd been about the Palestinians' story. Our church focused on the Chosen People—the Jews. But that type of favoritism never sat well with me. My God wouldn't play favorites. "Now I wish I'd known more before going to Israel. My visit would have been different."

Afshin brought the back of my hand to his lips. "You know, I talked to someone tonight, and he told me that Palestinians are citizens of Israel. I'm sorry for my mistake."

I turned on my side and nestled in the hollow of his shoulder. He pulled me closer and breathed in my scent as though it were the fragrance of forgiveness.

"I'm going to say my evening prayers," he said after a few moments.

"Would you teach me the prayer you say?" I asked.

"Why do you want to learn it?"

"Well, if terrorists ever kidnap me, I could pray in Arabic. Maybe they'd let me go." I grinned.

"It will be more useful for you to know '*Dast shui kojast?*' That's "Where's the bathroom?" He raised his eyebrows and grinned back at me. "But wait. Let me teach you something else for now. Listen: *La ellah ha ella lah*. Can you say it?"

I repeated the phrase and asked, "What does it mean?"

"There is one God—Allah."

I realized that the name Allah still made me slightly uncomfortable, after years of hearing it denigrated in the Baptist Church. But I liked the way my tongue clicked in my mouth as I repeated *La ellah ha ella lah* until Afshin climbed into bed with me.

Chapter 23

Friday morning I faced a blank document on my computer screen and started typing a memo to the Nutrition Committee about our upcoming meeting. As I typed the date on the fourth line, my eyes fixated on the numbers. Afshin and I had exactly one month left as husband and wife.

I left the computer and pulled a chair to the window. The apple tree with the crooked trunk had sprouted infant leaves. Next month it would wear flowers. I closed my eyes and shook my head in disbelief.

Miriam, stop it . . . you still have thirty days. Again, I envisioned Beth's way of treating her special cake—the closer she came to the end, the smaller the bites became and the longer she savored them. I could do that, too, with each coming day.

I stood and gazed at the tree a moment longer, then turned back abruptly to the computer.

Halfway through the meal that evening, Afshin said, "I called my mom today. She told me that the girl at her office is still interested in me." He shook his head. "I don't understand why. I didn't encourage her when I answered her letter."

He'd translated her letter for me, and she'd sounded like someone I'd like. "Maybe now you're not interested, but couldn't you be later?"

"She's too old."

"Too old?" A dragon breathed flames in my belly.

"Yes, she's twenty-six." He glanced at me, then casually returned his attention to the food on his plate.

I had an urge to whack him with the back of my hand, but nothing moved—except Afshin, who continued eating, oblivious to his role in the fire that raged in me. I told myself to take my time. He must have an explanation for what he'd just said, but at the moment I didn't want to talk. I kept eating. My fork moved up and down, as though on automatic.

At last we finished, and I pushed my plate aside. I crossed my arms on the table and leaned forward. "I'm angry about what you said." The words sounded hollow, but my chest burned hotter as I asked, "Would you explain why she's too old?"

He opened his mouth, but nothing came out for a second. "Well, she's out of college and probably set in her ways."

"You mean you don't want somebody with experience and maturity?" My voice vibrated. "You want someone you can mold to your ways?" I stared at him, trying to grasp what he was saying.

"I have enough maturity for two," he said with a wry smile. "And yes, I would enjoy teaching her some things. So someone younger would be better." He said it as though we were discussing a pet he'd be getting in the future.

I jumped up and started toward the stairs. Afshin gripped my arm, but I twisted free and ran to my room, snapping the door lock behind me.

I lunged onto the bed and wailed into the pillow, trying to rid myself of the monster's grip on my gut. But my crying brought no relief. He'd said that a twenty-six-year-old was too old. Had he forgotten the woman he'd caressed and made love to only last night? Had he forgotten her age?

The rapping on the door grew louder. "I love you. Please let me in. Please."

You love me? Suffer—suffer behind that door for a while. My fists tightened.

"You know how much I love you." He knocked harder. "We can talk it, can't we?"

I'm not ready, I thought, but Afshin's funny English—"talk it"—found my soft spot.

Slowly, I turned and curled up in a ball, my ear on the wet pillow.

The hammering on the door continued. "Please, let me see you. Let me tell you why . . ." I heard anguish in his voice.

Why hadn't he realized how his words would affect me?

Slowly, I unwound my body and spread one hand on the mattress. I propped myself up as I stared at the door. What else could he say? He'd already explained—a young woman would be easier to train to his way of thinking.

I hesitated for a while but needed to see him face-to-face. I made my way to the door, unlocked it, and stepped back. He clutched me as though to save me from falling over a precipice. I stood, arms tight at my side.

After a moment, he released his grip and held an open hand toward the bed. "Please, come sit."

He reached for my hand as we sat down, but I yanked it away and clasped it to the other. I stared down at my hands, folded as though ready to pray, but I was in no mood for talking to God.

Afshin clasped his own hands and kneaded thumb over thumb.

"I've told you how girls are in Iran—they are tied to their families."

I listened and hoped I'd be satisfied with his explanation.

"I don't want a wife like that. I want to marry one girl—not her whole family." He took a deep breath. "I thought that if I met someone who is still in college and away from her family, maybe I could convince her to live in a different part of Iran after we marry." He shifted toward me but continued to look down. "I need a wife who will understand the time and dedication it takes to be a good teacher, not one who'll say, 'If you loved me, you would spend less time at work.' In Iran that's often what a wife says, and her family backs her up."

I understood that part, and my hands relaxed.

He tried to catch my eye. "I don't want my wife's family to control me. I need the freedom to expand. Do you understand?" His eyes pleaded.

I remembered that he'd once told me that his mother hated visiting her husband's family because they constantly criticized her lifestyle. He'd said to me, "You don't have a family to tell us how to live. I like being married to an orphan." I understood that concern. What I didn't understand was what difference it made whether the woman was twenty or twenty-six.

"It's not the age that's better," he said, as though reading my thoughts, "but I think a younger girl will be more open to doing things differently." He paused. "Miriam, please . . . please forgive me. You know I never want to hurt you. It was stupid of me to say what I did."

I believed he hadn't meant to hurt me. I yearned to touch him but held back. A part of me didn't want to forgive so easily.

Miriam, I told myself, *you're only hurting yourself now.* I unclasped my hand and held it open to receive his.

"Do you really forgive me?" he asked, looking at me wide-eyed. "Are you not still angry?"

"No, but don't you see? I hate to think of you with another wife. I want to stay in that role." I almost added, "And when you say that you want a very young wife, I doubt that you really enjoy being with me." But, remembering how he'd reacted the last time I didn't trust his feelings for me, I avoided that trap.

"I'll always love you with a great love. You know that won't change." He bent forward and caught my eyes. "Don't you?"

"Too much *will* change."

"I'll always be only a phone call away. If you need me, I'll come to you—though you may have to buy the ticket," he added, watching my face for a smile.

His reassurance helped, but without warning, aftershocks shook me. *How can he speak with apparent ease of the change in our relationship?* I wanted a fellow mourner when our marriage ended.

"If we stayed married," he said, "I'd have to give up the chance of developing that math department in Iran. I can't give that up unless I can replace it with something as important."

Of course—his dream. How could he give that up?

But as we sat in silence, my heart sent out an SOS, as though from a ship in distress: I want to be your dream. I want to be your dream.

I strove to remind myself why this message was unrealistic. I'd been married, had children, and followed my dreams—but he was just beginning that journey. And besides, how much longer did I want to repress important parts of myself for love? Finally, how long would he find me attractive once my wrinkles deepened and my sexual drive waned?

This time I'd gotten myself into a good one, marrying a man half my age and then wishing it could last a lifetime. At least I was living fully. And, maybe Jacob and my other grandchildren would be proud of a grandmother who was willing to wander off the path of convention.

Afshin continued to hold me and asked again whether I'd really forgiven him. I had. The burning in my chest was just an ember now. But minor tremors continued for a while.

Later, during the night, I woke up and reviewed the reasons he'd given me for wanting a young wife in Iran. They made partial sense, especially because freedom was crucial for Afshin. No wonder he liked being married to an orphan, an orphan of twenty-five years standing—since Mamy died in that hospital on Staten Island.

The nurses are letting me stay overnight, again, in this empty bed. I prop a pillow against the wall and lean back on it so I can see Mamy in the other bed, nine feet away. She lies motionless, her mouth open, her skin sallow. Only five foot one, she weighs all of eighty pounds now. Her swollen abdomen forms a hill under the sheet. To think she once did hundreds of pirouettes and grand jetes on stage as a ballet dancer. I grab another pillow lying nearby and press it against my chest.

I'm pleased that last night she had just enough strength to sing, "You Are My Sunshine" for Greg into the tape recorder I'd brought. It might be her last message to her little grandson.

I struggle to stay awake. The solitary driving—a hundred and eight miles, four times a week for the past month—is wearing me down.

A stout, grey-haired nurse comes in and pats my outstretched leg. "Listen honey, you need to go home tonight. Get some rest."

I hesitate, but recall how badly I'd slept the night before. "Maybe you're right. But I'll be back in the morning." The room seems like a cavern. I don't want to leave Mamy alone. "Think she'll be all right?"

"She's sleeping. There's nothing you can do tonight." She gives a little nod and her caring eyes reassure me.

I tiptoe to Mamy's bed. She looks frail and helpless lying there. She's like a child, and I'm the mother now. How I wish I'd grown up in a family where hugs and kisses were an everyday occurrence. Yes, we kissed hello and goodbye, Belgian style: one, two, three, moving from cheek to cheek, but those were brushed kisses, not planted ones that grew flowers in the soul.

My hand lies on hers. I want to say, "Get up. Get better. What did you ever do to deserve this?" No, I need to calm down. "À demain, chère Mamy," I whisper and kiss her forehead lightly, afraid to disturb her precious sleep.

My steps resound all the way down the terrazzo corridor to the elevator, and I almost turn back when its doors open.

Outside, the drizzling rain shimmers in the lights of the parking lot as I walk to the car. I look up at Mamy's window. "God, be with her tonight."

In the morning, the phone rings while I'm eating breakfast with Greg in our apartment.

"This is Dr. Good. Is this Mrs. Valmont?"

My worry meter shoots up. "Yes."

"I'm sorry to have to tell you—your mother passed away during the night."

He goes on to reassure me that I had done all I could. I tell him I've already made funeral arrangements. After hanging up, I drop into a chair and pound my fist into my palm.

"Mom. Mom." Greg's small hand pats my arm. "Why are you crying?"

Afshin touched my shoulder. "I'm having a hard time sleeping. I can't forgive myself for causing you pain."

"*Azizam*, you've also caused me the greatest joy. Please stop worrying."

I rested my head on his chest. For now, *I* was his orphan. Hadn't he tried to teach me some things, too?

I smiled when, a few minutes later, his breathing deepened.

I was excited that Afshin had agreed to a trip to the Amish country. He'd see Americans who defy that all-American bumper-sticker motto: "Shop till you drop." Plus I'd have a full day to delight in his company.

Halfway through the drive to Lancaster Afshin turned to me, his eyes bright. "Could you come to Iran with me this summer?"

I jumped in my seat. "You mean it? That would be great!"

He glanced at me with an amused smile.

I would be in Afshin's country with his people. A tremor went through me at the thought of meeting his family, especially his mother. I had a feeling we would get along. What spunk she had! I pictured a scene Afshin had described. His mother had seen a young woman about to be arrested for selling outlawed newspapers on the street. She had yelled for the young woman to hop into her car, and they'd whizzed away.

I would get to eat the dishes Afshin had grown up eating. I might even discover his favorites, though food didn't play as large a role in his life as it did in mine. I started to salivate at the thought of my favorite childhood meal: sausages, mashed potatoes, and cauliflower with cheese sauce. And then I had an idea.

"Are you still planning to go to the math conference in Germany after your visit to Iran?"

"I'd like to, but I still have to get a visa."

"I'd love it if you could come to Belgium for a few days, too. I could show you where I grew up, and you could meet my cousins. What do you think?"

"All right, but that means another visa." He pressed his lips together briefly. "I'll call the embassies on Monday to find out what I need to do."

Visas to Germany and Belgium should be easy to obtain, I thought. Europe was friendlier toward Iran than we were. What a shame that so many Americans had demonized Iranians after the hostage crisis in '79.

"I want you to know Iran," Afshin said, reaching for my hand with his right while steering with his left. "You will see, people there are very different from what you've heard about them in the news here. You will be amazed at how much they love Americans."

We talked about things we could do together in Iran and Belgium, and when I spotted the exit sign for Lancaster, I gasped. With Afshin time flew.

Afshin paid the toll and pulled over so I could drive. I wanted him to be able to take in the sights. Twenty minutes later, we arrived on the outskirts of Lancaster. In the distance, I caught sight of an orange triangle on the back of a black box on wheels.

As we drew closer, I pointed, "Look, look—a horse and buggy. Try to see the people inside."

I eased my foot off the gas pedal as we passed the buggy. The Standardbred's hooves clip-clopped on the asphalt. I glanced at the man at the reins, who wore a wide-brimmed black hat, flat on top. His beard followed the contour of his face but, like other Amish, he'd shaved his mustache. Did they remove it to stay cleaner at mealtimes? I couldn't imagine they did so "the better to kiss you, my dear."

"This is the way they get around," I said. "They don't want cars because they don't see any reason to go far. They live close to each other in their community. You'll see, they don't use tractors for farming, either."

Afshin just shook his head.

"We'll go to the Visitors' Center first. They show a movie about the history of the Mennonites and the Amish. I think you'll like it," I said, knowing that he preferred absorbing information from pictures or movies rather than books.

A few seconds passed while he patted his thigh absentmindedly. "Why should we watch a movie about the people when we can see them right outside in real life?" he asked.

"Well, this will give you an overview of their lives, so you can better appreciate what you're looking at."

A little later, we arrived at the center and followed other tourists inside. I was relieved to see that the next showing of *Postcards from a Heritage of Faith* was starting in a few minutes. Afshin didn't like waiting for anything unless he was sure that the wait was going to pay off.

In the darkened room, the movie showed the history of the Amish and why they'd broken away from their original group, the Mennonites. Both groups came to Pennsylvania to escape religious persecution in Switzerland. The other "postcards" featured the Mennonites and their present activities. I noticed Afshin's knee was in jackhammer mode, but I didn't ask if he was bored. Even though I'd seen the movie before, I found it interesting.

"That was a good movie," he conceded afterward, as we returned to the car. "What's next?" He took the passenger seat again.

"You'll see. There's a place not far from here that I think you'll find interesting."

Fifteen minutes later, we pulled into the parking lot of the Bird-in-Hand Farmer's Market. There, amidst a field of cars, the Amish buggies stood out like time travelers. We joined shoppers squeezing through a door into a two-story white building.

Inside, dozens of stands lined the walls while others clustered in the center of the building. We strolled past displays of cheeses, shoofly pies, nuts, seeds, and local honeys. Afshin's eyes wandered over the goods and then lingered a few seconds on the merchants. He quickly looked away if the women looked in his direction. They wore ankle-length dresses covered with black aprons, and white organdy caps or black bonnets over their hair. Did they remind Afshin of women in Iran who also had to cover their hair?

"They are so modest. I like the way they dress," he said to me in a hushed tone. "What simple people."

I smiled. "I think that's what they call themselves."

As we wandered through the rest of the market, Afshin's constant look of wonder kept me entertained.

We left the market with our sole purchase, a bag of sunflower seed—the national snack of Iran, according to Afshin. We drove down a road bordered by cultivated fields. I slowed down as we passed a farmer grappling with a plow pulled by two sturdy Clydesdales. They reminded me of Belgian workhorses.

A couple of miles farther we saw a one-room schoolhouse. A couple of visitors were leaving as we arrived. After paying an entrance fee, Afshin stepped into the room ahead of me. He moved quietly, as though entering a class in session. If I hadn't known the boys and girls in the room were wax figures, I would have moved the same way. A teacher stood at the blackboard as though writing out math problems. A ten-year-old boy was standing by a wooden desk with forged iron legs. His hand was raised, ready to throw a wad of paper at another boy.

I stood next to Afshin at the rear of the classroom as he took it all in. For me, the scene had grown familiar from previous trips I'd made to show visitors this unique area.

"Do they still teach this way?" Afshin asked, not taking his eyes off the scene.

"I think they do." He had the look of a man who'd stepped into a cave and found it filled with ancient artifacts. I waited a while to let him experience whatever had him transfixed. He walked up to the teacher and, after examining her, continued on to the potbellied stove. I chuckled as he held his hands to it, as though warming himself. Finally, he came back and took my hand.

"Ready to move on?" I asked.

He looked at me as though I'd woken him from a dream. "Uh, yes. All right."

I drove west and turned onto a narrow road.

Beside a white clapboard farmhouse, one woman kneeled, curved over her vegetable garden, while another hung clean laundry on a clothesline. She'd already lined up black pants and aprons, and green, blue, and purple dresses. Where was the underwear? Did they wear any? Did they dry it out of sight?

"See that windmill? They use it for power. Notice there are no electric wires going to the houses." I said, touching Afshin's thigh. "They don't want television or radio to get in the way of family life. Even phones are off limits in their homes."

"Nooo. In *this* country?"

I laughed at his astonishment. "Yes. They'd rather visit each other and chat in person, instead of talking on the phone."

"Hmm," Afshin muttered, raising his eyebrows and nodding. "It's so different in this place. Is this America? People here work together, and I doubt that there is divorce." He paused. "Could I teach here? I would do it. I'm serious."

I tasted the yes in my mouth, but said, "I'm afraid not. Amish schools stop at eighth grade. They see no need for further education."

His eyes grew wide. "Really? What amazing people."

I was the one who was amazed. Even if only for a moment, something made him consider staying in the States. He must have been enthralled to see people living in a way he could admire. His question about teaching here probably gushed out before he thought about what he was saying. Surely, he wouldn't give up teaching in Iran so easily. Yet lately he'd expressed doubt about his ability to realize that hope. Ever since the loss of his thesis problem, he hadn't been his confident self.

"I'll show you a farm where I used to go with David occasionally. For about two years he had a job delivering packages near here once a month.

Sometimes I'd go along. We found this farm with a natural-food store on the property. It'll give you a close-up look at life on the farm."

"What a tour guide you are," he said, smiling at me.

After a couple of turns, I found Monterey Road and spotted the mailbox that read, "Christ Miller."

"Here we are. And no, Jesus doesn't live here. It's Christ with a short 'i.'"

Afshin ruffled the back of my hair. I liked it when he did that. I felt loved.

As we drove up the long drive, we saw a herd of cows grazing off to the left, and from a grassy spot on the right, two cows looked up at us. After passing the barn and the house, we parked in front of the store.

"We are closing in a few minutes," said a man with a German accent as we entered the dimly lit room.

Our clothes let him know we didn't speak Pennsylvania Dutch.

I hurried through the store and grabbed oatmeal and whole-wheat flour. The prices were much lower than those in Girton's natural-food store. Between the small windows and the kerosene lanterns—connected to a pipe running the length of the ceiling—there was just enough light to read the labels. Now and again I caught sight of Afshin closely observing two little girls helping their mother wrap up wedges of cheese.

Afshin's hand closed around my wrist as I passed him. "This is the way a family should be. Do you see how they work together?" He nodded, with an admiring smile, toward the farmer, his wife, and two daughters.

"Yes, yes, Afshin," I said as I slipped out of his grasp and continued dashing about the store.

The two girls watched as I paid their father for the food. I felt like asking them, "So what do you think about people like us? Do you wonder about our lives the way we wonder about yours?"

As we left the store, Afshin said, "I'm getting hungry. The sunflower seeds weren't enough."

I purposely hadn't brought a picnic so that we could eat Pennsylvania Dutch food. We headed west on Route 340 in the direction of home. A few miles down the road, a sign read, "The Amish Barn." This time Afshin would taste foods new to his palate.

Once inside, I noticed that, unlike many Pennsylvania Dutch restaurants, this one did not provide family-style seating. I was relieved because I doubted that Afshin would have been comfortable sitting at a long table with strangers. In any case, I didn't have to worry—the server led us into a dining room with private tables.

I described a few of the menu items to Afshin. He grimaced, in disgust, at the mention of pork sausage. Finally, we both ordered chicken pot pie with handmade noodles and a side of dried-corn pudding.

"What will I do in Iran?" he asked, while we waited for our meals. "I wonder if my dream will be possible." He curled an index finger around his chin and squinted at me. "What do you think I would be good at?"

"Teaching, of course."

"I wish I could stay in Girton. That town is heaven on earth," he said. "The only problem is that there are so many rich people there."

"You don't like the rich, do you?" I asked, keeping in mind that he considered people who I thought of as upper-middle class to be rich. "Why don't you like them?"

"It's hard, after the poverty I've seen. When I first came to America, I would hear people talk about their vacations, and I would get so angry. How could they go on silly vacations when people are starving? And then, the waste of food here . . . it still makes me sick."

"I know what you mean. Even after all this time in the States, I'm appalled when I see people throw out good food. I wonder if they forget about the preciousness of it, or figure that there's no correlation between throwing away food and letting people starve."

"Islam teaches us that we are responsible for the poor, and the rich are required to share." He paused with a question on his brow. "Do people here help the poor?"

"Of course, but usually through charitable organizations."

"I like giving directly. It's more human."

The server brought our meals, and Afshin gobbled up his pot pie.

After wiping the dish clean with a piece of bread, he asked, "Do you know why I think the U.S. is the Great Satan?"

"You said before that it's because of some actions our government took. Is there more?"

The question had come up at the latest meeting of the Sunday evening discussion group I'd been hosting for a few years. The topic was Islam, but at the end of the evening I still didn't understand why some Muslims call the U.S. "the great Satan." Now I could get a fuller answer.

"Yes, but I think it's also because Satan is the tempter, and so is the U.S. It tempts with pictures of beautiful naked women, fast foods, and fancy cars. It tempts all our senses. Most people are weak and give in. Too late they find they're still not happy."

"I see what you mean. A lot of advertising sends out shallow messages about how people can be happy. It's the price of capitalism, but please remember, not everyone buys into that."

"You don't, but who else?" he asked. "Americans don't know poverty. One of my aunts sold her kidney so she could pay for an operation for her son. *That's* poverty."

"Wow! That's amazing." Against the magnitude of his example, I felt unprepared to tell Afshin about all the Americans who lived in poverty.

We left the restaurant. "Will you drive?" I asked, holding the keys in front of him.

He took them, and I guided him back to the Pennsylvania Turnpike.

"Thank you," Afshin said, as he reached for my hand. "You are showing me that America is a place of many characters."

"That makes me happy. I could show you much more, but next year you'll be too busy to travel."

He nodded, and after a while his pensive eyes made me wonder whether he was still trying to figure out a way to become part of the community. An Amish Iranian. A picture of Afshin heading down the highway on a camel, instead of a horse and buggy, formed in my mind's eye, and I tightened my lips to keep from bursting out in laughter. He might not appreciate my humor when it came so close to American stereotypes of people from his part of the world.

Chapter 24

At dawn, Afshin was getting into his clothes when he noticed my eyes were open. He said that his mind was bursting with math problems and he couldn't sleep.

When he returned a couple of hours later, he paced the dining room and living room as I made an omelet for us.

I waited until he finished breakfast and then said, "Something's bothering you. What is it?"

His gaze dropped for a moment. "I'm feeling unsure about what to do after my Ph.D."

"But I thought you knew. What about the program you want to develop in Iran?"

He took a deep breath, closed his eyes and rubbed his forehead before answering. "It may take more of a math genius than I am to develop a superior math department."

The despair in his tone shook me as though he'd informed me of a death. Afshin and his dream were inseparable. Was he serious when he spoke of dropping it? The loss of his thesis had shaken his confidence more than I'd realized.

"Do you have suggestions for what I can do?" he asked, as though he expected an answer. After a pause, he added, "I could stay here and cut grass." I heard no humor in his voice.

I leaned forward, my eyes reaching into his. "You *know* you're a wonderful teacher," I said, my heart aching. "I see no other work for you."

He was quiet for a while. "I thought so, too. But now I'm not sure."

How disheartened he sounded, even depressed. I almost asked how he felt, but remembered that he thought depression was a Western fabrication for those who had too much time to think and not enough fortitude to overcome sadness through willpower.

The Bird and The Fish

He stared past the magnolia tree laden with plump pink buds outside the window. "I've done some thinking about your coming to Iran this summer..."

An invisible hand clenched my belly.

"Since I haven't seen my family for four years, we'll be doing a lot of talking—in Persian, of course. That would not be pleasant for you. I'm also going to look up friends, in different cities, and give a few lectures at my university in Tehran. What would you do during that time?"

I searched for an answer, but I heard what he wanted: freedom with the little time he'd have back in his homeland after a four-year absence. And sure, I could find a way to get around with a translator, but I wanted Afshin as my guide, sharing with me the places he loved and explaining the customs of his ancient homeland. "I guess it would be hard for me to stay with your mother and father since they don't speak English," I said, my voice flat.

"Yes, I think it's better if you go another time, when I've been home a while, and I can spend time with you." He looked in my eyes. "I would love for you to meet my family, see my country, and form your own impressions about it. You *know* how much I want that, don't you?"

The sting of disappointment kept spreading. "Yes, and I definitely want to see Iran before I commit to teaching English there."

"Oh, no. I'm afraid you would not want to go back then. I'm even afraid for myself. I've changed, and so has Iran." He leaned forward, resting his forehead on the tips of his fingers and thumb. "I wonder how this trip will affect me. Even Milad told me I shouldn't visit. He thinks I may decide never to return."

I waited for Afshin to say that he'd told Milad that he was crazy, but nothing followed. Instead, he volunteered to help me clean the house for the evening's visitors. I treaded the waters of my disappointment in silence for a while.

Not long before my Sunday discussion group was due to arrive, I slipped back into my clothes while Afshin took his required shower. The intensity of my physical response had been diminishing lately. I told myself that this was normal and that it mattered more that my love continued to grow.

I slid the glass pot into the coffee maker and gazed outside. I thrived with Afshin: his questions about my well-being, our conversations, his words of love, and his physical love acted as a tonic coursing through my veins.

"Hello-o. May we come in?"

Marvin and Martha, the two discussion group members who usually arrived first, stepped in from the foyer.

"Are you going to join us tonight?" Martha asked Afshin.

He'd joined us once, in January, during the last fifteen minutes of a video about Abraham and Isaac. I'd been proud of what he contributed to the discussion afterwards. It showed his intelligence and also the similar roots of Islam and Judaism. But no, by now I understood that he preferred to socialize with my friends as little as possible.

"Thank you very much," Afshin said in his formal voice, "but I need to do some work with my friend tonight."

Afshin left as the rest of the group members arrived. As always, over dinner we caught up on each other's lives. My marriage to Afshin had given an extra zing to these get-togethers over the last four months. The glint in these friends' eyes when they asked how Afshin was, made me wonder if they—especially the women—weren't really wanting to ask, "So . . . how is it to make love to a sexy young man?" I simply answered, "He's great," and perhaps they noticed the glint in my own eye and wondered at all the things I left unsaid.

At eight o'clock we gathered in the family room to watch *From Jesus to Christ*, a PBS series about Jesus and the first Christians.

After an hour, the video ended, and we looked around at one another. A lengthy discussion followed. I argued that Jesus was more unique than commentators stated, but when Joe and Marvin countered that many men claimed to be the messiah in those days, I realized I had no solid argument to prove Jesus's uniqueness.

At the end of the evening we took out our calendars to decide on the next meeting date. I was thinking about no longer hosting the group because I wasn't interested in philosophical discussions that focused on historical and scientific facts without allowing for some mysteries. Before Afshin moved in, I'd reveled in the discussions, but now they left me empty. Since Afshin had entered my life, God had slipped back into it, as well, and I felt ill at ease with people who knew me as an agnostic. If they knew I believed in God, they'd blame the change in my beliefs on a complete infatuation with Afshin, and I didn't want to admit that they could be right. But Afshin's God made life so simple, and Afshin's love for me made me a believer.

Before going to sleep, I snuggled with Afshin. "It's clearer to me than ever before—the most important thing for me is to love and be loved."

He drew me closer. "I've learned how to love from someone—you."

"I think your mother played a part in that too," I said, wanting to give credit to the one who'd shaped his early years.

"I love you," he whispered in my ear.

"Really and truly?"

"How can you question that?" he asked, each word a parcel of pain.

"I was joking," I blurted, but an inner voice didn't let me off so easily. *No you're not. You wonder if he married you to obtain Allah's forgiveness for some old sin*, it whispered.

"That's not something to joke about. You did this before. How could you doubt my love?"

I couldn't tell him that I wondered whether duty, more than love, prompted his amorous advances. Recently, I'd felt a jolt while reading about Islam at the library. I'd read that marrying a widow was considered a good deed, a *savob*—and good deeds erase sins. My guess was confirmed. Yet even if a desire to erase his sins had motivated Afshin to marry me, he'd shown his love in a thousand and one ways. Wasn't that what really mattered? I wasn't feeling disillusioned. He'd warned me, at the beginning, that he probably wouldn't feel the same passion for me that he'd feel for a younger woman. But this thought didn't disturb me, either. What mattered for me was how *I* felt: more consistently passionate than I'd ever felt in any other relationship.

"I'm sorry," I said because I didn't doubt his love; I doubted the extent of his sexual attraction.

"No, you're not."

"Yes, I am!" I said, as I sat up and stared down at him.

He laughed and cradled my face. "I meant—you don't need to be sorry. That's the way we phrase it in Persian."

How frustrating. If two people who love each other can miscommunicate so easily, no wonder world leaders get into trouble when they talk.

We rearranged our bodies with our heads touching just above our temples as we held each other.

"We are *hamsar*," Afshin said.

"What does that mean?"

"That we are husband and wife, but the word literally means 'joined at the head.'"

"Oh, I like that, but even more, I think we're joined at the heart."

The next evening, I agreed to watch television with Afshin. In this last month as *hamsar* I would take every opportunity to touch him, hear his voice, or listen to his breathing in the quiet of night.

When the show ended Afshin turned the TV off, and we lingered for a minute in silence. I was musing about Afshin being a typical male—he'd chosen to watch a program with lots of action and violence—when he turned and faced me squarely.

"What are my best and worst characteristics?"

"Hmm . . . let me think." But I didn't need to think long; I knew what stood out for me. "Your commitment and devotion to a person is your best. I've seen that with your mother, your friends, and me."

"Thank you." His whole face smiled his pleasure. "And my worst?"

"Your worst?" I raised my eyebrows at him.

I couldn't stand his black-and-white thinking. He had no sympathy for Iranians who left at the time of the Revolution, or for Judy and Henry's desire to erect a Stonehenge replica in Pennsylvania. He showed little tolerance for spiritual beliefs different from his own.

"Well, I think it's your inability to put yourself in someone else's shoes."

His features turned somber and he didn't deny it. My heart ached for him. He'd often told me that he wished he had my compassion.

I leaned forward. "Now tell me mine." Would the worst be my mistrust of his love or my habit of answering my own questions before giving him a chance to do so?

"Your best is your extreme forgiveness." And, with barely a pause, he added, "Not choosing to spend your time carefully is your worst."

My body slumped, and I stared. Had I heard him right? Me, not being careful about choosing how I spend my time? I was the one with a planner in which I listed and prioritized my activities each day. My friends teased me about it. Afshin must be teasing, too.

"What do you mean?" I asked.

"You're not as close to your children as you should be. You need to spend more time with them."

"Wait a minute! You're judging by Iranian standards. That's not fair. Yes, I wish Beth and I were closer, and I'm not giving up on that happening someday, but it won't work in the ways you've suggested." My stomach burned. *What nerve. He'd never even been a parent.* "And as far as Greg and Cal are concerned—we *are* close. We share feelings openly. You seem to think there's something wrong with that—unless they're happy feelings."

"But they don't call you often. Why don't they do more for you? You need help taking care of the garden and painting the house. They shouldn't wait for you to ask." A deep frown cut his forehead.

"I'd *love* it if they volunteered, but I taught them that each person should take care of himself. Maybe I taught them too well."

"I worry most about Beth," he said, shaking his head. "You and she should be close friends."

I didn't respond. He'd admonished me again and again about his concern. It was useless to explain, once more, why she and I weren't closer. Love without certain actions didn't exist in Afshin's dictionary of acceptable loving behavior. If the relationship between mothers and daughters in Iran is usually stronger, I could see why Afshin's concern was intense. In his eyes, Beth and I must have appeared estranged. What if he'd seen me with my mother? He would have judged our interactions as lacking in affection. Was that just my family or the Northern European way? We cared, but we weren't effusive.

He put his hand on my arm. "After I leave, I hope you'll spend your time in a worthwhile way."

"I will," I said, confident that I would—by my standards. When it came to my children, I couldn't promise any particular actions. Together, they and I would decide what we wanted.

Chapter 25

Beth bounced into the house. "I've been promoted to Junior Stylist!" We celebrated by having dinner together. She bubbled with the excitement of her promotion as she told me about co-workers and customers. I was thrilled by her chattiness. When she jumped up, unasked, to wash our dishes, I took it as a sign of better times ahead.

That evening, Afshin called from his office in New York. "My advisor didn't show up for our appointment," he said, in a tired voice.

"Not again!"

"It's all right. I love that man. Sometimes I wonder why—after all the appointments he has canceled with me." He paused. "Maybe it's his warmth, and he's so easygoing."

"I wish he'd show you more respect," I said.

"I forgive him," he said softly. "I love him like a father. We talk so easily together." He paused. "But the good news is—I have a tutoring job tomorrow. The guy is paying me two hundred dollars for six hours. Can you believe it? My father works two months to make that much."

"That's sad," I said, wondering whether Afshin felt guilty for his privilege.

"Would you mind if I stay in New York overnight?" he asked, with hesitation.

"I was so looking forward to seeing you." I heard the drop in my tone and added, "But go ahead, you need the money. I have that wedding shower tomorrow, so I'll be away until at least three o'clock. I miss you, I love you, I hug you."

"Ditto," he replied—a signal that colleagues had come within earshot.

I returned the receiver to its cradle, and a cloudburst of emotions showered me. I darted down the hall to Afshin's room and dove onto the futon. His blue soccer shirt lay nearby, and I sobbed into it. After a while, I quieted down. God, I can't stand it. I have such an easy life and yet there are people, like Afshin's father, who work long hours just for the basics. I turned over and stared at the ceiling. For a while, I lay fingering Afshin's nylon shirt. Afshin's mother, his aunt, his grandmother and his father had difficult lives, at least compared to mine. I couldn't go back to life as usual. How could I make a positive difference—one that could bring happiness to others (as well as to me)? *That's* what I could research after Afshin left. A sense of relief came over me.

I held Afshin's shirt to my nose and inhaled his scent again. Why did he touch me so deeply? Because he was different from any man I'd known? Because he helped me with chores that had no importance for him? Because of the way he expressed his love? Yes, all those reasons were important, but the most important—I felt cherished.

∽⚬⁀

Mother's Day. Afshin and I had made a brunch date at The Merry Widow's with Cal and Beth, and we stood waiting on the sidewalk in front. Within ten minutes, they both arrived. Each gave me a hug, and Afshin, a nod. Once inside, we perused the menu. After we all decided what we wanted, Cal and Beth started talking to me, but they didn't even look in Afshin's direction. My annoyance grew as the minutes passed. Couldn't they at least acknowledge his presence?

While Cal and Beth were speaking to each other, Afshin whispered, "I think I should go and leave you with your children."

"Please stay," I said, clasping his thigh. I wanted my mate by my side and was disappointed by my children. I'd never seen them ignore a companion of mine in this way. They seemed like strangers.

Cal and Beth each handed me a large envelope containing a Mother's Day card.

I read and lingered over what they'd written.

"I love what you wrote, but you don't have to buy such fancy cards. I'd be happy with a simple card."

Cal rolled his eyes. "Mom, why do you worry about what I spend? It's my money. Can't I decide what to do with it?"

"Sure. But it's *my* Mother's Day. Can't I tell you my preference?"

While Afshin gave his order to the server, I mouthed to Cal and Beth, "Talk to Afshin—be friendly."

After the server left, Cal turned to Afshin. "Do you argue with your mother?" he asked, in a cocky tone.

"Not really. My mother has enough worries. I don't want to add to them."

Cal frowned and pulled the corner of his mouth down. "I don't understand that."

"Islam teaches that a mother should get the highest respect from her children."

"I respect my mother, but that doesn't mean I can't disagree with her," Cal said, as he slipped his knife back and forth between the tines of his fork.

"I was taught that offending my mother is a serious sin."

"It's a good thing I wasn't brought up in Iran," Cal said, sounding more irritated.

Afshin probably thought Cal's response to my comment about the card was disrespectful. Though disappointed that Cal disregarded my request, I didn't hear a lack of respect in what he'd said. One could as easily have thought *I* was the disrespectful one.

Our food arrived, and the conversation turned to the mundane. Afshin observed in silence.

Later, as we left the restaurant and said our goodbyes, Cal turned to Afshin. "That was really a good conversation we had."

What good conversation? Was he serious or sarcastic? The latter, I thought.

Afshin and I reached our car, and he held my arm before I got in. "I'm afraid I've helped create distance between you and your children. I'm not going to join you for a meal again as long as they don't want me there."

I knew he was right, but while he played the leading role in my life, it would be hard to have him stay backstage. "Maybe it's better for now," I said, feeling downhearted.

On the ride home we exchanged few words, but back in our familiar surroundings, I said, "I wish Cal didn't act that way with you. I expect that type of behavior from Beth—she's friendly toward only a few people—but not from Cal. He's usually so easygoing."

"Don't worry about it. But I don't understand why they don't show you more respect. You're their mother! How can Cal say things that make you sad? That's a serious sin. When he asked me if I argue with my mother, I wanted to say, 'No, because I couldn't stand to hurt her.'"

We walked over to the love-seat, and I snuggled into his warmth.

"He didn't mean to hurt me. Besides, I *want* my children to tell me what they think."

"No, no. Not if it hurts you," he said. "But remember, if they don't always show their love, you still need to trust that they love you. When I become your son, I'll show you how much a son can love his mother," he said, stroking my hair.

The reference to the upcoming role-change stung, but the caring gave me comfort.

Afshin rose and inserted a tape in the stereo. *Ashokan Farewell*, our favorite waltz, started playing.

"Come, let's dance!" he said, holding out his hand to me.

I wrinkled my nose but reached for his hand. He pulled me close and, as we swayed, the tightness in my chest loosened; I felt like a rowboat moored in gentle waters.

When the dance ended, he said, "I told Milad I would help him with his paper today, so I better go."

"Go," I said, as I nudged him toward the door. "I feel full of your love, and it will hold me until you return."

Through the picture window, I watched him head toward his car. I closed my eyes and replayed his every move, embedding each one in my mind. Scenes of the past six months arose, and the joy of those times tasted bittersweet as the day of his departure approached. I looked forward to the camping trip we'd planned to take during the last three days of our marriage. We'd have concentrated time together.

A few hours later, I called Greg. After chatting a while, I reminded him that the end of my marriage was drawing near. We were saying our goodbyes when I heard, "Home, babe." I smiled at the greeting Afshin had been using regularly since learning that David greeted me that way.

"Gotta go, Greg. Thanks for the pep talk." I hung up the phone, grateful that Greg reminded me to live in the present.

A second later, Afshin stood next to me. "How have you been?" he asked, bending to check my eyes.

I shrugged and brushed past him on my way to the love seat.

He joined me and took my hand in his. "Have I been a good influence in your life?"

So that's what he wanted to be. "You've been a treasure. Your love convinces me that there must be a God." He smiled. "Also, my ideas about relationships have changed. The way you and your friends do big things for each other—it makes me want that kind of commitment with *my* friends."

"Anything else?"

"Well, yes. I've also felt the sacredness of marriage. I'm sad when I think of people having affairs. I wish couples would find a way to heal their marriage if they're unhappy, or get a divorce." I paused. "I feel so safe with you. I have no fear that you'd betray me. Do you realize how much comfort that has given me?"

He squeezed my hand.

I thought of all the time he'd spent with me when he could have been studying. "Are you sorry you married me?" I asked.

"Not at all." He looked taken aback.

"How has this marriage affected you?" I asked.

"I haven't examined it." He stroked his mustache. "I may not know until some time has passed. I learned a lot. I never thought I could love someone this much—the way I love you. You let me open the secret doors of my heart." He paused. "Should I say this?" My breath caught as I waited for him to go on. "At times this marriage was difficult because I had to deal with your past. I couldn't relate to it. In those moments, I felt a great imbalance."

He stopped for a minute, and my heart sped up.

"I dealt with it by trying to find out more about David so that I could love you with a pure love, the way he did."

So that's why he'd asked me about David so many times.

He stared at our intertwined hands resting on my lap and said, "Sometimes it was hard to hold hands with you in public, and I felt guilty for that."

"But you told me our age difference didn't matter. Did you lie then?"

"No. At first it didn't matter, but later I saw that, because of others, it did matter. If it were just you and me in the world, I wouldn't care."

He paused. His lips parted, but no words came.

"The discovery of your boyfriends was the hardest," he finally muttered. "I wanted to be the only one but, instead, I felt like just another link in a chain."

"No! How can you say that? You're unique. The love I experience with you is different. You're not a link in a chain—more like a key to a door. You've opened up a new way of seeing life for me."

He drew me close. His body quivered and a sob escaped. I couldn't hold back my tears.

Together we cried. I then understood the meaning of sweet sorrow.

After a while, he said, "I promise. I will love you as much as my mother—and that's a lot."

This time, what he said didn't hurt at all—perhaps because I was wrapped in a soft love cocoon. "And I wish that your next wife will be perfect for you. I believe you'll choose a person who values the meaningful things in life."

"I'll have you check her out," he said and then nuzzled into my neck.

Who'd believe this exchange was sincere? But I knew it was. The new affirmation I repeated almost daily was paying off: I'm able to bear the loss of this love for a new kind of love, and I'll create a meaningful, happy life.

Tuesday morning Afshin left early to visit consulates in New York City. He needed visas for two countries: Germany and—Belgium! I may not have been included on his trip to Iran this time, but at least I could meet him in Belgium after his math conference in Germany.

With Afshin away for the day, I decided to take the opportunity to talk with Cal. Whenever I thought of the way he'd acted toward Afshin on Mother's Day, I noticed an instant case of indigestion. I picked up the phone to see whether he and I could meet later in the afternoon.

When he arrived, we walked around to the patio and sat facing each other. The fragrance from a neighbor's lilac bush revived memories of spring in Belgium. Normally I savored childhood memories, but I was distracted by more recent memories of Cal.

"I'm wondering . . . Do you have something against Afshin?" I asked.

"No, but I don't have anything to talk to him about. He's too serious."

"He has a great sense of humor. You're not giving him a chance. And, worse than that—on Sunday, you seemed to take pleasure in trying to provoke him."

"I don't like his ideas. He thinks his way is the only right way." He slumped into the chair.

"I like his ways."

His head pulled back. "Mom, what is happening to you?"

"Nothing," I almost yelled. "I like the way Afshin loves me—with total commitment, and . . ."

"Then why doesn't he marry you forever?" He bolted forward, palms heavenward.

I couldn't answer for a moment, but then said, "There are reasons—and he'll still love me after our marriage. He believes in total devotion."

"Total devotion? Where's the freedom in that?"

"Oh, Cal." But though I didn't admit it, Cal named what I wanted to ignore. Was Afshin so dedicated to devotion that he ignored his needs? I feared that he might later resent not having fulfilled other aspirations because he was busy being devoted to me.

Cal stayed a little longer, but our usual camaraderie didn't surface that afternoon. After he left, I realized he was right: Afshin *did* think his ways were the best. Cal had learned, from me, to leave room for error and mystery. Yet here I was, loving a man who thought in terms of black and white. Were love hormones blocking pathways in my brain?

I inhaled the fragrance of lilacs, and it soothed me.

Like Beth, Cal wanted to protect me from the pain he saw coming, but he was probably even more disturbed by experiencing a mother who acted "crazy in love" and wasn't the person he knew. No wonder he wasn't friendly toward Afshin. And soon I would present Cal with another challenge—my next role in Afshin's life. I couldn't imagine Cal welcoming Afshin as a brother. Fortunately *that* role was not part of the deal.

―――

In the evening, I drove to the train station, straining to see through a spring downpour. As I approached the covered walkway at the station, I spotted Afshin, standing with his arms crossed, protected from the rain. He jumped into the car and stared ahead.

"The stupid Belgian consulate!" His fist struck his thigh. "Before giving a visa, they want me to prove that I'll have a hundred dollars a day while I'm there, and they want a copy of your cousin's bank statement. The woman was so mean—you wouldn't believe it! Is it because I'm Iranian? Do they think I'm a terrorist? Is that why I'm treated without respect?"

I reached for the back of his neck. "Afshin, there are ignorant people everywhere. It's not about you. I went to that consulate once and a woman acted very unfriendly to me, too. Maybe it's the same one."

I wanted to show Afshin the land of my childhood—the park where I played, the spot where my house once stood, the school with its center courtyard, and the remnant of family I still had. He'd get his visa; we just had to persevere.

I gripped the steering wheel and plowed through the puddles. If people could travel freely within a country, why not throughout the world? When were borders invented anyway?

"I just found out that Belgium had a colony in Africa and that the stories about Tin Tin take place there," Afshin said, his tone more irritated. "I hate Tin Tin. He's a racist. Do you notice how Africans are shown in those books? They're like silly children."

I felt embarrassed to admit that I hadn't noticed that aspect of the comic book stories I'd loved as a child.

"The German consulate people were difficult, too," he continued. Like a deflating balloon, he blew out a stream of air. "Because I'm from an 'unfavored nation,' the list of requirements for a visa is very long." He paused. "I may have to give up on going out of the country this summer. I don't know how I can do everything they want."

"Afshin, no." I clasped his hand. "Your family will be so disappointed. And what about the conference? Isn't there *some* way?"

"Don't worry, I can handle it," he said, his tone resolute.

Of course. He couldn't be disappointed. It was a sin. He *had* to be strong.

Chapter 26

Afshin's frustration about his European travel plans still clung to me when I got home the next afternoon. We both needed lighthearted moments in the few days we had left together. I had an idea and trotted out to the garage for the rollerblades I'd recently bought. After lacing them, I rose unsteadily and stood near the door. Just then, Afshin's car screeched into the driveway. He stepped out and I rolled toward him, knees bent and arms stretched out like plane wings.

"Is this how my landlady greets me?" he laughed, as he caught me.

"Would you teach me how to rollerblade?" I asked.

"Not now. Let's eat." He marched toward the house.

I lowered myself on the spot to take off the skates and wondered how to spend the evening. Tomorrow afternoon, we'd take off for a three-day camping trip; tonight might be our last supper at home as *hamsar*. I hoped we could make it cheerful, but the Afshin who'd constantly injected humor into our days was a serious man now. No wonder. First, he'd lost his thesis problem, and then he'd been treated like a pariah by the staff at the consulates.

By the time I got to the kitchen, Afshin had turned on the water for spaghetti and was getting a bell pepper and mushrooms from the refrigerator. I wouldn't have traded our traditional meal for one from a five-star restaurant. After he washed the mushrooms, I sliced them with special care. How long ago it seemed since I'd first questioned Afshin about Iran as he cooked the same dish—for himself alone.

He ladled sauce over two plates of spaghetti, and set them at our places. I reached for his hand, and for a moment we sat in silent gratitude. I then picked up my fork and chewed each mouthful as though taking part in a ritual.

Over tea, we discussed the visa impasse. "Why can Americans travel so easily without a visa, and yet this society is the most violent in the world?"

He stared outside for a moment. "I'll go to the consulate in the morning and try one more time," he added, looking back at me.

"But Afshin, tomorrow we're leaving for our trip around noon. I doubt that you could make it there and back in time."

"When can I go then?" His hands flew up. "Next week I'll be at the math conference."

"What? Did you forget? You agreed not to go." A tide of disappointment rose in my belly. "It will be your last week here."

"I'm just going for part of it." He shot up out of his chair and fled downstairs. A second later the television blared.

I rushed to it and turned down the volume. "We should get our things ready for the trip."

"I want to watch this," he said, looking straight ahead. "We have plenty of time to get ready."

My jaw tightened. "Ask me now if you're a good husband." He glared at me and refocused on the television. Why act like this and ruin our last few days? Fuming, I sat down at arm's length from Afshin. I wasn't about to go pack alone.

After watching the news, he went to pray, and I got ready for bed. A little later, he climbed into bed with me, wearing his clothes.

"Go ahead. Go to the conference," I said. I realized I'd been so consumed with spending every last moment with him that I hadn't left room for what *he* wanted. No sooner had the words left my mouth than another wave of sadness rose in me. I reached up and switched the light out so he wouldn't see my face. He moved close and his hand reached across my chest. Tears coursed into my ears. My hunger for time with him bordered on starvation. He turned the light back on, looked at me, and turned it off.

His clothes dropped to the floor, and soon his hands caressed me. I wasn't in the mood for love-making but, after a few moments, I responded. I wondered, though, whether he acted only to avoid God's displeasure. Our lovemaking stopped my tears, but I couldn't smile when he teased me with, "The road wasn't well paved tonight."

I struggled to accept that Afshin didn't need the kind of closure I did at this transition time. I kissed him goodnight and turned on my side. He molded his body to mine, and I snuggled into his warmth.

At the hospital the next morning, I gasped when I saw the number of cases assigned to me. Throughout the morning I tried to hurry, but the patients required more time than usual.

I called Afshin. "I have tons of work, but I'll try to be home by twelve-thirty."

After I saw the last patient, I looked at my watch. Ten after one! I grabbed a phone. "Afshin, you wouldn't believe the crazy day I'm having. I'm really sorry, but it looks like I won't get home until about two o'clock."

"I could have gone to the consulate today," he snapped.

"I know, but this is unusual."

I rushed into the hospital kitchen and handed my written instructions for special food requests for patients to the diet aide. By then, the tightness in my stomach had grown painful. Before leaving work I still had to enter data into the computer. Finally, I sped home.

Afshin met me at the door, "Let's go, let's go," he fired at me.

"Afshin," I said, my voice rising, "We didn't pack last night, so . . . " I raced up the stairs and flung my clothes and toiletries into a duffel bag. I then raced to the kitchen and gathered all the food we needed. On my way to the garage to collect the rest of the camping equipment, I passed Afshin pacing the dining-room floor like an animal behind bars. Had my lateness annoyed him *that* much? I'd expected him to help me, but he wasn't offering.

"Will you take these to the car?" I asked, handing him two sleeping bags.

He grabbed them, and when I came back with the tent, he said, "I'm not in the mood to go now. All my excitement for this trip is gone. Let's leave in the morning."

I started up the stairs for the shelter of my room, but my hand tightened on the banister. No! I wouldn't let Afshin's mood ruin our plans. I turned to him and struggled to control my voice. "If we go tomorrow, it's not worth going at all."

"Then we can walk in this area," he said, making an arc with his arm.

"What? How can you say that?" Tears stung my eyes. "Doesn't this trip mean anything to you?"

"If you really want to go, I'll go," he said, his voice flat.

I hesitated. Could I deal with the disappointment of a ruined trip if Afshin stayed in his present mood? I'd take that chance—I wouldn't give in by staying home. "Let's go," I said, grabbing the keys from the hook and flinging them at him. "You drive."

After five minutes of riding in smoldering silence, I stuck a cassette in the player. By the fifth song, the singer had cajoled me into singing along. A few minutes later, Afshin joined in. I looked at him, wide-eyed.

He reached for my hand. "Thank you for pushing me to come."

By the time we reached the campground in the Catskills, I wondered whether we'd be able to get our tent up before dark. Across the way, Slide Mountain rose some 4,000 feet; on the left, Woodland Creek gurgled past. Only a few tents stood among dark tree trunks. Far above our heads, the trees' leafy canopies fluttered.

We chose a secluded site and pitched our tent as daylight faded. The last campers at our site had left a stack of logs nearby, and Afshin gathered twigs and branches for a fire. I handed him an old newspaper I found in the trunk of the car.

Crouching in a spot where a previous fire had burned, he balled up strips of newspaper and built a pyramid from the paper balls. I watched as he placed twigs and branches geometrically around it. When he was satisfied with the pyramid, he struck a match and lit it. As it blazed, he retreated and sat on the ground, a few feet away, wearing a contented smile. For a long time, he stared at the dancing flames and then at the sky. The smell of burning wood drifted past me. I sat quietly, at a distance, happy to see Afshin calm for the first time in days. I had an urge to throw my arms around him, but I held back—nature needed more time for her healing work.

The air grew cool and my body tired. I unrolled my sleeping bag on the bench of the picnic table and lay on my back. Afshin came over and stepped up on the table. He stood still for a moment, his eyes and palms raised to heaven. Then he uttered, *"Allāhu Akbar."* From "God is great," he continued the prayer, bending at the waist with hands on knees, until, at the incantation, he sat on his heels. From my vantage point, he stood out like an ethereal being against the backdrop of a zillion stars puncturing the ebony sky. I loved to watch him pray. Each movement symbolized his respect for a Higher Power, and I respected his devotion.

I whispered, "Thank you Infinite Everything, Creator, Higher Power, Allah, Yahweh, for the beauty of nature and the love Afshin and I share."

Afshin stepped down and stood by the flames lapping the cool night air. "I wish I could stay up all night to watch this fire," he said.

"It *is* beautiful, but I have to go to sleep." I sat up and hugged my thighs to my chest.

"Would you like to hear about Zeus and Prometheus as your bedtime story?" he asked.

"Yes, yes."

Afshin straddled the bench in front of me and placed his hands on my knees. "Once, a long time ago, Zeus . . . " I drifted back to when he'd first told me the story, months before, but suddenly his words caught my attention: "And then, one day, Zeus punished Prometheus because she had played a trick on her father." I smiled, hearing Afshin change Prometheus from a son into a daughter.

"Zeus knew that she liked the humans who lived at the base of Mt. Olympus, and he told her that he would not give them fire. Prometheus became sad, but then decided that she'd deliver fire to the humans herself. When Zeus wasn't looking, she stole a burning charcoal and hid it in the hollow of a giant fennel stalk. She raced down the mountain and gave it to the humans.

That night, when Zeus saw dozens of fires burning at the base of the mountain, he was furious. He caught Prometheus climbing back from her expedition and ordered that she be hung on the Caucasus Mountains. During the day an eagle came and nibbled at her liver, and each night the missing part of her liver grew back. After a minor god e-mailed the Iranians to tell them of her fate, a brave Iranian went to the Caucasus Mountains, killed the eagle, and released Prometheus."

I chuckled at each new twist in the myth and delighted in Afshin's returning sense of humor.

Neither one of us moved for a while. The water swirling over the rocks, a dozen feet away, sang a mountain lullaby. Afshin got up and sauntered to the fire. It crackled and spit sparks as he added logs. Guessing he needed time alone, I carefully unzipped the door flap on the tent and crawled inside.

After I undressed and slipped into my sleeping bag, Afshin stepped into the tent. He bent down and kissed my lips lightly. I reached around his neck and smelled the fire's smoke as I pulled him close. We lay facing each other, our foreheads touching. As he exhaled, I breathed in his breath. After a while, he slid into his own sleeping bag and we kissed goodnight. The pressure of his kiss conveyed affection, not desire.

The hard ground kept me awake. I turned on my stomach, but then my neck hurt. I turned to my side—but no, that wouldn't do, either.

Afshin tapped my shoulder. "Here, roll to your side," he said, pushing his foam pad under my sleeping bag.

"You need it," I said.

"I'm a man, and I've slept on harder floors."

Morning took a long time coming as I awakened, again and again. When dawn shed its first light, Afshin left the tent as though summoned by a friend. I stuck my head outside and saw him hunched on hands and knees, blowing the embers over which he'd placed a few twigs. I got dressed and stepped into the chilly mountain air. Afshin was watching the flames like a proud father.

I poured granola, sunflower seeds, and dried fruit into tin bowls.

We ate to the crunchy sound of our breakfast. After taking down the tent, we drove to the parking lot at the foot of the mountain trail. I looked forward to sleeping near its summit that night. Just Afshin and me—away from the rest of the world.

As we left the car, each shouldering a full backpack, sunrays poked through a gathering of gray clouds. Once on the trail, I pointed to a marker on a tree. "Afshin, we need to keep an eye out for markers like that or we'll lose our way."

"Let's not use them," he said. "It's too unnatural."

I didn't argue, but I kept checking the trees for trail markers anyway. Getting lost in these woods could pose a danger—black bears roamed the Catskills.

Although Afshin carried two-thirds of our equipment, my shoulders ached under the weight of my pack. An image of Afshin leaving for New York City the following week flashed before my eyes, and my physical ache diminished as my heartache grew. I grasped at the beauty around me for relief. The trail was covered by last autumn's leaves and bordered by fresh green ones, unfurling into hundreds of new plants.

No one passed us on the trail. And the next time I searched for a marker—I found none. "Afshin, we lost the trail! We better turn back."

He turned around. "Don't worry. We'll find it. It can't be far."

We retraced our steps and followed paths that resembled trails, but each one faded into the forest floor. The straps of the backpack dug into my muscles. "Afshin, I can't keep going like this."

"Here, sit on this rock." He patted a boulder. "I'll go look for the trail."

"Wait. What if you can't find me later?"

"We'll keep calling to each other. I won't go farther than your voice."

I freed myself from my backpack and climbed onto the three-foot boulder. Afshin's voice grew faint, and I grew uneasy. "Aaaafshin!" I heard a distant response and a few minutes later, he reappeared.

"I think I found a trail," he said with excitement.

But when we reached the so-called trail, it wasn't as well defined as I'd hoped. No markers appeared as we continued uphill.

"I have to . . . stop for a while." I trudged to a fallen tree and unloaded my pack. "Let's have some lunch. I need fuel to keep going."

Afshin nodded, and lowered his backpack onto the ground.

I pulled out a can of sardines, bread, peanut butter, and jam. We made sandwiches and ate them with gusto. When the last bite was gone, we continued our climb, stopping only when we heard rushing water. Following the sound, we came to a rivulet running down the mountain. At last, a landmark! Afshin pulled the map from my pack, and we located our starting point, as well as the small stream. We guessed at our present position along its course.

"Let's follow the stream to its beginning," Afshin said. "It must be near the top of the mountain."

Just then, helicopter blades whirled overhead and I waved. "Hey, over here! Come save us!" But I was just having fun playing the damsel in distress—the spring foliage overhead hid us well.

Afshin led the way up the steep incline, littered with rocks and boulders. I searched for a large, well-placed rock for each step. My heart pounded and my breath labored, but I clambered on. The distance between us increased. Noticing, Afshin said, "Come on, you can do it." Every few minutes after that, he stopped and said, "I love you," instead, as though those words would give me strength. And they did.

Seven hours after starting, we reached a flat area encircled halfway by a wall of rock fifteen feet high. A carpet of green hues covered the floor of this haven.

"It's beautiful," I said. "Let's camp here."

"We better find a trail and water first."

I hated leaving the idyllic spot, but I examined the map. "Let's go northwest." We'd gone about two hundred feet in that direction when I looked down in surprise, realizing I'd just stepped onto a trail.

"Hurray!" We hugged with the excitement of explorers reaching their destination.

The loss of the trail markers had given us an adventure we'd never forget. Smiling proudly, Afshin said, "You see, we didn't need those unnatural markers."

We decided to continue on to a campsite with drinking water. After walking downhill for about twenty-five minutes, we came to a plateau on which tents stood in solitary spots among the trees. At one end, there were no tents. We dropped our packs there to claim our domain.

Before setting up our tent, we snaked through nearby trees and shrubs and found ourselves on a rocky ledge. I gaped at the sight of the sun casting orange hues over clouds and hills. We reached around each other's waists and stood, taking in the panorama, for a few minutes.

Racing against nightfall, again, we set up our tent and gathered wood. With the same enthusiasm and precision he'd shown the previous night, Afshin arranged twigs and branches for the fire. Meanwhile, I prepared supper.

"You're a great travel partner," he said, looking at me through the flames. "In fact, you're a great partner in every way."

I just smiled and swallowed my words: *If I'm so great, why is our marriage ending tomorrow?*

As we settled down to eat, encircled by darkness, the flames lit our faces. A strong wind gusted and the fire blazed. Sparks landed on a shrub nearby, and Afshin rushed over to it. Bending its branches away from the fire, he spoke to it: "I'm sorry. Hope you'll be all right."

After tea and dates, we placed all the food in a plastic bag. I tied it to one end of a twenty-foot rope and secured a rock to the other end. Afshin flung the bag over a branch and wrapped the rope around the trunk. As he wound the rope, the bag lifted out of reach. The guidebook warned that bears might come through at night, and we weren't about to invite them to join us by leaving out a tasty snack.

Exhausted, we crawled into our tent and cuddled. "I'm sorry I've been so impatient," Afshin said. "When I'm tired and hungry, I get irritable. You're so patient and compassionate." He kissed my forehead. "Let's pray."

Our fingers intertwined, and I said, "God, I'm grateful for our marriage and the love we've shared and the things we've learned. Now help us with the change, and may our love grow in its new expression."

Afshin added his thanks, and we lay silently, facing each other, our hands clasped between our chests.

Thunder rumbled in the distance as I waited for sleep to come.

Afshin's grasp on my shoulder woke me. "Listen!" he whispered urgently.

I heard twigs snapping outside the tent.

His lips touched my ear, "Is it a bear?"

"I think so." My heart raced, and my breathing grew shallow.

We snuggled, and I heard snorting near the flap of the tent. We gripped each other's hands. For the longest time, no muscle moved as we strained to decipher every sound. Raindrops came, lightly at first, and then like a bag of rice being poured by heaven. After many minutes, we let out a nervous half-laugh. I concentrated on the raindrops and finally fell asleep.

Even with my eyes closed, I couldn't shut out the inevitable: the light shining through my eyelids announced that the last day of our marriage had dawned. I longed for Afshin's warm body, molded to mine. Darn these sleeping bags! I rolled on my side and gazed at his sleeping face. He had no awareness yet of the significance of the day. It had loomed in my consciousness like a long dreaded exam.

With lips parted, Afshin seemed about to speak. I wished his heart would move those lips to say, "I can't leave you—to hell with the rest of the world." But, by midnight I'd be what he needed me to be—his mother. We'd walk a new path. I couldn't imagine pulling down the shade on a marriage at night, and raising it, the next morning, to . . . to this other relationship. I'd seen his iron will when he lost his thesis, but this new challenge to his will power was different—it involved shutting off basic sexual urges.

Afshin's eyelids twitched. I waited until his eyes stayed open. "We haven't made love these past two days," I said. "I hope this afternoon we can—for the last time."

"The 'lion' has been quiet, but later he'll show you how alive he is." His eyes smiled and I felt relieved. For the past two days we'd seemed to be slipping into our next relationship, and I'd started to grow anxious. Where was our usual intimacy? Now, reassured by both his words and his eyes, I knew that once we were back in the familiar surroundings of home, we'd recapture it.

The rain had stopped. I straddled Afshin and poked my head outside. No bears—only the fragrance of pine and freshly soaked soil. We took down the tent, ate some granola, gathered our belongings, and stuffed them into our backpacks. As we started down the trail, I turned and blew a kiss to the campsite.

All the way down the mountain, the trail markers jumped out at me. I couldn't imagine how I'd lost track of them on the way up.

Three and a half hours later, we reached the parking lot at the base of the mountain, packed our things in the trunk, and drove away. Afshin suggested we stop for lunch in the village ahead, and I gladly agreed.

The Bird and The Fish

We crossed a bridge over the Esopus River into Phoenicia. Near a building on the left, I saw stacks of huge inner tubes, ready for summer tourists. After driving only one short block down the main street, I pointed to a restaurant with a packed parking lot. Afshin pulled in and created another parking space along the fence.

As we waited, first for a table, then for our omelets, I expected that at any moment I'd have to pretend to be calm, while a gray whirlwind swept through me. But pretending wasn't necessary. My heart beat regularly, my chest filled and emptied easily, and no tears surfaced. I looked around at the other patrons and imagined myself an actor on location for a film. Otherwise, this scene couldn't have been real.

Forty minutes later, as we drove out of the mountains onto a six-lane highway, sadness made her late entrance. I turned and stared at the passing landscape.

Afshin laid his hand on my thigh. "This weekend was really good for me. Thank you." He pointed to a bumper sticker on the car ahead: JESUS IS COMING AGAIN. "We believe our Twelfth Imam is coming back, too. He was sinless, like Jesus, and he disappeared more than 1,100 years ago. Someday, God will allow him to come back and establish the kingdom of Allah on earth. Some people thought that Ayatollah Khomeini was the Hidden Imam." Afshin shook his head. "We are told that the world will be full of injustice and terror in the last days, but the Twelfth Imam will bring justice and equality to the world."

My mouth was agape. He could have been describing the Second Coming of Jesus that I'd learned about in church. "So where is he now?" I asked.

"He is hidden in the spirit world."

I stared outside again. In my college history class and in my Sunday evening discussion group, I'd discovered many other similarities among different religions. If only we could meld all the world's religions into one… then maybe our fighting would stop.

Halfway home I offered to drive, but Afshin refused. That was fine with me. I welcomed anything that could make life easier at that point. Every now and then, my stomach tightened when a glance at the speedometer showed we were traveling between seventy and eighty miles per hour.

"Tomorrow morning I need to leave by five to catch the train," Afshin said.

Ah, yes, the math conference.

"On Wednesday I'll go to the German Embassy, again, to see about a visa, and then I'll come back to celebrate your birthday," he continued.

A week later was his birthday, too, but he placed no importance on celebrating it.

"Don't do that for my sake. The conference means a lot to you, and you'll miss a whole day if you go to the embassy and then come home."

"I'll come back," he repeated. As I heard his determination, I was touched by his willingness to honor the importance I attached to being with him for our birthdays.

I glanced at my watch—five forty-five. The heavy traffic had added over an hour to our trip. I had an urge to turn back the hands on the clock—the same urge I'd had when my mother-in-law told me of David's death.

As soon as we arrived home Afshin said, "I'm going to take a shower. Would you join me?"

I nodded, eagerly, and followed him into the bathroom. While I undressed, I turned away, conscious of a new shyness. Pushing the curtain aside, I stepped into the bathtub at one end; Afshin came in from the other end. He picked up the soap, worked up a lather in his hands, and then spread it on my shoulders and down my arms. He moved to my waist and slowly sculpted the lather up to my breasts. The "lion" was awake.

"Let's go to the bedroom," I said.

He stepped onto the bath mat and handed me a towel. "I have to give Milad a call," he said as he dried himself.

I stood, stunned for a second, as he headed for the phone in the bedroom. I wrapped the towel around my torso and followed. With my basic Persian, I understood "dinner" and "very good." Though I loved the sound of the language, especially when Afshin spoke it, I wanted to understand more of what he and Milad were saying.

He covered the mouthpiece. "Milad invites us for dinner." He made no sign that he wanted to refuse the invitation. "Or we could ask him here? What do you think?"

"How can you even think of doing that during our last hours together?" Milad may have heard me, but I didn't care.

Afshin declined the invitation and hung up the receiver. "We have to eat, anyway, and it would be quick."

If he needed an explanation for my refusal of Milad's invitation, we occupied different planets indeed. With my emotions like crystal glasses on the edge of a card table, I wasn't about to attempt to get Afshin to tell me what was motivating his behavior—the attempt would be futile, as always.

"I'm going to get dressed," I said, grasping the bath towel to my chin.

Six months earlier we'd plunged from a normal existence into a freefall of joy and sorrow. Like a parachute, the camping trip slowed the fall, but as we approached the ground, I was drawing my knees up to keep from making contact, if only for a few more moments, while Afshin seemed ready for the roll into our new relationship.

"I'm going to pray," he said, giving my head a caress.

I went to the closet and pulled a denim skirt and my favorite blouse from their hangers. My Gauguin blouse—like a painting of tropical flowers—had accompanied me at other major events since Diane gave it to me nineteen years ago.

I had insisted I didn't want to move out of our marriage gradually. I wanted to savor the relationship until the last second. But maybe that wasn't realistic. The trip did provide a space for us to ease out of our marriage. Maybe I was asking for more pain than necessary, while Afshin was trying to make it easier for me.

I'd just finished dressing when Afshin came in and enveloped me in his arms. Then he stepped back for a moment. His eyes softened and glistened. Slowly, he unbuttoned my blouse. He cupped my breast, for an instant, before he reached down and kissed it. My breath caught. We moved to the bed and I lay back, trying to focus on every sensation as we kissed and caressed each other. But I felt myself going numb. Damn the sadness!

As though sensing the change, Afshin sat up. "If we do this now, I'll have to take another shower before the last prayer. Let's go eat."

You'll have to take another shower? So what?

My mind craved physical union with Afshin even though my body was uncooperative. Four hours until midnight. We still had time.

We stepped into the hoagie shop and ordered our usual sandwiches. The men behind the counter greeted Afshin as though he kept them in business, and then smiled briefly at me. They had to wonder at the kind of relationship this young Middle Eastern man had with a middle-aged American woman.

We ate our sandwiches on the bench near the shop. As he finished eating, Afshin said, "I should go check my e-mail. I could do it now or later. What do you think?"

"Do it now so it's off your mind."

He dropped me off at home and left for the university computer room. I leaned against the foyer wall for a while. I wished we could express what we were feeling and why.

Forty minutes later, he returned. "Let's drink some strong tea so we can stay up all night."

I brightened up, hearing that he saw this night as special. He made the tea and I prepared sandwiches for him to take to the math conference. I avoided his face because floodwaters pressed my eyelids.

Afshin came over and made me face him. "Why do you look so sad? Don't you see? I can love you forever the way I have these past two days." He drew me close.

But that wasn't what I wanted, and I'd made it clear. He was cheating me of the last bite.

"By the way," he continued. "I just received bad news. Some students are having trouble getting a visa to get back in this country. My friends are warning me not to leave the U.S. until my thesis is done."

"But your mother! How will she feel?"

"She's strong, and I'll tell her I have a mother here."

"Don't tell her that. She'll be hurt."

"No, she won't," he said, shaking his head as though trying to empty his ears of my words. "She wants the best for me."

My eyes closed.

"It's your bedtime," Afshin said.

The phrase he'd used when he wanted to make love didn't fit my mood, but I nodded and wondered if I could feel sexual again in the next half hour, before the clock struck midnight. I started up the stairs, but stopped.

"Let's dance first," I suggested.

He looked puzzled and hesitated, but then said, "I'll get my shoes."

He returned a minute later, pressed the button on the CD player, and rushed toward me as the Cajun music of Beau Soleil surrounded us. He clutched me and broke down in a sob. A long moment passed, and then I heard, "Mama." A sharp twist wrung my gut.

Why had I suggested a dance before lovemaking? I suddenly realized why he'd looked puzzled. Weeks before, we'd agreed to end our marriage with a dance, so when I suggested dancing, he thought I was ready to formally mark the end. I should have explained that my motive was exactly the opposite: I wanted to dance right away because I *assumed* we'd be making love, and I thought I'd lack the energy to come downstairs for a dance afterward.

But now—poof! As though a magician had waved his wand over me, Miriam, the wife and lover had disappeared. "Mama" stood in her place. What a crazy romantic I'd been to envision the ending as an ideal celebration—a passionate love scene and then a dance.

Afshin gathered me in waltz position. I looked up at his smile and tears. If he let go, I was sure I'd fall to the floor. We danced at half time until our bodies swung in unison.

I can do this. I can. The flames lapped my breastbone less fiercely.

Suddenly, he stepped back into the full beat of the music. His hands shot toward the ceiling while his feet danced the rhythm into the hardwood floor. I tried to match his pace, but felt five-pound weights strapped around each ankle. What propelled him? Was it relief from the duty of being a devoted husband? Tears ran down Afshin's cheeks. Mine were dry. I smiled at the face I'd come to love ferociously. We were doing what had to be done.

As soon as the song ended, we fell into each other's arms. I kept wanting to ask: "Why don't we make love one last time?" But how could "Mama" ask such a thing? I hated to give up the ending I'd imagined, but there was no kindred spirit to whom I could appeal. We weren't simply in different scenes—we were in different movies.

Afshin held out the ring hanging from his neck on the leather strap. "I'm not giving this back," he said before he led me up the stairs. "Call me when you're ready for bed." He left me standing in front of my bedroom door, arms heavy at my side.

I shook my head and inhaled deeply. From the dresser drawer, I picked out a huge T-shirt and pulled it over my head. The wide surface of the bed lay before me and my gut contracted. As though swallowing a bitter medicine, I hurried and scrambled under the covers.

Afshin appeared at the door and stood there, for a second, before coming toward me. I noticed a new body language: arms hanging at his sides and head tilted down, as a show of respect. I felt ill. He sat on the edge of the bed, in that place that belonged to him. Lifting my hand, he pressed warm lips on the backs of my fingers.

"I'll sit on the chair over there until you're asleep. I have to leave so early for the train that I've decided to stay up all night."

He rose to his feet, bent over me, and lightly kissed my forehead. "*Bekhob*, sweet Mama. Sleep."

This is so odd. But the love is the same. Afshin had said it would be. The love would be the same.

Part 3

My Son:
The Last Three Months

Chapter 27

Throughout the night, my mind replayed scenes of my time with Afshin. Morning finally came, and I looked toward the chair, now empty. It was past six o'clock, so Afshin was on his way to the conference. I longed to feel close to him and headed for his room, prepared to curl up on his empty futon, but there he was, sleeping on his stomach. Kneeling near him, I whispered, *Thank you God, for the depth of love I've experienced with him.* It would be easier if my love hadn't deepened over the past six months. How can my heart contain so much love and grief at the same time? The familiar discomfort rose from my heart to my throat.

"Afshin, you missed your train," I said, curving my hand over his cool shoulder.

"I'm not going. I'll explain later," he mumbled, before pulling the blanket over his head.

I went to work early and, as if in a dream, walked the long empty hall to my office. Once inside, I burst into tears. Knowing I couldn't face anyone, I locked the door, grateful for a quiet, solitary place. For almost an hour, I struggled for control over my emotions. Thinking I'd achieved it, I opened the door to face the workday, but another sob rose. *God, please send me some inner calm*, I prayed. I called Diane and, as she listened to me, the heaviness lifted. I washed my face and set off to see patients.

A few times during the day, I rushed into a nearby restroom when tears threatened to spill. Around four-thirty, I steered my car out of the parking lot and down the road toward home, passing the same houses, the same fields, the same woods I'd passed every working day for five years. "How can you stand there, oblivious? Don't you know that everything has changed?" I screamed.

I met Afshin at our front door. "So why didn't you go to the conference?"

He took me in an embrace for a few seconds, stepped back, and held my elbows. "I tried to stay awake by eating and listening to music, and when that didn't work, I went for a walk. While walking, I realized it would be crazy to go today. I can't leave you when you're feeling like this," he said, shaking his head and looking sideways at the floor. "I'll go tomorrow."

My shoulders dropped. This time I wouldn't encourage him to leave.

While I changed into a casual cotton dress, Afshin called up, "Let's go get some food."

Hand-in-hand, we walked the few blocks to the shopping center. Every few minutes he stopped and kissed my temple. I felt as though I were recuperating from major surgery. More than anything else, I needed caring.

On the way home, my back started hurting, and each step became more painful. I decided to stay off my feet for a day. Maybe I'd strained a muscle when I'd slipped and landed on my rump during the hike down the mountain. I left a message for my boss explaining why I wouldn't be at work the next day.

While Afshin made dinner, I lay on the sofa. Whenever he talked to me, it was "Mama this" or "Mama that." I wanted to stick my fingers in my ears. Then, like a melody amid traffic noise, I heard my name, but he quickly corrected himself.

"Why can't you call me Miriam?"

He stopped setting the table and looked toward me with a worried expression. "We are mother and son now. Do your children call you Miriam?" He sounded so damn logical. "We must be careful. We cannot mix this relationship with our marriage or the change won't work."

Yes, each "Mama" was another cinder block in the wall being built between our former relationship and this one. However, Afshin needed his emotional safety net. I put myself in his shoes: if I truly believed that touching the opposite sex—outside of marriage—was a sin, I'd also find ways to get around that ban and avoid feeling guilty.

He pulled a piece of paper from the buffet drawer. Carefully, he wrote on it and showed me a word: *PESARAM*.

"It means, 'my son,'" he said, as though proffering a great honor.

My eyes fixated on the word.

The paper he'd handed me during our marriage vows had given me wings; this one clipped them. I would never treasure this note as I did the other. He undoubtedly envisioned a mother-son relationship that would bring me great happiness—greater than the joy I experienced with my sons.

But I had never longed for that—I had only longed for a husband. He didn't understand.

"*Pesaram*. Would you say it?" he asked, with an expectant look.

"*Pe-sa-ram.*" I enunciated each syllable.

His face lit up, and he lifted my hand to his lips. The Persian word that meant the world to him held no meaning for me. I was relieved he didn't ask me to say it in English.

I'd stepped out of my society's norm with a short-term marriage, but this new relationship felt like a trip to Mars.

By nine o'clock, we both had trouble keeping our eyes open.

"Mama, you look sick," he said, examining my face with concern. "May I sleep on the floor in your room?"

"Yes, I'd like that."

I wondered if he missed his wife or if he was sleeping near me to make sure I wouldn't cry. Whatever the reason, his nearness acted like a heating pad on my aching heart, and when he brought his sleeping bag and placed it at the foot of the bed, I couldn't help but smile as I imagined myself a queen with a bodyguard.

I turned out the light, and the truth of the moment hit home. *Near and yet so far.*

Twelve hours later, I sat up and yelped as a pain zapped my lower back. Afshin moaned and stretched.

"You're still here?" I asked. "Aren't you going to the conference?"

He stumbled over and plunked himself down next to me. "No, I decided to skip the whole thing."

"Please, don't do that," I said, sitting up carefully. "I know how much you've been looking forward to this conference."

"I'm *not* going." He stared at me for a few seconds. "How is it going for you? Do you love me like a son?" he asked, in a gentle voice.

I held his gaze while I wished his eyes could see the vast vacant place in my soul where a husband had lived. "I'm working on it. For just having lost another husband, I think I'm doing well. It takes time. Don't you understand?"

"But our love is the same," he said, looking at me as though *I* had a problem understanding the situation clearly. "*I'm* not sad." After a moment, he asked, "Did you cry yesterday?" The concern in his voice touched me.

I nodded.

"Don't cry. Please. I feel it's my fault."

"It's *not* your fault," I said, my fists slamming my thighs. "I can hardly control my tears now, but that's normal. Stop feeling you're to blame."

"If your heart is not in this change, it won't work," he said, sounding discouraged.

"It *will* work. Give me time. I'll stop crying soon."

A resounding silence followed.

"Are you sorry we were married?" he asked.

"Sorry? Never! It changed me for the better."

"I'm also glad I married you."

"Will you tell a future wife?"

"I'll tell her about you, and you can stay with us whenever you want." He took hold of my hands. "Come, I'll make breakfast," he said as he gently pulled me up.

Yes, I thought, but will you tell her of our marriage?

After breakfast, he kissed me on the cheek before setting out for the math library to continue his search for a thesis problem. To treat my back and soothe myself, I decided to get a massage.

I lay on the padded table, soothed by the New Age music playing in the background. As the massage therapist kneaded muscle after muscle, I thought about the love I'd experienced with David and Afshin, and my gratitude grew. Their love would fuel my future. I got off the table with renewed hope.

After I arrived home, the phone rang. "How are you? I've been worried," Ana said.

My throat swelled with sadness and a sweet ache at her caring. "I'm doing my best with it, but it's so hard when he calls me 'Mama.'"

"He's crazy! How can he expect this of you? It's ridiculous. You're not his mother and never will be."

"I know, I know, but I don't like the other option. I want his love and affection. I'm not ready to risk losing that."

"But you could have stayed married until the day he left," she said, each word carrying more agitation.

"No. That wouldn't work." Again, I explained the reasons we'd ended the marriage when we did.

"If you love each other, I don't understand why you can't stay together," she said, her tone so adamant that I wondered if she'd heard a word of what I'd just said. No. She probably only heard my pain, and my reasons blew away like chaff in the wind.

I told her that I couldn't talk more about Afshin and me aa I untwisted the telephone cord from my hand. I didn't have the energy to hear her heart's outrage or answer her questions. I'd already asked those questions of myself dozens of times and had come to terms with the remaining mystery.

Later, Rachel called. Her voice sounded even sadder than mine. "I feel so bad for you. How can you stand it?"

"I'm grateful for what I had. Experiencing this love has changed me."

"I think I know what you mean, but do you want to tell me?"

"I see Muslims differently—especially Iranians. Now that I've gotten to know a few of them, I see that they follow their religion as little or as much as we follow Christianity or Judaism." I paused a couple of seconds, listening to the voice within that insisted: It's the love. It's the love. "But the love he's shown me—that's what has really changed me. I'll never settle for less again."

"Yes, you're fortunate. Few people experience love the way you have."

"Thank you for understanding." I didn't want pity. I didn't want to hear that Afshin should stay. He'd kept our agreement. I simply wanted to celebrate what I'd had—the laughter, the passion, the fulfillment of the Qu'ranic verse Afshin had given me: "We created you male and female and put you into nations and tribes that you may know each other." Oh yes, I'd come to know him, this man from another nation, and I'd come to love him.

Late that afternoon, Afshin walked in as I came up from the family room. Our eyes met for an instant in a familiar way, but when he rushed over and hugged me, he bent forward, keeping the "lion" from touching me. I pressed my eyes shut and bit my lip.

As we watched *Nikita* later that evening, he reached for my hand and held it between us. It throbbed and took on gigantic proportions as the rest of my body faded into the background. He lifted my fingers to his mouth and nibbled at my ring. A desire to hold him threatened to overpower me. I sat statue-like. Did he realize what he was doing?

At bedtime, he said, "Mama, I'm going to sleep near you again, if you don't mind."

I nodded and slipped into bed. Afshin came over and kissed me goodnight—on the forehead. How bizzare. We'd made love here dozens of times, but now the word "Mama" punctuated nearly every sentence.

Fortunately, his frequent utterances of "I love you" soothed me like applications of a potent balm.

"I feel loved when you hold my hand and hug me," I said, wanting to make clear what I needed at the time.

"Yes, but my love is much deeper than what I can show that way. Even though I haven't held my mother in four years, my love for her is strong."

I smiled at his transparent attempt to make sure I knew he now loved me as "Mama" and that love is not dependent on physical presence.

Newly hatched birds peeped for their breakfast somewhere in the back yard. Oh, for their simple existence. I propped myself up and gazed at Afshin, sleeping on the floor a few feet away. I wanted to cuddle but squelched the urge. I headed for the shower and stood under its warm spray longer than usual before wrapping myself in a terrycloth robe. When I tiptoed toward the closet, Afshin stirred. I knelt and brushed his forehead with a kiss. He squinted, smiled, and mumbled a good morning. After slipping into khaki shorts and my Gauguin blouse, I left for the kitchen and started breakfast.

Afshin soon joined me. "How are you feeling today?" he asked, his tone conveying an expectation of good news.

"I'm amazed, but I'm feeling better," I said, wondering if the gratitude and hope I had felt on the massage table still buoyed me.

"We're doing it!" he exclaimed, with more enthusiasm than his morning voice usually carried.

He was clearly in a hurry to make our transition a swift, successful one. How I wished I could see the workings of his mind and heart. But thank God he showered me with affection—it was my lifesaver.

My back still ached, and as long as emotional pain didn't allow me time off from work, I was grateful for the physical pain. I could take another guilt-free day at home to recover.

After breakfast, Afshin started packing for his move to New York City. I'd dreaded this time, but felt at peace. Maybe his leaving hadn't registered yet. He'd be back on weekends, and now that he'd canceled his visit to Iran, there was a chance he'd come back on the first of July, after teaching his early summer course.

I stepped over the small prayer carpet lying near the door and joined him in his sunlit room. We sorted out winter clothes to store in the garage. A part of him would stay with me. I folded the sweater he'd worn for our wedding celebration and held it to my heart.

He caressed my head. "Mama, you're so beautiful."

I turned away. Not beautiful enough. My eyes fell on the picture of a mosque in Isfahan that hung above his desk. Afshin had told me that the mosque with the huge square in front of it was the most beautiful spot in the world. I could see why he thought so. An intricate design of mostly sky-blue mosaic covered that place of worship.

Afshin reached for the frame and handed me the picture. "For you. Would you like it?"

My eyes stung with tears. He was offering me his home. What other object did he have to remind him of the land of his childhood? I received it with an ache in my heart.

Afshin gazed at a crocheted doily. "My grandmother made this," he said. He kissed it and offered it to me.

Her hands had fashioned it. How could he part with it? It wasn't a time to ask. I had a feeling that he wanted to share what he held most dear. Perhaps he also wanted these items out of sight because of the memories and sadness they elicited in him.

"I'm going to call my mother," he said, buckling his suitcase.

He headed down the hall toward the phone. I caught a few words I recognized.

He hung up and turned to me. "I told her I have a mom here now. She said, 'I hope you can find one in New York, too,' and I said to her, 'What? Do you think it's easy to find a mother?'"

"Doesn't it bother her that you're calling someone else 'Mama'?"

"Oh, no! She's happy for me."

He entwined his fingers with mine and led the way down the stairs.

"Wait here." He pointed to a dining-room chair and then trotted toward the garage. A minute later, he came back holding a pair of rollerblades in each hand. "Let's go. *Aré?*"

I hesitated—not the best thing for my back, but when would I have this chance again?

We slipped into the rollerblades and protective gear, and skated down the street. My legs vibrated over the rough asphalt until we reached a recently paved section. I balanced from one foot to the other with unexpected steadiness, but when I noticed that we were approaching a downhill stretch, I grimaced and came to a halt.

"Don't worry," Afshin said. "I'm going to teach you how to stop. Look. Just bend at the knees as if you're going to sit down and put one leg forward with your heel dragging."

I practiced on a flat surface until I could stop, and then headed for the slope.

Afshin skated ahead. Near the bottom he whirled one hundred eighty degrees and stopped, ready to catch me. Two hundred feet beyond him, cars passed through an intersection. My muscles tensed and my arms shot out as I pushed off.

Afshin laughed and yelled, "I wish I had a camera."

As I zoomed toward him, I stuck my heel forward, but dared not apply too much pressure. I kept moving. Afshin rushed into my path and caught me.

"You can do it," he said. "Try again."

Determined, I trudged back up the hill for another try. Coming down, I gathered more speed than the first time. When Afshin reached for me, I fell back, and he landed on top of me. He stayed immobile for a second, his frightened eyes staring at me. Though my back and buttocks pulsated with pain, I assured him that I was all right; I wanted to show him I was tough. After three more tries, my braking technique improved. My wet shirt clung to me and my calves ached, but I loved the wind on my face. And I loved conquering my fear.

Nearly an hour passed before we headed home. My back pain had diminished. I suspected that part of that pain had been emotionally induced and that connecting with my strength while rollerblading had been therapeutic. In the months ahead, I would need to be able to tap into courage.

In the evening, we decided to celebrate our birthdays with cake at a café in town. I picked up my large handbag, in which I'd hidden a present for Afshin eralier in the day, and we left the house.

At the coffee shop, I ordered a piece of raspberry-chocolate cake and a café latté; Afshin, ordered a large almond cookie and coffee. After getting our food, we had to wait for a table.

We stood with our coffee and dessert, being entertained by a group of boisterous university students. The young women's complexions glowed—not a wrinkle in sight. They spoke of graduation and I thought about their adult lives just beginning. How long ago that was for me. How much I'd learned since then. Like the students, Afshin still had those years ahead of him.

A couple left their seats near the window, and we hurried over.

"Happy Birthday, to my forever young Mama," he said as I was about to take my first bite.

Afshin made a couple of innocuous comments about the "chicks" standing near the door. I'd explained to him once why the term "chick" might bother some women, but it didn't bother me. He wasn't using the word out of a lack of respect. Just as the word *pesaram* carried no true meaning for me, the word "chick" carried little for him. He had said he liked the sound of it. I joined him by making lighthearted comments about the young women. I thought this might be an effective way to desensitize myself for the day when he would find his next love. Like an allergy shot.

A few minutes later, I noticed Afshin's face turning grim.

"When I look at you, I miss my mother more," he said.

I covered his hand with mine. "I remember that picture you showed me where your mother and grandmother held up the Qu'ran, like a bridge, over your head. What a wonderful send-off for a safe trip to the United States." He looked down for a moment. "Now that you have an American Mama, I thought you'd like to learn a little about the religion that influenced her life," I continued, pulling a Bible from my handbag and handing it to him.

Afshin opened the black, fine-grained leather Bible.

"It's in Persian!" He stared at it in surprise.

"Of course. You are my Persian son, aren't you?" I added those words as an extra gift.

"Yes," he beamed, but then his expression grew serious. "You never tried to convert me before."

"And I'm not trying to now, but the words in this book have shaped the West for nearly two thousand years. I'd like you to understand more about Christianity, and I want to continue learning about Islam."

"You don't need to do that. It's what is between us that's important." He waved a hand back and forth between his chest and mine.

Ah, yes. That was true, but we didn't reside in our bodies alone; the spirits of our ancestors lived within us, too.

Afshin closed the Bible. "Uh, thank you. You're very kind." His tone didn't convey any excitement, which is what I'd expected. Yet, I hoped that in the future he might get curious and read it.

We finished our drinks and left. I was relieved to get away from the crowd of Afshin's peers. We strolled past the fancy shops that lined the town square. As we rounded a corner, I noticed a teenaged girl sitting on the curb. Her head rested on her arms, which were crossed over her knees.

"Go talk to her." Afshin lifted his chin in her direction. "She looks sad."

I drew back, reluctant to intrude, but Afshin prodded, "Why don't you go? She needs help."

Yes, why not? I bent down next to her and asked, "Are you all right?"

She looked up, startled, and forced a smile. "I'll be OK. Thanks," she said.

I rejoined Afshin, who had waited a few feet away. "Why," he asked, "didn't you put a hand on her shoulder when you spoke to her?"

"Afshin, if I touched her, I'm afraid it would be seen as overstepping a boundary."

"I don't understand this society," he said, shaking his head. "How can a loving action be wrong?"

Afshin's question rang true. Yes, indeed. I'd wanted to put my arm around her. For all the wonderful aspects of the Northeast, I dreamed of cohesive communities where showing caring with physical touch was welcome, not labeled as "crossing boundaries."

While eating lunch the next day, Afshin and I took turns yawning.

"Let's take a nap," he said.

Five minutes later, I lay on the bed, and he, on the floor. A neighbor's lawnmower droned incessantly, and I was about to shut the window when Afshin sprang up and stretched out next to me. His head lay near mine and he took a deep breath as I exhaled. "I love your smell," he said and kissed my neck.

The familiar tingles scurried through me. I savored the feeling, turned, and kissed his face, staying clear of his lips. If his conscience accepted these actions, I wouldn't remind him that he'd crossed into forbidden territory. I glanced at his crotch and saw a rounded mound. So this was difficult for him, too. I smiled and closed my eyes.

The Bird and The Fish

A knock at the front door jarred me awake. I looked toward the clock, guessing twenty minutes had passed, but sat up with a start when I realized it had been over an hour. I trotted downstairs and flung open the door. Cal displayed a knowing smile when he saw me.

"Hey, Mama, did you forget I was coming?"

I'd loved it when Cal had switched from calling me Mom to calling me Mama a few years back. It was more distinctive. I was glad that Cal pronounced "Mama" with the emphasis on the first syllable rather than the last, the way Afshin pronounced it. At least something was different.

"No, I didn't forget. I was resting and fell asleep."

I led Cal toward the dining room, hoping he wouldn't see Afshin leave my room. With what I was about to tell Cal, he didn't need to see something that would confuse him even more.

We chatted for a few minutes, and then I said, "You know Afshin and I ended our marriage last Sunday . . ."

"Y-esss," he said, sounding afraid about what he might hear next.

"Did I tell you he wants us to be 'mother and son' now?"

His faced contorted to one side, and I expected to be told we were crazy. Instead, he said in a deadpan tone, "You hinted at it before . . ." He stopped himself. "Whatever makes you happy," came from his mouth, but I heard, *Mom, you've gone overboard this time.*

"I know it sounds completely weird, but let me explain."

Even as I explained why I was willing to go along with being Mama, the words sounded hollow. I wasn't used to pretense, and Cal was clearly upset at seeing it in me. As soon as I finished, he changed the subject.

Afshin didn't come downstairs until Calvin left.

"Are you going to start telling people now that we're mother and son?" Afshin asked.

We'd never discussed who would be privy to our latest relationship. Though I could tell my children and close friends, I felt reluctant to tell acquaintances and co-workers who'd known of our marriage. How would I explain why I agreed to the role? But without further thinking, I said yes to Afshin.

Later, I lay in bed and imagined telling someone about the new roles. Would person after person react as Ana had—if not with outspoken disbelief, then with a volley of critical thoughts? It would have been easier if I didn't care about their thoughts, but those thoughts could affect the way they behaved toward me—and that mattered. I needed to effectively convey the reasons Afshin and I were willing to follow this unusual script. Maybe people would understand.

It was beyond me how a man as intelligent as Afshin could think that people would believe the roles we played, but he sought emotional equilibrium, and then, so did I. Few people would understand unless they'd lived with my yearnings, my disappointments, and finally, my fulfillment in Afshin's love.

The last full day arrived before Afshin's move to a temporary rental in New York City. After he packed his last few things, we sat at the dining-room table eating leftover vegetarian lasagna. I was gazing out at nothing in particular when a couple walked by, hand-in-hand. The food stuck in my throat. Afshin ate with relish. After his last bite, he went to the kitchen cupboard and brought out the butter biscuits.

Holding them up, he asked, "*Chaii mee Khai?*"

"*Aré, azizam,*" I said, smiling at his invitation. I loved the sound of the words that had invited me to share tea with him dozens of times during our marriage.

A while later, I watched him swallow the last of the amber, unsweetened tea. He got up and, giving me a passing caress, went up the stairs. "I'm going to take a shower."

By ten o'clock, I dragged myself up the stairs, noticing the lack of my usual energy. When I slid into bed, Afshin came in and sat facing me. With eyes on mine, he placed his hands on my shoulders. Suddenly, he pulled me into a crushing embrace. My tears gushed out.

He leaned back. "No, please! You don't need to cry. I'll be back on Friday," he said, tears coursing down *his* cheeks. "Promise me you won't cry this week."

I shook my head. His lips found the hollow of my eyes, where, resting momentarily in each one, he placed a kiss, but his eyes averted mine before he turned the light out and moved to his floor mat.

I wondered what made him able to cry while telling me that I shouldn't.

A few minutes passed and from the darkness, arms gripped me. "Mama, I love you so much."

I held him tightly. "I love you." *So much that my heart is aching.*

Was he transitioning to "son" any better than I was to "mother?" I doubted it, but how could I know? The kisses and embraces he gave me now may have been the same kind he once gave his mother.

After a few moments, he returned to his mat.

"Let's go! I'll miss the train."

He slipped the travel bag over one shoulder, and grabbed his ancient suitcase. Opening the front door, he stepped out. "Mama. Come on, come on."

I followed him out, locking the door behind me. As I drove, I paid special attention to the road and the cars. Soon, the train station came into view. How many couples had stood under its eaves clasped to each other before a separation? I pulled into a parking space and turned off the engine.

Afshin looked at me for a few seconds. He didn't smile. "Don't get out. The train will be here soon."

He leaned over and kissed my cheek. Simultaneously, we reached across the emergency brake handle, and held each other in an awkward embrace. He sprang out of the car, retrieved his suitcase from the trunk, and walked briskly toward the ticket machine. I backed the car out and drove away.

I didn't cry. He would've been proud.

Chapter 28

After work every day that week, I practiced rollerblading. As I skated, I felt alive in a way that made me trust that all would be well.

Although friends called often and invited me over for dinner, I declined. I craved solitude and time to grieve my loss.

Friday arrived. In late afternoon, as many commuters poured from the train with pinched faces, Afshin hopped onto the platform looking young and fresh with the haircut I'd given him before he left. His free arm clamped me to his side. We held each other's gaze for a moment, then broke into joy-filled laughter.

"I'm so happy to be back here," Afshin said, as we pranced toward the car. "First, I want to stop for a hoagie."

I reveled in our conversation, which continued non-stop until we reached home.

"I found some low-fat ice creams that aren't too bad," I said, wondering whether he'd been indulging in Coke since we canceled our earlier agreement about our "vices."

"Don't get low-fat. Everyone has to have a passion—get the ice cream you love."

Of course. A small amount of what I enjoyed passionately—hmm, much better than a large amount of mediocre stuff.

After dinner, we were cuddling on the sofa, watching a documentary about the universe, when I heard Beth come in. I pulled away from Afshin. She passed behind us with a brief greeting before going into her room.

"What's the matter?" Afshin asked, as his brow crinkled. "Wouldn't you sit like this with Cal?"

"Never!" I couldn't even imagine sitting this close, much less having our arms wrapped around each other.

"You *did* tell Beth that we're mother and son now?"

"Yes, but she can't understand it. Few people can."

"You do, don't you?" A look akin to fear colored his eyes.

"I do." I understood the reasons he'd given me, but I wondered whether having a Mama nearby didn't also give him a way to express love for the Iranian mother he missed. Then I caught myself. I was always trying to figure out why people did what they did. But who could know? Even Afshin might be unaware of his motivations.

"Why is it that I was born in the desert so far from here, and yet you and I are so close in our thinking?" He put his arm around me and pulled me back to his side.

Yes, in many respects we were alike—tribe mates—yet, with regard to our mother-son relationship, my ways lay a world away from his. Anyhow, I strongly doubted that changing from wife to mother was an Iranian custom. An Indian co-worker of mine, also a Muslim, found the idea repugnant.

But why repugnant? Afshin was simply getting what he originally wanted. And why shouldn't he? I'd gotten what I wanted. Wouldn't it have been unreasonable for me to want more? How long could I have kept up with the sexual appetite of a man twenty-five years my junior? And even if I'd been able to, wouldn't Afshin's attraction to me have taken flight after menopause? I hadn't wanted to test that possibility. I preferred to continue experiencing love, even in a context that I'd never imagined for an ex-lover.

I snuggled closer, and he brought my head to his shoulder.

When bedtime came, we had our usual chat time in my room. Then, before leaving for his bed, he lifted the sheet covering my feet and gently kissed them. I drew my legs up.

He looked hurt. "Mama, it's a sign of respect."

"It feels strange to me. Would you let me kiss *your* feet?"

"Nooo. A mother shouldn't kiss her son's feet," he said, as though even the suggestion were inconceivable.

"I don't like being on a pedestal."

"A pedestal?"

"Yes. You're putting me at a higher level than you. We're equal. I like being equals."

"Mothers are always above their sons," he said with conviction.

I couldn't persuade him to the contrary. After saying goodnight, I switched off the light.

The red numbers on the clock read 2:34 when Afshin climbed into bed with me and nudged me over. "I can't sleep. I'm tense from being in New York City. It's so crazy there."

In the past he'd experienced relief from tension when we had sex, but I repressed the urge to reach out to him in that way. Instead, I massaged his back, grateful that I still could express my love with touch.

After a few minutes he said, "I'm feeling better. Thank you," and he returned to his mat.

~~~

Sunday evening, Milad came over for dinner. When he went upstairs to wash his hands, Afshin said, "I'm going to tell him that you're my mother now."

My stomach contracted. "Do you really want to tell him *now*?"

"Why not?"

I waved a hand as if to say, "Never mind."

A part of me hoped for a miracle that would reunite us as husband and wife, but once Milad learned of our new relationship, how could we ever turn back?

Milad returned, and we sat down to eat. I passed a steaming dish of rice and lima beans to him, and he spooned a mound onto his plate.

"We're mother and son now," Afshin said, fanning the air between us.

Milad smiled at us, Buddha-like. "That's very nice." He scooped up some rice and chewed.

How could he react so calmly? Why hadn't he said, "Are you sure you want to do that? You seemed so happy as husband and wife."

Afshin and Milad were soon talking about Seiberg-Witten equations and the Yang-Mills theory. Although they spoke in English, they may as well have been speaking in Persian; I understood nothing.

My ears perked up, however, when Afshin mentioned Ferdowsi's *Shahnameh - The Book of Kings*. In *The Iranians*, I'd read about people's love for this epic tenth-century poem, four times longer than *The Iliad*. Even illiterate Iranians can recite stanza after stanza from it. I was amazed at what people are willing to do to feel pride in their roots. Perhaps Ferdowsi had written *The Book of Kings* in response to an Arab invasion that was designed to squash Persian culture.

"Have you heard of Ferdowsi?" Milad asked.

He must have noticed my interest. "Yes, I have."

I didn't feel like talking and was grateful that Afshin picked up the conversation at that point. When we finished eating, I gathered our plates and carried them to the kitchen.

A few minutes later Milad brought the empty serving dish to the sink and said, "I'm so happy to have dinner here."

"I'm glad you came," I said, forcing a smile.

"That you are glad means you are a good person," he said in a quiet tone.

I sensed his attempt at making me feel better and almost cried.

He rejoined Afshin and, ten minutes later, said goodnight. Afshin came up behind me at the kitchen sink. His hands clasped my arms. "You looked sad all evening. What's wrong? If you have pain, I want to know the cause."

I closed my eyes. The tenderness in his voice made it hard for me to answer.

"Don't worry. It will work itself out," I finally said, keeping my eyes on the dishwater.

"Remember, you said there should be no secrets between us. Wouldn't you want me to tell you the reason if I had pain?"

I wanted to say, "Yes, but you've been in pain and unwilling to talk about it with me," but I knew what he'd say: "I have good reasons. Remember, sometimes it is better that I keep things in my chest."

He stepped around to my side and scrutinized my face. "Mama, talk it."

How I'd cherished every time he'd said, "Miriam, talk it," but now I had a gag in my mouth. I scrubbed the pot harder.

Afshin didn't move as I finished. "Before God—I will stay up all night until you tell me why you are sad."

I looked at him, but words wouldn't come. I emptied the dishpan and turned to go upstairs, but Afshin grabbed my hand and led me to the staircase. He gestured for me to sit beside him on the top step.

Tears gathered, and I covered my face.

"It's all right," he said as he brought my hands down. "Cry if you want."

Just then, Beth opened the front door and walked in, facing us. I brought my emotions to a screeching halt. Her expression of surprise transformed into a sliver of a smile that seemed to say, *You two are too much*. But she didn't say anything as she clomped downstairs, and I was relieved when her bedroom door clicked shut.

"Let's go to my old room," Afshin said.

Bare now, except for the futon still covered with a sheet, the room awaited its next occupant, due to move in the following week. We plopped down on the mattress and I blurted, "I'm not used to this new role. I had what I wanted for six months, and now you have what you want for the rest of your life—me as your mother."

His expression turned serious. "Why does that make you sad?"

I stared at the hardwood floor. I couldn't bring myself to say aloud, "No longer having the same kind of intimacy with you." I'd made an agreement, and our marriage was over.

"I love you so much," I said. "I'm sad now, but eventually I'll be happy again. I'm sure of it."

His features quivered. Suddenly, he clasped me, and I felt his tears on my neck.

"What's the matter?" I asked.

"For a moment, I saw my mother. I love you as much as I love her," he murmured before kissing my face in a half dozen places.

My heart leaped. He missed his real Mama more than he admitted to himself.

Neither one of us moved for a while. Then he said, "Let's go sleep," and we went to my room. After he kissed me goodnight, I breathed a sigh of relief.

While trying to fall asleep, my eyelids snapped open. *What if, because he loves his mother deeply, he'd been acting the role of my husband with only eighty percent of his heart, while the other twenty percent had been enjoying a reminder of his connection with his mother? Maybe after we stopped having sex, the love of a son for a mother resurfaced like a ball released from being held underwater.*

Through these painful thoughts, I was grateful that we agreed on one thing: At its core, love is love.

Back home again the following Friday, Afshin said, "Let's go out for dinner. I'm bored. How about that Mexican restaurant where you go with Ana?"

On the way there, he referred to himself a few times as my son.

"Would you please stop referring to yourself constantly as my son?" I asked. "It sounds like you're trying to convince me."

He stared ahead and didn't respond.

When we arrived at the restaurant, I gave my name to the hostess, and Afshin and I waited on a bench for a table.

I admired Afshin's well-formed physique, shown to advantage through his emerald green polo shirt, and noticed his gaze follow a slim young woman who swaggered by.

"Do you think she's attractive?" I asked, wanting to show I understood his interest in beautiful women.

He averted my eyes and hesitated a second. "Yes, if I may say so."

"Sure," I said, grateful that, for some reason, I didn't feel jealous.

The hostess led us to a table for two against the far wall.

After we placed our orders, Afshin asked, "So, Mama, are you going to look for a chick for me?"

My stomach twisted. I stared at him as I picked up my water glass and took a long drink. *Acknowledging that you appreciate a beautiful woman was easy*, I thought, *but finding one for you to embrace . . . no, you have no idea what you're asking of me.* My free arm hugged my waist. He must know I still have feelings for him. If he's trying to "clean my heart out"—that metaphor he'd used to mean letting go of emotional attachments—well, the detergent he used was too harsh.

I wanted to avoid a heated discussion and kept my astonishment to myself. "I wouldn't know where to find a woman who would be good for you. I think it will be easier to find one at the university. Yet, selfishly, I'd prefer you met someone later, so I can have more time with you while you're here."

"But all three of us could spend time together," he said, as though stating the obvious.

His naiveté struck me. "I doubt she'd want to."

A few minutes passed, and we started eating without further discussion. I could tell that he was upset, but I kept quiet and sent comforting thoughts to my wounded heart.

As soon as we climbed into the car, Afshin snapped, "I don't understand how you can talk of selfishness with love. If you love me, doesn't my happiness come first? That's how I feel for you."

Hmm. Something doesn't sound right here.

"In the purest form of love, it's true. I'm not wishing you unhappiness— only that I hope a new relationship might be put off for a while—at least until your thesis is done."

"I don't agree," he said sternly.

My gut tightened and boiled. "Afshin, it will take time for my emotions to change."

He looked in the distance for a second. "If you don't leave the other relationship behind, it could come up again in a year, or ten years, and that would not be good."

"I've told you—I need more time. It's only been a month."

I hoped someday I would love again, but now I needed Afshin's love—even in its new expression. I started the engine and drove toward the university without saying a word. Afshin reached for my hand and kissed the back of it. I ignored him.

I pulled into a parking lot near the math building.

"Oh, bullshit! All right . . . so I *don't* love you perfectly." I liked speaking out in my authentic voice—the one that didn't make a priority of short-term harmony. "But I love you as much as I can. You're expecting too much. And you're not even *trying* to understand *my* feelings."

He stared at me for a moment, and a smile hovered on his lips. "Maybe you're right."

We sat quietly for a few moments. Hearing him admit that I might be right made me wonder: Had I made a mistake by tiptoeing around his assertions so often for the sake of a blissful six-month marriage? Perhaps adding my own assertions to the mix wouldn't have made the soufflé flop. I regretted my caution.

He squeezed my shoulder, and made a face as though saying: I know I'm difficult sometimes. He got out and disappeared between the boxwood hedges for his other world. I hoped a new thesis problem would surface during his research. Maybe his humor and laughter would return.

With each passing day, the separation from Afshin became easier. I didn't slip back into my previous lifestyle, but found peace in reading books on meditation by Eknath Easwaran, meditating daily, taking long walks along the canal, and writing in my journal. I also started writing the story of Afshin and me. And because I wanted to test Afshin's idea that I should be closer to my children, Cal and Beth saw more of me.

One evening I heard a knock at the door, and when I opened it, Milad bowed slightly.

"I came to get the book Afshin is giving me and to say goodbye to you. I'm leaving for Iran tomorrow."

I handed him a math book that Afshin had left for him and, as I wished him well, my eyes filled with tears. Though he talked too much for my taste and gave advice without being asked, I loved his intention—to be helpful.

"Don't be sad," he said. "People are never really separated."

So, it wasn't just Afshin who thought that way.

A few days later, as I drove to work, a pain stabbed my chest. I reached my office and lowered myself in a chair, afraid to breathe too deeply. I called a nurse to contact the doctor on duty. He sent me to the lab for an EKG.

The nurse told me to lie down, and she placed electrodes on my arms, legs and chest. I heard the machine printing out the results and braced myself for the worst.

"Everything looks normal to me," the nurse said, "but the doctor will look at it, too. Why don't you go home and rest?"

How can everything be normal? This pain is intense.

Back home, I climbed into bed. Maybe I'd struggled too long to restrain my grief. I wasn't about to lose my health, not even for Afshin. I closed my eyes and invited sorrow to surface. In no time, the sadness that had accumulated in my heart gushed forth in a howling torrent. When it finally stopped, my abdomen ached. At last, I fell asleep.

When I woke up, the pain was gone.

Just before July 4th, Afshin finished teaching his summer course. With his advisor in Europe until September, Afshin decided to stay in Girton until then. But first he wanted to spend the holiday weekend with his friends, Kamran and Bijan, in Boston. Upon hearing that we'd be living together for two more months, I scheduled three weeks off over the summer. Perhaps we could spend a couple of days in Cape May. The Victorian town hugging the ocean would be a new sight for Afshin.

I found myself singing again—often.

"I had a great time with my friends in Boston," Afshin said as we were preparing dinner on Sunday evening. "I talked to them about you. May I show them a picture of you next time I see them?"

"Of course," I said, happy that he wanted to show them what I looked like, yet surprised that he was asking permission.

"The only problem with them is that they only have Iranian friends. Their English is hardly improving. You know, I've noticed that there are two kinds of people—those who try to recreate their home when they're away from it—and those who seek out new things. I'm the second kind."

"I love that about you." It was a trait we shared.

Afshin turned the flame down under the rice and leaned back against the counter. I chopped the onions faster. I couldn't wait to tell him what I'd done during the week. What a great way to show him that my love wasn't selfish. I'd plunged into unknown waters and had come up without drowning. He'd see just how strong I was. I'd proven to myself that I could act my part in our new roles. More importantly, I hoped my ability to adjust would desensitize me from the pain I'd feel if I ever saw Afshin with another woman.

The onions and chicken strips sizzled as I slid them into the pan. I turned to him with a satisfied smile.

"I thought I'd found a woman at work you might be interested in dating. She's tall and loves soccer. But when I told her you planned to go back to Iran she said, 'No, thanks.'"

Afshin sprang forward, hands to heaven, "Tell her I'm negotiable about Iran."

For someone he hadn't even met, his life's dream was negotiable!

"Ask if she'll go on one date."

A bowling ball had just smashed into my chest, but I stood firm. I wasn't about to ruin my opportunity to show him that I was learning to be a good mother. "I thought you only wanted to date women whom you might want to marry. Did I misunderstand?"

"I may be changing," he said, throwing up his hands again and grinning.

No! This can't be true. I gaped at him for a second and turned away. The chicken and onions looked done. Afshin, the man I loved—changing? The man I admired because of his strong principles. The man who only three weeks ago had insited on coming home from New York at two-thirty in the morning to support me in dealing with a tenant partying with his friends downstairs and ignoring my requests for quiet.

Now Afshin seemed oblivious to my feelings.

Over dinner we spoke about other things, but something I hadn't wanted to recognize became apparent—for all the maturity Afshin expressed, he carried an adolescent inside.

"Since I have a few days off from work, why don't we go to the shore? There's a place I'd like to show you—Cape May." I explained a little about its uniqueness. "What do you think?"

"If you like," he said without enthusiasm.

Confident that he'd like it once he was there, I didn't ask why he didn't sound interested. Besides, I was still clinging to my desire—a block of time with him, away from everyone and everything familiar.

By the time Afshin brought in our after-dinner tea, my pain over his earlier reaction had dissipated. As before, when he'd told me that a twenty-six year-old woman would be too old for him, he hadn't meant to hurt me. If I told him how his words affected me, he'd be stunned and remorseful. I didn't want to take that route again. Let him go there with another life traveler. I cherished the love he could show and held it to my heart.

Chapter 29

Two days later, the car trunk stuffed with travel bags and camping equipment, we flew down a country road, cutting through the Pinelands of southern New Jersey toward our destination: Cape May. Next to me, Afshin was perusing some math papers he'd picked up earlier at Milad's former Girton University office.

After a minute Afshin said, "When I met Milad at the airport yesterday to say goodbye, I asked what he thought of my marriage. He told me that when he saw us happy, he was happy, too, but when we ended the marriage, he was concerned. He said, 'I wonder if this is not very heavy for her.' I told him that I don't think it is, but I want *you* to tell me."

My mouth froze for an instant. "Not right now."

"Oh no! I just wanted a short answer."

"I can't give you that." I took an extra deep breath.

Two and a half hours later, we reached the campground near Cape May. After setting up our tent and changing into bathing suits, we asked the camp manager where we could find a good beach.

"There's a nice one in town, or, if you walk to the end of this road, there's a beach on the bay side. But you'd better hold on to him if you go there," he said to me, nodding toward Afshin.

"Why don't we see what's right here?" I suggested, as we walked out of the office. "Then we won't have to drive back to town."

"OK," Afshin agreed. "But what did he mean by 'hold onto him'?" His brow furrowed.

"I don't know. Maybe it's a nude beach." Afshin's eyes widened, and I didn't explain that the beach might be popular with gay men.

We ambled down a country road toward the bay. On either side of us, knee-high grass danced intermittently with the breeze. Here and there, gnarled pine trees stood like spectators.

For a man used to seeing women in chadors, I was surprised at his willingness to go to a nude beach and allow his eyes to fall on masses of bare skin. Surely, guilt would smother him.

"I see nothing wrong with nude beaches," I said, as we came to a path to the beach.

"Nudity in public is wrong," Afshin said, watching the sand engulf his sneakers with each step. "It should be saved for the intimacy that makes it special between two people."

"Hmm . . . I like that idea."

We plodded our way through the short dunes and reached the wide spread of light gray sand. After a few minutes of walking south, I noticed a cluster of people nestled in the dunes about fifty yards ahead. As we approached, I could see that all of them were men—without a shred of fabric on their bronze skin. One of them stretched and walked toward the water. A moment later, he turned and headed in our direction.

"Don't look," Afshin ordered, looking down.

I didn't turn my head, and my eyes strained to catch a glimpse of the man's penis.

We walked a few more yards. "Let's go back," I said, imagining Afshin's discomfort.

Without a word, Afshin did an about-face.

Squawks of seagulls accompanied us back to the path. I wondered at the voices squawking inside Afshin. A reminder that God had nothing against nudity might help.

"Adam and Eve were naked . . ." I started.

His right hand pressed my upper back while his left landed firmly over my mouth. His eyes bore into mine as though offering me a glimpse of his soul. A long moment passed before he slowly lowered his hands. We resumed walking. Not a word left our lips for the next twenty minutes. Normally, I'd be furious if anyone put their hand over my mouth, but imagining Afshin's extreme discomfort on the nude beach, I felt only compassion.

As soon as we got back to the campsite, Afshin said, "I'm going to take a shower."

I was surprised. He'd taken a shower in the morning. Did he need to cleanse himself after the "sin" he'd witnessed? Hoping to add to his comfort, I also took a shower, and afterwards we returned to our campsite.

The late afternoon sun, the bright blue two-person tent set on top of a sandy rise, and the pine trees surrounding the site created a perfect picture. I loved it—and so did the mosquitoes. After spreading my towel over a branch, I sat on the picnic table with my feet on the bench.

Afshin walked over and stood in front of me, his hands deep in the pockets of his jeans. "I'm sorry. I'll try to get out of this bad mood."

I smiled slightly and nodded.

"Let's get wood for a fire," he said, pointing to the woods adjacent to the tent.

We gathered a pile of twigs and branches, and then Afshin motioned for me to sit, again, on the picnic table. He faced me with arms crossed.

"Do you have feelings of jealousy when I talk about chicks?"

His question shook me. I'd expected the question that Milad had asked about the role change being "heavy" for me. But no, he was asking me about jealousy after all my efforts to stay light-hearted, and even joke with him about "chicks."

"Why do you ask that?"

"If I brought someone home and said that she was going to be your daughter-in-law, how would you feel?"

I stared at him for a minute. *Why was he pushing me? Was this a test? I couldn't fail. I wouldn't. Could I answer honestly: "I'd be really hurt. I'd wonder if you cared at all about my feelings." No, no. Wrong answer.* My chest tightened. "Happy for you and . . . I'm not sure. I have to wait and see."

"Why couldn't you feel the same as you'd feel if Calvin brought a girl home?"

"Because I wasn't married to Calvin," I said, shocked. *This man is not an idiot, yet . . .*

"That shouldn't make a difference," he said.

"Maybe it *shouldn't*, but it does." What kind of robot had Afshin become? Where was the sensitive man of the past nine months? "The only time I felt hurt was when you said I should tell that girl at work that going to Iran was negotiable for you. You never told *me* that."

"Don't you know me well enough to know that I was joking?"

Joking? He'd sounded serious.

"And if you thought I was serious," he added, "if you thought I lied to you, how could you still love me?"

"I didn't think you meant to be dishonest. But it made me wonder whether you'd decided that you'd be willing to stay in the U.S. if the right woman came along."

He shook his head and stared at the ground.

I continued hesitantly. "The change in our relationship was harder for me, because I was more into the marriage."

"You think I wasn't?" He leaned forward with a bewildered look.

"You seemed relieved that our marriage was over. You acted loving, but maybe you didn't feel the love the way I did."

"How could you think I wasn't sincere?" His voice quivered, and he bolted into the woods.

I was stunned, and my heart pounded at marathon speed.

A few minutes later he reappeared, poker-faced.

I climbed down and approached him on rubbery legs. "Maybe the kind of love I felt during our marriage was not necessarily true for you . . ."

"There's no need to talk about it anymore. That guy is dead."

His words siphoned through me, draining any hope I had for us to come to an understanding. I remembered the last time he'd used that expression—"That guy is dead"—about the man he'd once been who had committed some sin he wouldn't mention.

"What do you mean?" I asked.

"That guy had pride and joy in the husband he was." He paused. "He's gone now," he said as though talking to himself.

I felt like collapsing but tried, instead, to bring the dead man back to life. "You brought me tremendous joy. You were an *excellent* husband," I stressed.

"How can you say that if you thought I was not sincere?" he asked in a whisper.

His despair pumped up the pressure in my chest. Before it could burst out, I darted off between the pine trees, and dropped on my haunches at the end of the path. Being a good husband had meant so much to Afshin. Why had I expressed my doubt?

He caught up with me. "Don't cry, don't cry," he said as he ran his hand up and down my back.

"It hurts so much to hear you say that the husband you were is dead." I caught my breath. "Our marriage was wonderful. I want you to have a good memory of it—as I will."

"Mama, please don't cry. I will have a good memory, but I'll never have this kind of marriage again. I loved you completely, but at times it was hard work to be a good husband."

I could understand that, but how I wished he could understand that it was hard for me to be a good mother—a mother at all—to him.

"Mama, I love you—that *hasn't* changed."

With a hand on my back, he kept repeating that our marriage and our love were special. Gradually, I breathed freely again.

"I'm glad you can talk through difficult things to the end," I said, imagining how lonely I would have felt if he hadn't followed me down the path.

He pulled me to my feet and held my head to his chest. I could have stayed there for hours. Near the end of our marriage, we'd had another sweet embrace—when he'd feared being only a link in a chain of men I'd loved. We'd cried together. I had no doubt of his love then, and it wasn't the love of a son.

A couple of minutes passed. Simultaneously, we took a deep breath and looked at each other, smiling. "Let's go eat," he said.

We drove to Wildwood and found a small Greek restaurant on the boardwalk where we ate souvlaki. Afterwards, Afshin insisted we find a pint of New York Super Fudge Chunk ice cream. Back at the campground, we made a fire and snuggled as we ate the ice cream and the mosquitoes ate us. I struggled to keep my eyes open.

"We need sleep. Come," Afshin said, offering a hand.

I dragged myself to the tent. After changing—with our backs to each other—we lay on our sleeping bags. Afshin's arm brushed mine and my heart quickened. Mind games didn't fool my heart.

The next day we climbed to the top of the lighthouse, strolled on the boardwalk through the bird sanctuary, swam in the ocean, and then left for Girton. It had become clear to me that Afshin wasn't enjoying himself—so how could I? We had seven weeks of living together again . . . probably for the last time. How could this time serve our connection rather than destroy it?

That connection came naturally over those next precious weeks. Afshin and I tended our time together like gardeners nurturing a fragile plant. We taught each other French and Persian. We shared the thrill of the hunt at yard sales as we found items to send to Iran. We danced and sang, and exchanged thoughts and feelings over meals and in the bedroom we still shared. That closeness, in turn, nurtured us while we learned to suppress the expression of our sexual feelings, an effort at which we were mostly successful, although I occasionally experienced slight slips on Afshin's part.

About halfway through that period, as we lay in bed—in pajamas—Afshin turned and inhaled deeply, just below my ear. "I'm going to miss your smell this coming month when I go to sleep," he murmured.

I stared at his face, washed by the moonlight. "You mean—we can't sleep together anymore?"

"Not with the new tenant moving in."

"But when you came home for weekends in June and the other tenant was still here, we slept together. And besides, I thought you didn't care what people think," I said, recalling the time he'd gotten upset because I hadn't introduced him as my son to a neighbor. Hadn't he told me I shouldn't care what others think?

He raised himself on one elbow and looked down at me. "That guy was never home at night. And your neighbors—they have no reason to have bad thoughts, but this guy will if he sees that we sleep in the same room. We should be careful." He was quiet for a minute and I tried to make sense of his logic. Then, he shot up. "I'm so tired of this topic. It makes me angry, depressed, and lonely. Maybe I need to move." He took a deep breath and stared into the sky through the window behind me. "If you want, you don't have to introduce me as your son." He paused and fell back onto the pillow. "Sometimes, I wish I'd never left my mom."

His voice, like that of a homesick child, gripped my heart and I clasped his arm. A moment later I grasped his idea. "Do you mean we could keep our new relationship just between us?"

"*You* have to decide." The sudden strength in his voice surprised me. "Either we keep it between us that we are mother and son, but then I will not be affectionate with you in public, or, you can introduce me as your son, and I can be affectionate any time. It's your choice. Let me know." He caressed my cheek.

So he *does* care what people think, I thought, smiling to myself. Did he really think that my neighbors wouldn't be surprised to see us holding hands, as long as I'd told them that we were mother and son?

"Our different backgrounds are giving us problems, but we'll work this out," I said.

Between my counseling sessions with patients the following day, Afshin's two choices tugged at my thoughts. As I considered what each of us wanted from the relationship, I didn't see a good option. At lunchtime I plopped onto my office chair and closed my eyes. What to do? My concern about the neighbors' judgments paled in comparison to the prospect of being deprived of Afshin's affection anywhere, anytime.

Outside my office door, I heard the voices of co-workers as they passed by on their way to the cafeteria. Before going to join them, I imagined myself introducing Afshin as my son. It would stick in my throat, but I could do it. I could explain that we'd adopted one another.

"Help me with this, all right, God?" I took a deep breath, and opened my palms to the ceiling.

As soon as Afshin stepped into the house that evening, I walked proudly toward him and said, "I've decided—I want to go public as your mother, and this time, I mean it."

He wrapped his arms around me, lifted me off the floor, and covered my face with kisses. His joy reverberated through me. At bedtime, as I lay with a wall separating me from Afshin, asleep in the guest room, the satisfaction of my decision carried me to a peaceful sleep.

Chapter 30

Our final evening arrived. After this night we would no longer share a home—not the next day, the next month, or the next forever.

At work, I grew irritated by issues I usually took in stride. I wanted to be home with my beloved "son," and any activity that kept me from going there made me grumpy. But since I'd already used all my vacation time, I forged through the rest of the workday.

When I got home, Afshin led me to the sofa and told me to rest while he made dinner.

I stretched out and closed my eyes. Rachel's outcry in reference to my marriage came to mind: I could never do that!

Could I ever do it again?

I'd loved being married to Afshin. I'd had joy and sorrow, just as Khalil Gibran had described:

"When you are joyous, look deep into
your heart and you shall find it is only that
which has given you sorrow that is giving
you joy.
When you are sorrowful look again in
your heart, and you shall see that in truth
you are weeping for that which has been
your delight."

How true. Knowing an end would come, sorrow had accompanied me daily. In the past I'd been familiar with such ideas only by reading books, including *The Prophet*. Now I'd been following Gibran's advice and had confidence that I could live in the way he described. And wow! Did I ever learn how important it was for me to have a fully committed partner—even in the short-term. Afshin's love and devotion had filled a void that I'd carried since David died.

As a bonus, I'd made discoveries about cultural and religious differences. My huge desire for understanding and connecting with people from different cultures had been satisfied, at least for now. Maybe living in my grandmother's boarding house, with residents from all over, had instilled that desire in me. Every day, a new adventure. And time with Afshin was my ultimate adventure. I looked toward the kitchen and caught sight of his form moving across the doorway opening. A smile spread over my face.

My sweet, stubborn, post-revolutionary Iranian. You practice devotion to please Allah and are satisfied when you see me pleased. I wish I could have shown you more smiles and fewer tears.

He called me to the table, and I took a moment to finish my reflections before making my way to the dining room. As the evening progressed, I noticed how attentive he was to my needs.

After watching the news, he gazed at me for a few seconds. "May I sleep with you tonight?"

He didn't have to ask twice.

Later, as I climbed into bed, I made sure my long T-shirt covered my hips. Afshin immediately followed and lay on the sheet, pulling the summer bedspread to his waist.

"Do you love me like a son?"

The familiar refrain sent a jolt through me. I'd played my part rather well, I thought. Better than he played his. Why did he still question me? Did he need constant reassurance to relieve his guilt about my sadness—knowing this wasn't the first time I was losing a husband? But how could I offer him peace of mind and keep my own? I hated lying.

My answer came slowly. "I love you like a son as much as I can for having started out with you full grown." I couldn't say, 'for having started out with you as a husband.' By then, it sounded bizarre, even to me.

"I love you, Mama," he said. And again: "I love you, Mama. I love you, Mama," over and over, as we fell asleep in each other's arms.

Afshin's bulging suitcase, plus a travel bag, two boxes, a stuffed 50-gallon garbage bag, and a dorm-room refrigerator stood in a row in front of the garage when I pulled into the driveway after work the next afternoon. I braked and cut the engine. For a moment I sat, staring straight ahead. A blur in front of the car—Afshin rushing back and forth—drew my attention away from the lineup that indicated his departure. I stepped out of the car and our eyes met, but we quickly looked away.

"You were able to leave work early. That's good," he said, opening the trunk.

I took a deep breath and followed him to his belongings.

Together, we packed the car. We tried, every which way, to squeeze the refrigerator between the back of the passenger seat and the doorjamb to get it onto the back seat, but it was impossible.

"I'll sit in the back," Afshin said. "The refrigerator will have to sit next to you."

I grimaced but saw no other solution. We barely talked during the drive to New York City.

When we arrived at Afshin's student residence, I compared my feelings to those I'd experienced when taking Cal to his dorm for the first time. I'd been glad to see friendly, attractive, and intelligent-looking girls carrying their belongings into the building. Cal would make friends, including girlfriends. This time, the girls inspired only envy.

Afshin swung open the door to his tiny room with the pride of new ownership. A couple of students stopped by, and Afshin introduced me as his mother, without further explanation.

When they left, I said, "Afshin. You're the one with the accent. Isn't it usually the other way around?"

"We're an unusual pair." He flashed me a conspiratorial smile.

He opened his suitcase and my heart jumped at the sight of our lamb puppet's head looking out from one corner. He, too, could be sentimental, after all.

I noticed how energetic he seemed as he unpacked. Was he excited about his next adventure? Although his mood seemed to clash with mine, I shared his love of exploring new territories. What adventures lay ahead for us?

After plugging in the refrigerator, I opened it to store the hoagie we'd brought from the hoagie shop in Girton. Within twenty minutes, we had all his belongings in place. We locked the door behind us and headed for Central Park, rollerblades in hand.

A half-hour later, we reached the park and found a road where people jogged, biked, and skated past us. An empty bench offered us a spot to switch to our skates. I was lacing mine up when I felt Afshin's hand on my back. "I love you as much as my other mother."

I looked up into his eyes. "A man who loves his mother makes a good husband." No pain accompanied my assertion. Yes! I thought. I'll be OK.

"And for me, a wife is not better than a mother."

My eyes must have doubled in size, but if it meant that even when Afshin found a wife, his love for me, though different, could continue as strong as ever, I was satisfied. I stood, gave his arm a squeeze, and skated away. Soon, I steadied myself as I traveled beside men, women, and children of all colors and sizes. Afshin skated next to me until I was gliding with ease. He then surged ahead, but circled back a few times to check on me.

When we took a short break, Afshin said, "Don't ever say that you're getting old when you can rollerblade like that. You are forever young."

I felt that way. Maybe that's why I'd been able to marry a younger man.

After skating, we took a subway back to the dorm. I opened the refrigerator and brought out the hoagie. The aroma of vinegar and oregano revived the memories of all the times we'd eaten one together—sitting in the dining room, on a concrete step on Main Street, on a street bench, in the car.

As though performing a ritual, he carried the hoagie to Washington Square Park. We found a bench facing the fountain. In the amber light of dusk, we unwrapped our dinner and ate quietly. Our paths were about to diverge—I could no longer avoid it. Each bite became harder to swallow.

"I guess I should go," I finally said softly.

"I'll ride with you as far as I can."

We found the car and rode through Greenwich Village in silence. Saying anything would have been like banging on pots in a sacred space. Afshin's hand gripped mine. When the entrance to the tunnel came into view, a couple of blocks ahead, I pulled over to the curb. A streetlight lit up Afshin's face, and my chest tightened.

"I feel so close to you," Afshin said. "I know we can stay in touch now, but even if we couldn't, I would continue to feel this close."

"We are tribe mates," I said, covering his hand with mine. He reached over and kissed my cheek, then leaned away, but returned to meet my lips for an instant.

Before I knew it, he was standing outside the car. I didn't want to drive away. Couldn't we stay together—forever?

He stepped back, hands in his pockets. I shifted into first gear and pressed the gas pedal. The car crawled into the street, but I braked and turned my head in time to see Afshin's back as he walked up the deserted sidewalk. My eyes swallowed the last morsel of his form before the night took him from view. There goes the man I love, not as a husband, not as a son, but as a mysterious treasure who once leaped into my heart and would live there forever.

I steered the car toward the Holland Tunnel and New Jersey. In the tunnel, far below the Hudson River, Afshin's physical absence began to sink in. I wailed once, then again—and again. As my exhausted body quieted, I heard a gentle whisper: *Don't worry,* said my heart. *You'll be all right.*

I drove toward the Turnpike entrance and the beginning of a new chapter in my life—richer for the chapter that Afshin and I had lived—and now closed—together.

END

Author's Note

I have changed the names of the characters and locations in this story. I value the privacy of all the people described here, especially that of the Iranians. For a large part of their history, Iranians have had to stay out of the limelight in order to thrive or survive. The popular American pastime of exposing one's private life (as evidenced through social media and countless "reality" TV shows) is not one in which most Iranians can comfortably participate.

Otherwise, I have tried to describe the events in the story accurately, mindful of the fact that we all view our experiences through our own filters. My interpretation of what motivated Afshin's surprising actions may be inaccurate; perhaps at times I have inadvertently misrepresented him. I would be interested in reading his version of our story; I'm guessing there would be scenes in which I would not recognize myself. My hope is that if Afshin reads my account, he can say, "She got it mostly right."

Afshin gave me a poster of the following poem after our marriage. I wish I'd written it.

Underneath We're All The Same—By Amy Maddox

He prayed—it wasn't my religion.
He ate—it wasn't what I ate.
He spoke—it wasn't my language.
He dressed—it wasn't what I wore.
He took my hand—it wasn't the color of his hand.
But when he laughed—it was how I laughed
and when he cried—it was how I cried.

Acknowledgments

I yearned to tell this story about my year with Afshin, even though I didn't think my skills at writing were adequate. Therefore I attended a writers' retreat in New York and met my first writing teacher, Pat Carr. She didn't laugh at my first draft, written in a spiral notebook. Instead, she offered encouragement. Next came Areta Parle, whose patient editorial guidance and compassion for the characters helped me continue to shape the story. Angela Watrous, who shares my love of Nonviolent Communication (NVC), supported my getting to the heart of the story by suggesting how to prune it. Finally, Kathy Wilcox helped me fine-tune the wording for greater clarity.

Without the collaboration of many willing contributors, I'm sure I would not have succeeded in getting the manuscript to a publishable form. My immense gratitude goes out to Christine D., who also knows the challenges and joys of an American-Iranian marriage, and to Azar A., for her Persian perspective on the story. Arlene B., Emily C., Jamie C., Sandra C., Pauline D., Richard F., Barbara H., Shelley K., Katie L., Abigail M., Brownlee M., Jane M., Susan M., Toni M., Stacy S., Anand S., Rosemary S., Gail T., Julia W., Nancy W. and Morton Z. helped by either reading drafts, providing feedback, giving worthwhile advice, or providing editorial support. Thank you. Merci. Gracias.

Big hugs to the friends who listened and supported me on this writing journey.

It came as no surprise to me that my children, Gregory, Calvin, and Beth, were supportive during the writing of the book. They readily allowed me to write about them and the interactions we had during Afshin's time in my life. I'm grateful beyond words for their acceptance and love.

Miriam Valmont

All of those named here, as well as any others I may have inadvertently failed to mention, supported me in voicing something incredibly important to me—the ways we often create enemies, country to country, and how we can create friends, human being to human being.

Lastly, to Pete S., my special friend and late partner: I carry you in my heart. It's getting crowded in there, but I trust you understand that there's room for everyone—for you, for David, and for Afshin—wherever Love has opened the door.

Reader's Guide

1. How do you feel about the term "marriage" used in reference to the six-month intimate relationship Afshin and Miriam had? Did assigning that name to the relationship make it more real in their eyes? Would giving it another name have accomplished the same thing?

2. Why do you think Miriam was drawn to Afshin and vice versa?

3. Why do you think Afshin suggested a short-term marriage?

4. Why do you think Miriam was willing to agree to a short-term marriage, and how did you feel about it?

5. Do you view Miriam as a woman who makes things happen or lets things happen? Why? What in the story made you come to that conclusion?

6. Do you think that Miriam felt isolated from others during the relationship with Afshin? Does that often happen when a couple is first together? Or, was it more of an issue because of their age difference?

7. Do you think that Afshin would have wanted to stay married to Miriam if he didn't have a calling to return to Iran to teach? Why or why not?

8. Do you think that Miriam would have wanted to stay married if Afshin had said that he would like to stay with her in the US? Why or why not?

9. Do you have a different viewpoint regarding Iranians (not their government) after reading this story?

Miriam Valmont

10. Miriam refers to herself and Afshin as "tribe mates." Why do you think that is?

11. Were you shocked at Afshin's insistence that they switch to a mother-son relationship? Did you come to accept the reason that he gave for wanting that definition of their new relationship? Did you accept the reason Miriam gave for going along with Afshin's wish?

12. Afshin wanted Miriam to introduce him to her neighbors as her son. Why?

13. Do you wonder why Afshin didn't change more of his ways of thinking or doing things? Why did Miriam willingly adjust to so many of his ways?

14. Do you think Miriam benefitted from the relationship? Did Afshin?

Made in the USA
Lexington, KY
12 December 2016